ISBN 978-0-243-95372-1
PIBN 10805810

1 MONTH OF
FREE
READING

at

www.ForgottenBooks.com

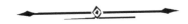

By purchasing this book you are eligible for one month membership to ForgottenBooks.com, giving you unlimited access to our entire collection of over 700,000 titles via our web site and mobile apps.

To claim your free month visit:

www.forgottenbooks.com/free805810

English
Français
Deutsche
Italiano
Español
Português

www.forgottenbooks.com

Mythology Photography **Fiction**
Fishing Christianity **Art** Cooking
Essays Buddhism Freemasonry
Medicine **Biology** Music **Ancient**
Egypt Evolution Carpentry Physics
Dance Geology **Mathematics** Fitness
Shakespeare **Folklore** Yoga Marketing
Confidence Immortality Biographies
Poetry **Psychology** Witchcraft
Electronics Chemistry History **Law**
Accounting **Philosophy** Anthropology
Alchemy Drama Quantum Mechanics
Atheism Sexual Health **Ancient History**
Entrepreneurship Languages Sport
Paleontology Needlework Islam
Metaphysics Investment Archaeology
Parenting Statistics Criminology
Motivational

THE
SALT-CELLARS.

BEING A COLLECTION OF PROVERBS,

TOGETHER WITH

HOMELY NOTES THEREON.

BY

C. H. SPURGEON.

*THESE THREE THINGS GO TO THE MAKING OF
A PROVERB:*

Shortness, Sense, and Salt.

VOL. II.—M TO Z.

London:
PASSMORE AND ALABASTER, PATERNOSTER BUILDINGS.
1889.

ALABASTER, PASSMORE, AND SONS,
PRINTERS,
FANN STREET, ALDERSGATE STREET, LONDON, E.C.

Proverbs and Quaint Sayings.

AD bulls cannot be tied up with a pack-thread.

Far greater restraints are needed. Obstinate people must be held in with strong measures. Our corrupt human nature in its madness is not to be ruled by mere resolves, nor by any power less than divine.

" Some men demand rough treatment everywhere :
Will apples tempt a wild boar to a sty ?
You cannot with a whistle tame a bear :
You cannot with a beckon lure a fly."—*S. C. Hall.*

Mad dogs cannot live long.

The furiously wicked have but a short career. Bad for them, but good for the universe.

Mad folk are not to be argued with.

Any more than mad bulls. They are not in a condition of mind to appreciate argument, and should be let alone. To stand reasoning with a wild bull would be very absurd, and it is equally so to debate with a hot-headed partisan.

Mad people think others mad.

The judgments of men are warped by their own follies, and we should not pay too much heed to them. When a man is "mad as a hatter," or "mad as a March hare," his opinion of others is of small consequence.

Maidens should be mild and meek,
Swift to hear and slow to speak.

The same advice will apply to men also ; but the men like advising the women, better than doing right themselves.

Make all sure, and keep all pure.

Make every bargain clear and plain,
That none may afterwards complain.

> This would save a world of heart-burning, and greatly tend to peace and quietness. If possible, put it down in black and white that there may be no after quibbling.

Make good cheese, if you make little.

> Keep up the quality of your work, even if you cannot excel in the quantity of it.

Make great excuses for people in love.

> They have not all their wits about them. A temporary insanity possesses them.
>
> > " Love is a dizziness :
> > It winna let a poor body
> > Gang about his business."

Make haste slowly.

> A wise Eastern proverb says, "Hurry is of the devil, but slow advancing comes from God." What is done hastily is seldom done well; and being ill done, it has to be undone, and this wastes time. "With eager feeding food will choke the eater."

Make hay while the sun shines.

> You cannot make it when it is pouring with rain, therefore seize on the season, and, like the busy bee, improve each shining hour.
>
> > " Make your hay fine
> > While sun doth shine."

Make home happy, and you will be happy at home.

> A golden sentence. When any one ceases to care for his home, it is one of the worst possible signs of moral sickness.

Make matters of care matters of prayer.

> This is the wisdom of the anxious. To lay the matter before the Lord is to take the sting out of trial.

Make much of little.

> By economy use a small income well; by grateful praise express your value of the least of God's mercies; and by charitable judgment come to a favourable conclusion concerning those in whom you see even a little grace. One can see the sky in a single drop of rain, and a work of grace in a tear of repentance.

Make no debts, and lay no bets.

A debtor is a slave, and a bettor is no better; for before long his losses will bring him into the same condition of bondage. *Rowland Hill* said, " I never pay my debts, and for the best of reasons—*I never have any debts to pay.*"

Make not another's shoes by your own foot.

For that which suits you very well may be quite unsuitable for another person. Every foot needs a last of its own. Allow latitude of thought and manner within the bounds of truth and holiness. Avoid Chinese shoes both for yourself and others.

Make not fish of one and flesh of another.

Unless they are really distinct. Give equal justice to all; but yet discriminate, and judge none sweepingly.

Make not friends with an angry man or a drinking man.

The first is Solomon's advice; the second does not need a Solomon to see its common sense. We grow like our friends; therefore let us choose them with care.

Make not much of little.

That is to say, when finding fault, don't make mountains of molehills, nor crimes out of blunders. This is the apparent reverse of a proverb a little back; but then it applies to another set of things.

Make not thy tail broader than thy wings.

Have not more show than substance, more outgoings than incomings, more promise than ability to perform.

Make not two sorrows of one.

Do not so worry as to create a second sorrow, nor so sin as to involve a repetition, and perhaps an aggravation, of your grief.

Make not your holiday an unholy day.

Make one wrong step, and down you go.

This may be the case at any time; therefore cry unto "him who is able to keep you from stumbling." With certain uncharitable people this proverb is bitterly true; for all your years of acceptable service will be forgotten if, for once in your life, you give them the least cause for complaint.

Make others happy, and you will be happy yourself.

When out for a holiday, a sour-visaged lady said to another, "Are you enjoying yourself? I am sure I am not." "No," said her friend, "I did not come out to enjoy myself, but to enjoy other people, and I am doing it heartily." This is a surer way to pleasure than self-consideration.

> "For the sake of those who love us,
> For the sake of God above us,
> Each and all should do their best
> To make music for the rest."

Make short the miles with talk and smiles.

Cheerful conversation causes time to fly by unnoticed.

Make speed to-day, you may be stopped to-morrow.

Whenever we have a chance for undisturbed work, let us use it, for there are many hinderers. If the train does not get over the ground where there are few stations to stop at, it will certainly make small speed upon other parts of the road.

Make sure of nothing, but that God is true.

Make the best of a bad bargain.

Say as little as you can about it, or you will be injuring your own reputation for good judgment. If you have entered upon marriage, and find yourself mistaken, "bear and forbear." In all trying cases, among a trying people, say—

> "I'll not willingly offend,
> Nor be easily offended;
> What's amiss I'll strive to mend,
> And endure what can't be mended."

Make the plaster as large as the sore.

If you have given offence, let the apology and, if need be, the reparation, be ample. Make it up; leave no back reckonings.

Make your hay as best you may.

If the season is wet, watch the intervals between the showers, and use them with diligence. If we cannot alter our circumstances, we must do the best under them.

Make your mark, but mind what the mark is.

Too many seem eager for mere notoriety; but if we are not famous for goodness we are practically infamous.

Make your pudding according to your plums.

> Arrange your whole plan of life so as to suit your means, and thus avoid debt, and other forms of failure. Some men try to do too much, and do it to their ruin.

Make your will without delay,
For death may come on any day.

> Great sorrow has been brought on families by neglect in the making of wills. It is cruelty to one's own flesh and blood to leave one's affairs unsettled. Yet some persons have a strange aversion to do what ought to be done by every sane man. Do they think that it will be signing their death-warrant, to sign their will? Reader, are you one of these wilful waiters?
>
> > Come, swallow the pill,
> > And draw up your will.

Make yourself an ass, and everyone will lay his sack on you.

> Too great softness is a rare fault, but a fault it is. We need not invite all the world to impose upon us. They will burden us if they can, and it is as well to let them see that we are not quite so stupid as they suppose. When the sheep is too meek, all the lambs suck it.

Malice is mental murder.

Man by nature is poor, proud, peevish and pig-headed.

> You cannot slander human nature; it is worse than words can paint it. Man is an animal that sins. He is often a wolf to man, a serpent to God, and a scorpion to himself.

Man does not grow perfect in a hundred years; but in one day he becomes corrupt.

Man is a puff of wind and a pile of dust.

> Yet "all men think all men mortal but themselves." In truth, "Life's but a walking shadow." We rather seem to be than really exist. Our life's a shade.

Man proposes, but God disposes.

> Napoleon boasted that he proposed and disposed too, but God's answer was given when Napoleon was deposed.

Man's saying is only saying; but God's saying is doing.

> With men, "between saying and doing many a pair of shoes is worn out"; but God speaks and it is done. *Dictum, factum.*

Man's security is Satan's opportunity.

When we think ourselves wise and strong, our enemy soon trips us up, and proves us silly and weak. Carnal security is a strange fatuity. He is not safe who thinks himself so.

Man's twelve is not so good as the devil's dozen.

He is older and craftier than we are. How can we hope to cope with one whose experience is so wide, and of so long a duration?

Man's work lasts till set of sun; Woman's work is never done.

She has to prepare the meal before the man goes out, and also to have another ready when he comes home, and even through the night the children demand her care. It is as *Tusser* wrote :—

"Some respite to husband the seasons may send ;
But housewife's affairs have never an end."

Manners maketh man.

Not money, nor birth, nor office, but behaviour makes the man among his fellows. To the proverb above is generally added the words, " Quoth William of Wickham."

Manners you may have though you have no manors.

The man who has not a foot of land, nor a pound in money, may yet be a perfect gentleman. In certain cases we might justly say, " He hath of manors and manners, none at all."

Many a child is hungry because the brewer is rich.

What should have been spent in bread and butter has gone in malt and hops. A little fellow was asked by a lady, " Why do you not come for cold victuals any more ?" and replied, " Because father's signed the pledge, and we get hot victuals at home." This story was told by *J. B. Gough.*

Many a cloudy morning leads on to a fine day.

So that we may live in hopes of its clearing up. Carry your umbrella, but don't always put it up. Be careful, but not fearful.

Many a cow stands in the meadow and looks wistfully at the common.

Anxious to go from better to worse! Men often envy those whom they should pity. Mice outside envy those in the trap.

Many a dog is dead since you were a whelp.

You are not so young as you would wish me to think you.

Many a fine dish has nothing on it.

Many a person who is comely is also a dummy. An open countenance and a noble head may only be an apology for absent intelligence. We must not judge of men by their elegant appearance. A dish of finest ware only mocks a hungry man, if it brings him no food; and many a learned discourse is of this nature.

Many a good drop of broth may come out of an old pot.

An old text, an old minister, an old book, an old friend, an old experience, may yet yield us consolation.

Many a good tale is spoilt in the telling.

Let the speaker be too long, too loud, too low, or too lofty, and the best story will be sadly marred in the telling. It is a pity when it is so with the gospel.

Many a man cuts a stick to break his own head.

He, unknowingly, does that which will be to his own serious injury. A man's folly is his worst foe.

**Many a one for land,
Takes a fool by the hand.**

Marrying property instead of wedding a sensible wife is a great absurdity. Surely, if the woman who is chosen for her land turns out a fool, there is a pair of them!

Many a one is good because he can do no mischief.

Involuntary virtue wins no commendation. He who would do mischief if he could, should remember that in a bad as well as in a good sense, the will is often taken for the deed.

**Many a pang has been incurred
Through a single hasty word.**

Many a pearl is still hidden in its oyster.

No doubt there are as good pearls in the sea as ever came out of it. Let us not despair for the times. God has jewels in hiding.

Many a stroke must fell an oak.

Many a true word is spoken in jest.

That which was the subject of mirth turns out to be a real cause for sorrow. We are all, at times, unconscious prophets.

Many acres will not make a wiseacre.

Broad lands and breadth of wisdom do not necessarily go together, and yet many seem to think that everything a rich man says is eminently important. Yet in the parable the rich man was a fool. Riches cannot really cover folly, neither can they make an empty mouth speak golden words.

Many are betrayed with a kiss.

Judas did this with our Lord, and we need not wonder if others do so with us. Yet let us not be betrayed by the kiss of Delilah: that form of kiss we *can* refuse.

Many are brave when the enemy flies.

They pursue to share the spoil. Win you the victory alone, and thousands will then fight the battle o'er again.

Many are lighter in the heels than in the heart.

They dance with their feet, but they limp in spirit. They have a fantastic toe, but a fainting heart. Grief is all the more oppressive when it is forced to wear the mask of cheerfulness.

Many are wise in jest, but fools in earnest.

It is a small attainment to be great in foolery, and to be useless for all practical purposes; yet many are in that condition.

Many beat the sack and mean the miller.

They find fault with the sermon, but really dislike the preacher. They have a personal animosity which prevents their speaking well of what the good man does or says.

Many can get money; few can use it well.

Even to keep it is not easy. Many of the silliest investments have been made by men who, in their own business, were shrewd to the highest degree. It is harder to weave than to gather wool.

Many can help one.

Without hurting themselves they can put their littles together, and aid a friend in the day of his need.

Many can make bricks, but cannot build.

They lack the organizing faculty, though otherwise good workers.

Many captains, and the ship goes on the rocks.

Divided authority is as bad as none at all. What would a man do with two heads differing in thought? "There can only be one captain to a ship," one central source of rule.

Masters two,
Will not do.

Many commit sin, and blame Satan.

Just as Eve said, "The serpent beguiled me, and I did eat." Satan has quite enough sin of his own, without having our iniquities fathered upon him. Even the evil one can be libelled.

Many cut broad thongs out of other people's leather.

Preachers and authors make bountiful extracts. Servants help themselves lavishly to sugar and butter at their master's expense: and, in general, men are very generous with that which costs them nothing. Find a man in coals, and he will keep up a great fire at midsummer: pay his travelling expenses, and he will become a globe-trotter, and go nine times round the world.

Many dogs soon eat up a horse.

A number of fellows drinking and feasting at the expense of a man of means, will soon devour his fortune, as hounds will swallow a dead horse. These dogs are always prowling about.

Many drops make a shower.

Combinations of littles may accomplish great results.

Many find fault without any end,
And yet do nothing at all to mend.

Many give an egg to get an ox.

Or a sprat to catch a mackerel. This is the Oriental manner of giving presents to great men, to get a large return.

Many go out for clothes and come home stript.

Especially when they invest in a Limited Company, and the concern gets into liquidation.

Many good purposes lie in the churchyard.

Dead and buried, like those who brought them forth. What we should be if we did but carry out our good resolves!

Many hands make light work : this is clear.
Many hands make slight work : this I fear.

Many have come to port after a great storm.

Especially if they have taken on board the pilot of the Galilean lake. Courage, ye who are tost with tempest, and not comforted!

Many hostlers starve the mare.

"What!" say the Kashmiri, "eleven grooms for a one-eyed mare!" Alas, for the creature whose welfare depends on many! The business of many is the concern of none.

Unless you leave the work to one,
I'm pretty sure it won't be done.

Many hounds are the death of the hare.

She might baffle the pursuit of one dog; but when another and another join in the hunt, what can she do? Many cares, pains, and losses, coming close upon one another, prove too much for weak minds. If God help not, the many hounds will kill the hare.

Many leaves fade in summer, and many men die soon.

Many lick before they bite.

This I know by experience: and the worst lick-spittles bite the most venomously.

Many littles make a mickle.

Drop by drop the sea is filled. Add small to small, and it comes to great. Little grains make up the terrible quicksand.

Many love our persons for our purses.

Hear what the man said: "Leave you, dear girl! No, never; so long as you have a shilling."

" Sage Plutarch said in ancient days :
' When the strong box contains no more,
And when the kitchen fire is out,
Both friends and flatterers shun the door.' "

Many make straight things crooked, but few make crooked things straight.

> Most true. But the former is a far easier task than the latter. To make crooked things straight is the peculiar work of God's grace and providence. This he has promised to do.

Many men, many minds.

Many men mean mending, but more need it.

Many patients die of the doctor.

> This is what people say when they are well. Then they talk of having no doctor, but "dying a natural death"; but, after a little pain, they pitifully cry out, "Send for the doctor."

Many persons think they are wise, when they are only windy.

> During a stormy discussion, a gentleman rose to settle the matter in dispute. Waving his hands majestically over the excited disputants, he began: "Gentlemen, all I want is common-sense——" "Exactly," Douglas Jerrold interrupted; "that is precisely what you do want." The discussion was finished in a burst of laughter.

Many rendings need many mendings.

> Applicable, not only to garments, but to communities, to churches, and to the lives of men.

Many save their silver, but lose their souls.

> Many a man's soul has been ruined by his great love of money, although he had but little money to love.

Many sin like David, but do not repent like David.

> Yet they readily quote David's faults as their excuse. If, like David, I am defiled, let me, like David, be washed.

Many speak much, but few speak well.

> And those who speak well are not eager to speak much. From mountains of labouring words there may only come a mouse of sense.

Many suffer long, but are not longsuffering.

> Because they suffer unwillingly, and are angry and impatient.

Many talk like philosophers, and live like fools.

Many talk of *Robin Hood,* that never shot with his bow,
And many talk of *Little John,* that never did him know.

> Of course, talk goes ahead mightily. If you cannot do any-
> thing great yourself, it is something to say that you know those
> who are famous, or, at least, that you know their cousin's grand-
> mother's housemaid.

Many tickle with one hand, to strike with the other.

> Pleasing in order to betray. The flatterer is a vile reptile; like
> a boa-constrictor, he covers his victim with saliva, and then pro-
> ceeds to swallow him.

Many words will not fill a bushel.

> They are but wind at the best. The Scotch say, "Meikle crack
> fills nae sack."

Many would run away if they had courage enough.

> Strange to say, fear has kept many men from playing the coward.

Mar not what marred cannot be mended.

> If the mischief cannot be undone, we must avoid it with tenfold
> care. Do not break the shell if you wish to save the egg, for there
> is no repairing the damage.

March comes in like a lamb, and goes out like a lion; or it
    comes in like a lion, and goes out like a lamb.

> It seems ordained at one part or the other to rage and roar with
> tremendous wind. In this it resembles the lives of different men:
> some begin with peace and end with trial, and others commence
> roughly, but end in tranquillity.

March has many weathers, and life has many changes.

March is a lion or a lamb;
Which it will be uncertain I am.

> If this month comes in with raging winds, it often finishes
> delightfully; and, on the other hand, if it opens gently, it will
> rave before it is over. The month is near the vernal equinox,
> when wind is to be expected. We leave prophecies about the
> weather to Old Moore and Zadkiel, who know as much about it as
> the dead crow knows about the sea-serpent.

March winds and April showers,
Bring forth May flowers.

> Sorrows and troubles produce lovely graces when God sanctifies
> *them to that end.*

Mark this, one and all :
Pride will surely have a fall.

A striking instance was given in the life of Elizabeth Stuart, sister of Charles I. When her husband, the Elector Palatine, hesitated to accept the Bohemian crown, she exclaimed, "Let me rather eat dry bread at a king's table, than feast at the board of an Elector"; and, as *Mrs. Jameson* says, "it seems as if some avenging demon hovered in the air, to take her literally at her word; for she and her family lived to eat dry bread—ay, and to beg it before they ate it—but she would be a queen."

Marriage for love is risky, but it's right.

Without love marriage is wicked. But love must not be blind or mad. True love will not drag its object into hopeless poverty. Where love reigns supreme, the married life will be joyful, whether in wealth or in poverty: yet love is apt to fly out of the window when the wolf of want comes in at the door.

Marriage is either kill or cure.

It is either mar age or merry age, as the case may be.

> "O matrimony ! thou art like
> To Jeremiah's figs—
> The good are very good indeed ;
> The bad too sour for pigs !"

Yet people will venture upon it still, so long as the world standeth. Aunt Rachel said it was a solemn thing to be married; but her niece replied that it was a great deal more solemn not to be.

Marry a man, not a clothes-horse.

Fops, who give their whole mind to a hat or a waistcoat, are not worth looking after. As well marry one of the dummies in a tailor's window. It is a great pity when the man who should be the head figure is a mere figure-head. In such a case it is a mercy if the grey mare is much the better horse.

> Says Giles, "My wife and I are one,
> Yet, truth, I know not why, sir."
> Quoth Jack, "If I think right, you're ten:
> She's one, and you're a cipher."

Marry for love, and work for the lucre.

The prudent father said: "Do not marry for money, but only for love; yet let not your love go where there is no money." Our proverb is better advice by far. When a couple are united in love, then their joint exertions can be given to obtain the supply of their necessities, and in general they will succeed.

Marry for love, but only love that which is lovely.

Marry in a hurry, and live in a worry.

> Marriage is harness for a pair, and it should be adjusted with care, blinkers and kicking-straps included, wherever they are required. This harness should be put on with due deliberation. Take time to do that which time cannot undo.

Marry in haste, and repent at leisure.

> Marriage is a desperate thing. "The frogs in Æsop were extremely wise : they had a great mind to some water, but they would not leap into the well because they could not get out again." Blessed is the man who can say, after twenty years :
>
> > "I did commit no act of folly,
> > When I married my sweet Molly."

Marry not without love, but love not without reason.

Marry your first love if you can,
And hope to be a happy man.

Marrying is easy, but housekeeping is hard.

> Thoughtless young people need to be reminded that they cannot live upon love, nor keep house upon none-pence a day.

Masters and mistresses are the greatest servants in the house.

> On them lies the care of providing and directing, and they often lie awake when Sarah and Ann are sound asleep.

Matches may be made in heaven, but they are *sold* on earth.

> That is to say, they are too often a matter of bargain, and the lowest motives are brought into play.
>
> > Many a match is made for gold :
> > The bride is bought—the bridegroom sold.

Match-making is a dangerous business.

> Literally it is so ; for these little light-makers are apt to burn. The allusion is, however, to marriage. Match-makers often burn their fingers. If a mistake is made, the couple are apt to blame the persons who brought them together, and led them into matrimony. To recommend anyone for a husband or a wife is a very *responsible business*, and it is, as a rule, best let alone.

Matrimony should not be a matter of money.

He that marries for gold is bought and sold. Yet, even in the old times, men did such mercenary things; for the rhyme ran:—
"Bring something, lass, along with thee,
If thou intend my wife to be."

This also is a curious memorandum:

	£	s.	d.
The girl was worth	1,000		
The man wasn't worth	...	1	
And when she found that he had	...	...	0
To wed she was unwilling.			

"May-be" is very well, but "must" is the master.

May good digestion wait on appetite, and health on both!

A good wish, having far more in it than at first appears. The joy of life depends more on digestion than on any other earthly thing. He that would have a good life must have a good liver. A great deal of misery is born of the stomach.

May that flirt soon light on a limed twig.

May he or she be caught, and held fast, so that the indecency of flippant flirting may be finally finished, in that case at least.

Measure men around the heart.

A man of great soul and large heart is a man worth knowing.

Measure three times before you cut once.

For you cannot uncut it, and you may waste the material.

Medicines are not meant to feed on.

"Mirth," according to Solomon, "doeth good like a medicine." It should not be our daily bread, but it should be measured out in proper quantities as a tonic, and not as a constant food.

Meekness is not weakness.

On the contrary, it is a sign of strength, and a cause of it. The ox lies still while the geese are hissing. The mastiff is quiet while curs are yelping. As an instance among men: Moses was king in Israel because of his great meekness among a provoking people.

Men are strong and hale without strong ale.

Lions and horses drink water, and so did Samson. It is a popular fallacy that there is strength in strong drink.

**Men are seldom rashly bold
When they save a little gold.**

A conservative tendency takes the desire for risk out of them, and they had rather let things be as they are. A Socialist was advocating an equal division of property. "And how much," asked a Scotchman, "wad there be for ilka ane?" "Oh, maybe near a hundred pounds!" "Then I'll na gang alang wi' ye, for I've saved a matter o' a hundred and twenty mysel'."

Men hate where they hurt.

Men love best those whom they have benefited, and hate those whom they have injured.

Men, like puppies, are born blind, but they do not so soon have their eyes opened.

> "Man, a poor deluded bubble,
>   Wanders in a mist of lies;
> Seeing false, or seeing double,
>   Who would trust to such weak eyes?
>
> "Yet, presuming on his senses,
>   On he goes, most wondrous wise;
> Doubts the truth, believes pretences,
>   Lost in error, lives and dies."

Men make houses, but women make homes.

Ruskin says: "Wherever a true woman comes, home is always around her. The stars may be over her head, the glow-worms in the night-cold grass may be the fire at her foot; but home is where she is; and for a noble woman it stretches far around her, better than houses ceiled with cedar, or painted with vermilion, shedding its quiet light far for those who else are homeless."

Men may bear till their backs break.

But they very seldom do. They are generally more ready to put their backs up if you would lay a single ounce upon them.

Men may die of the plague, though the spots never appear.

Alas! sin may reign in the heart unto eternal death, and yet the life may appear free from grave moral fault. This leprosy lies deep within, and is fatal even when unseen.

Men muse as they use.

They think of others as they are and do themselves. They *weigh other* folk's meat with their own steel-yard.

Men praise themselves, to save praising others.

None are more unjust in their judgments of others than those who have a high opinion of themselves. He who is greedy of applause never gives a cheer for a rival.

Men rattle their chains to show that they are free.

The wicked, who are slaves to sin, make much noise and shouting, that they may appear to be happy and at ease.

Men readily believe what they wish to be true.

The wish is father to the thought, and the thought is father to the belief. Hence we should be jealous of our beliefs when they coincide with our personal interests.

Men who carry honesty in their faces are often rogues.

I remember a very eminent bubble-blower, whom I mistook for an Essex farmer of the most plain and outspoken sort; and after looking at his honest face, and hearing his bluff speech and jolly laugh, I never wondered that people believed in him. An honest manner is essential to the success of a great rascal.

Men who have weak heads are generally headstrong.

So that if you forbid them a thing they will be sure to do it! Of such we have to say, "He that will to Cupar maun to Cupar." There's no keeping fools from hurting themselves.

Men will blame themselves for the purpose of being praised.

This is called "fishing for compliments," and it is not even so profitable a business as fishing for sticklebacks.

Men with nought in purse to spare
Go most quickly through the fair.

So do some pass through life with less of hankering for the world by reason of their poverty.

Mendings are honourable; rags are abominable.

Women who are worth their salt will use their needle to darn and patch. *Tom Fuller* says: "Needle means ne idle, or not idle", but surely rags mean rogues.

Mercies and miseries seldom come alone.

These fly in flocks. It never rains but it pours.

Mercy to the criminal may be cruelty to the innocent.

Gentleness to those who commit burglary with violence is certainly cruelty to their victims; and there are many other cases equally to the point. We shall be glad to do away with the infliction of death when murderers set the example.

Mere wishes are bony fishes.

There is nothing solid and sustaining about mere dreams and schemes. The wishing-gate opens into nothing.

Merit only can measure merit.

A Sanscrit writer says:

"No man can others' virtues know,
While he himself has none to show."

Mice have tails.

Meaning that something may follow by way of consequence, even out of a trifling action. We should consider the results of little acts, for these may be greater than at first appears.

Mice must not play with kittens.

Nor must men toy with temptations, for they are not able to resist them.

Miles test the horse, and years prove the man.

They say, "It is the pace which kills," and it may be so; but it is far easier to make a great rush than to plod steadily on through a long life. Roasting before a slow fire is worse than burning.

Mind how you feed, especially when you feed your mind.

For as the silkworm is coloured by the leaf it feeds on, so do men take the hue of their reading. As we would not eat carrion, let us not read garbage. *Thackeray* once said to a visitor: "I read very few novels. I am a pastry-cook. I bake tarts and sell them. I do not eat them myself: I eat bread and butter."

Mind your " p's " and " q's."

These letters are exactly alike, save that one is turned one way, and the other the other. If mistakes are made in them even a peer is queer. Great errors may arise from carelessness in little things. *Mind etiquette*, or you will have the wrong ticket.

Mind that no doubting mind undermines your mind.

> A danger very pressing just now. For many are the deceivers
> "Who, wheedling round, with metaphysic art,
> Steal true religion from the unguarded heart."

Mind that *porter* does not carry you off.

> Double stout, though said to be nourishing, may readily carry a man half seas over. "*Porter* was a name given in the last century to a new mixture of malt liquors, which was at first chiefly drunk by porters; but it has twice earned its name by the tendency it displays of carrying heavy burdens and placing them upon men's hearts, and by the success it has attained in carrying men from their homes, reason from the brains, money from the pocket, love from the bosom, peace from the conscience, reputation from the character, and too often life from its victim."

Mind the corner where life's road turns.

> For as you turn that point, so will you be likely to continue. If one foot should there be placed awry, many a day may have to rue it.

Mind the main chance.

> But what is it? Take care to answer this question wisely, and then obey the proverb.

Mind the paint! Keep clear of the face that wears it.

> What good can you get from a picture painted on flesh? Paint is the outward and visible sign of inward and spiritual deceit.
> When a woman is painted up to the eyes,
> She's a Jezebel even the dogs will despise.

Mind *what* is preached, more than *how* it is preached.

> Meat is more than its carving, and truth is more than oratory.

Mind *what* you do, and *how* you do it.

> Let the matter be good, and let the manner befit it.

Mind you get the right sow by the ear.

> Don't blame the innocent, nor pounce upon a person whom you ought not to assail. Leave all piggies' ears alone, rather than seize upon the wrong one.

Mind your courting does not end in court.

> Breach of promise has overthrown many a promising young man.

Mind your own business, and you will be sure
To avoid many troubles which others endure.

Men who mind their own business will be very likely to succeed; for there is very little competition in that line. You will do better at your own business than at anything else: "Every man can blow best on his own horn." Let every tailor keep to his goose.

Mind your till, and till your mind.

Look to your business, its takings and makings; but do not forget the nobler part of your being. Don't put your soul along with the coppers; keep it cultivated with reading and thought.

Mind your work, and God will find your wages.

If not to-day, nor to-morrow, yet very certainly and abundantly, according to his grace, he will reward every good work.

Mirth should never run into mischief.

Boisterous boys should take heed to this. Mirth has its bounds. When we meet merrily, let us so act that we may part merrily too. There is an old saying not often quoted, but very true: "No mirth is good without God."

Misers' hearts are as hard as their hard cash.

Of such a man it could be said:

> " Iron was his safe,
>   Iron was its door;
>   His hand was iron,
>   His heart was more."

Misery hath strange bed-fellows.

In a common calamity men of different classes are thrown together without question of rank or character.

Misfortune comes on horseback, and goes away on foot.

Adversity pounces upon us like an eagle; but to retrieve a disaster is slow work. Sorrow seems to linger long.

Misreckoning is no payment.

This is clear enough in trade, and it is equally so in morals. Because a man thinks well of himself, is it therefore well with him? If a man's conscience reckons amiss, this does not make a breach of the law an innocent thing.

Mistress Margery, do not scold,
It makes you look so very old.

> *Ovid* wrote :
>> " Look in the glass when you with anger glow,
>> And you'll confess you scarce yourself would know."

Misunderstanding brings lies to town.

> People are apt to misinterpret those whom they dislike, and then the misrepresentation leads on to libel and slander.

Mock not a cobbler for his black thumbs.

> His disfigurement comes of honest labour, and, therefore, it is no theme for jest. Napoleon said, " Respect the burden," and truly all labour, and all that necessarily comes of labour, deserves to be had in honour. In the cobbler's case be very generous; for you ought to remember that while other trades take an earlier turn, he has to wait for his *last.*

Modest dogs miss much meat.

> No doubt one can stand in his own light by extreme bashfulness. Some puppies we know of never lose a mouthful from this cause.

Moles and misers live in their graves.

> Scarcely can we say this of moles; but they are of the earth earthy, and so is the man whose heap of yellow dust is all he cares for: he is buried in the earth he has scraped together.

Moles don't see what their neighbours are doing.

> Some persons are so absorbed in their own earth-grubbing, that they know nothing of anybody else. This selfish isolation is, on the whole, not so mischievous as perpetual interfering.

Monday religion is better than Sunday profession.

Money answers everything,
Save a guilty conscience sting.

> Golden ointment is no cure for a wound of the heart. Ready money is ready medicine, but not for the sting of remorse. Some call it " the one thing needful," but they know not what they say.

Money borrowed is soon sorrowed.

> He that lends it begins to sorrow, even if the borrower does not; for, in general, he may mourn that he has parted from it to meet no more.

Money burns many.

> They are injured by their wealth. Some by bribes are burned; for
>> When money's taken,
>> Freedom's forsaken.

Money calls, but does not stay;
It is round and rolls away.

> It makes the mill to go, but it goes faster than the mill-wheel.
> It is no more to be kept in the purse than snow in an oven ; at
> least, so I find it. But why should we wish it to stay? It is the
> circulating medium! why should we detain it? If it rests it
> rusts. Let it go about doing good.

Money gained on Sabbath-day
Is a loss, I dare to say.

> No blessing can come with that which comes to us, on the devil's
> back, by our wilful disobedience of God's law. The loss of health
> by neglect of rest, and the loss of soul by neglect of hearing the
> gospel, soon turn all seeming profit into real loss.

Money gilds over guilt.

> Money is said to be a composition for taking out stains in character ;
> but, in that capacity, it is a failure. Those characters which can
> be thus gilded must surely be of the gingerbread order.

Money has no blood relations.

> There is no friendship in business. Sad that this should be a
> proverb in any land, but so it is. The Chinese say: "Though
> brothers are closely akin, it is each for himself in money matters."
> They also say: "Top and bottom teeth sometimes come into
> awkward collision." So little power has relationship in the savage
> customs of business that, in some instances, one hand would skin the
> other, if it could make a profit by it.

Money is a good servant, but a bad master.

> Even as a servant it is not easy to keep it in due subordination. If
> "money makes dogs dance," it makes men proud. If we make
> money our god, it will rule us like the devil.

Money is often lost for want of money.

> It is so when men cannot get their rights, from inability to pay
> legal charges. Yet if one had plenty of cash, it would not be wise
> to throw away good money after bad.

Money is the best bait to fish for man with.

He bites greedily at a gold or silver bait : but is the creature which is thus taken worth the catching?

He who can be bought,
I think is worth nought.

Money is the servant of the wise, and the master of fools.

Money makes money.

The goose that lays the golden eggs likes to lay where there are eggs already ; perhaps because it is a goose. The lard comes to the fat hog. Capital grows by interest, or by wise use it brings in profit, and thus increases. Money is money's brother. " If riches increase, set not your heart upon them."—Ps. lxii. 10.

Money makes the mare to go and the dog to dance.

Pecuniæ obediunt omnia. " All things obey money." This saying comes from the Latin, but it is true in English. A little palm oil will gain entrance where nothing else will do it. Officials are greatly mollified when their hands are crossed with silver. In a more allowable sense, a good wife would be happier and more active if her allowance could be increased. If she has too little money to keep house upon, it takes the " go " out of her.

Money often unmakes the men who make it.

It has a defiling and degrading power over the mind which thinks too much of it.

" Money and men a mutual falsehood show ;
Men make false money ; money makes men so."

Money speaks more powerfully than eloquence.

Too often, because the speaker is a rich man he commands attention, and secures the approbation of persons who see no sound sense spoken by one who has no money bags. This is very well put in the following verse :—

The man of means is eloquent :
Brave, handsome, noble, wise ;
All qualities with gold are sent,
And vanish where it flies.

Money spent on the brain
Is never spent in vain.

Pour your money into your brain, and you will never lose it all. Education is such a gain, that it is worth all that it costs, and more. Yet some fellows learn nothing in the schools. Many a father, when his son returns from the University, might say, " I put in gold into the furnace, and there came out this calf."

Money will make the pot boil, though the devil should pour water on the fire.

But such fuel is not to be depended on. We need something better than mere money to keep our pot a-boiling. Such boiling is apt to scald a man sooner or later.

Money wins where merit fails.

It is a pity it should be so; but, with worldly minds, to be rich is to be good. This vulgar error is long in dying. "The boy in yellow wins the day." Canaries are still the favourite birds.
"This is the golden age: all worship gold:
Honours are purchased; love and beauty sold."

Monk's-hood is very poisonous. Beware!

Whenever a smell of Romanism is discernible, be on the watch.

More belongs to riding than a pair of boots.

So in most things there is much to be learned, and the thing is not so easy as it looks. Even in pastimes this is true, as the proverb saith, "More belongs to dancing than a pair of pumps."

More die of idleness than of hard work.

A very small burial-ground will hold those who kill themselves with excessive industry; but the cemetery at Idler's End covers many acres, and the ground is rapidly filling up.

More die of overfeeding than of underfeeding.

Death feeds himself at banquets, but fares ill where there are short-commons. Lean ribs last longer than fat collops. More die of suppers than of the sword.
When other forms of physic fail,
Try if fasting will avail.

More flies are caught with honey than with vinegar.

Gentleness and cheerfulness attract more to religion and virtue than severe solemnity, or stern manners.
There's but little power,
In religion sour.

More have repented of speech than of silence.

How seldom are men sorry for holding their tongues! How often have they had to bite their tongues with anguish at the memory of *unguarded speech!* Say nothing, and none can criticize thee.

More know Tom Fool than Tom Fool knows.

Public characters are known by thousands, but they cannot know thousands themselves. "Don't you know me? I heard you speak at Exeter Hall." Wonderful argument!

More light, more life, more love.

Worthy to be a common wish, and to grow into a holy proverb.

Light without life is a candle in a tomb;
Life without love is a garden without bloom.

More meat, and less mustard.

Often we would like more solid argument and fewer angry words; more gospel and less controversy; more wages and less scolding; more gifts of charity and less lecturing upon thrift.

More pith and less pride.

Generally your boaster has nothing in him of true grit. The more of the solid there is in a man, the less does he act the balloon.

More potatoes and fewer potations.

A capital motto for a labouring man. *Father Matthew* and plenty of *murphies* will be of more use to the Irish than all the whisky of all the stills in the Emerald Isle.

More than we use, is more than we want.

Except so far as we make reasonable store, like Solomon's ant, whose ways he bids us consider and be wise.

More words than one go to a bargain.

Because one man says he would like it to be so, it does not follow that the matter is settled for both sides. It takes two to make a binding agreement; and that agreement should be well talked over by both parties before it is finally decided.

Morning dew is good for the eyes.

Our forefathers thought much of dew in May; hence the rhyme:

" The fair maid who, the first of May,
Goes to the fields at break of day,
And washes in dew from the hawthorn tree,
Will ever after handsome be."

But early rising at any time is beneficial to body and soul. "The muses love the morning," and so do the graces.

Most felt, least said.

Deep and true feeling often causes an eloquent silence. The frost of the mouth goes with the thaw of the soul. Waters that are deep do not babble as they flow.

Most horses that are very fat have fed by night as well as by day.

This is an insinuation that those persons who have amassed great riches have done things which would not bear the light. Let it be hoped that this is not largely true. It is true in a measure.

Most men get as good a wife as they deserve.

And some get a great deal better.

Most things are difficult before they are easy.

Most trees have enough rotten wood about them to burn them.

We have enough of evil tendency in our nature to ruin us.

Motherless husband makes happy wife.

We don't believe it. This is a shot at mothers-in-law, who are constantly made a butt of. Some of them deserve it, but many do not. Why not abuse fathers-in-law?

Mothers make men.

They have the formation of their boys' characters.

Mother's love is the cream of love.

It is most pure, holy, and unselfish. "A mother's heart is always with her children." Hence the return on the part of her sons of the sweet proverb, "The mother's breath is aye sweet," and that other: "There is no mother like the mother that bore us."

Mother's truth makes constant youth.

Doubtless a good man generally comes of a good mother. It was usually so in Scriptural times, and it is so still.

Mourning tendeth to mending.

Sorrow is salutary, and when blest to us by God's Spirit it leads to thought, and to our seeking for salvation.

Mouth and heart should never part.

True men speak only what they believe and feel. When the mouth is white and the heart black, the man has a plague upon him.

> When tongue and heart go different ways,
> The very soul of man decays.

Mr. Facing-both-ways is not to be trusted.

If we can scarcely trust an honest man, we ought by no means to put confidence in the double-faced.

Mr. Too-good is not Mr. Good-enough.

Those that think that they are a little better than there is need to be, may be sure that they are far below what they ought to be.

Mrs. Chatterbox is the mother of mischief.

They say that when ten portions of speech were given out, the women seized on nine of them; and, really, it would seem to be true of certain of them, though not more so than of the same order of men. Mr. Chatterbox is a worse mischief maker than his wife.

Much ado and little done.

Often the case; great horn-blowing, and yet no hunting. All sound and fury, and there's an end of it.

> The King of France with might and main,
> Marched up a hill and down again.

Much banqueting, quick bankruptcy.

No doubt the kitchen fire has often burned up the house, and the table has devoured the estate.

Much broth is often made with little meat.

Long talk and short sense often meet in one. A very long story is often concocted out of a very tender supply of fact. Lengthy discourses are also manufactured out of the tiniest measure of thought and doctrine.

Much chatter, little wit; much talk, little work.

Pope says :
> "Words are like leaves, and where they most abound
> Much fruit of sense beneath is rarely found."

Much din and little done.

Often the case in religious movements, and political contests.

Much haste, much waste; much drink, little chink.

Much illness is caused by the want of pure air:
To open your windows be ever your care.

> The fear of draughts leads many foolish people to live like rats in a drain. They dread fresh air, which is one of God's best gifts. Would they not have been happy in the Black Hole of Calcutta?

Much in bed, dull in head.

> Unnecessary sleep prevents men from fully waking up at any time. Many walk in their sleep all day long.

Much is expected where much is entrusted.

> Most justly and rightly so. "Unto whomsoever much is given, of him shall be much required."—Luke xii. 48.

Much kindred, much hindered.

> Demands from a large family and numerous poor relations, tend to keep a man poor. Still, there is a blessing in helping one's kin.

Much laughter, little wit.

> The flame is fast and furious when the fuel is light and unsubstantial. A bush blazes greatly, but the flame is soon over, and nothing remains. When people laugh at their own jokes their wit is very small beer, and is lost in its own froth.

Much rust needs a rough file.

> Hence the sharp afflictions which some of us require to put us in a right condition.

Much to read, and nought to understand,
Is to hunt much and nothing take by hand.

> It is possible for a great reader to become a donkey loaded with paper. Brains can be buried under a pile of books.

Much water runs by while the miller sleeps.

> Many opportunities are lost by neglect, and others by necessity; for there is a sleep which is needful as well as a slumber which is slothful. Be it how it may, the past is passed, and we can do nothing with it. The Poet was right when, listening to the clicking of the mill-wheel, he wrote—
>
> > "And a proverb haunts my mind,
> >   And as a spell is cast;
> > The mill will never grind
> >   With the water that is past."

Much would have more, and lost all.

Mud chokes no eels.

> They have lived in it too long to feel its foulness. Use is second nature. People who dwell in filth lose sensitiveness, and grow used to abominations. No doubt, to a fox his hole is sweet, and pigs think they are cleaning themselves in the mud. People should be clean now that soap is so advertised. Let us hope so.

Muddle at home
Makes husbands roam.

> Slatternly wives drive their husbands from the fireside; and if they go where they waste the money in drink, their wives may thank themselves for it.

Muddy spring, muddy stream.

> "Who can bring a clean thing out of an unclean?" A depraved parentage cannot bring forth perfect children. Impure motives produce unholy actions. Impure amusements create vice.

Music will not cure the toothache.

> Much less the headache. "Music has charms to soothe a savage breast;" but in great grief it becomes a trial rather than a solace, and we think the man who offers it "more fool than fiddler."

Must is a hard nut.

> There's no cracking it. We must even let it alone.

Must is for THE KING.

> He alone can say that so a thing must be: yet even he for our sakes came under a necessity of love. "He must needs go through Samaria."—John iv. 4. "I must work the works of him that sent me, while it is day."—John ix. 4.

Muzzle not the ox which treadeth out the corn.

> Don't starve the man who works hard to find you spiritual food.

Muzzled dogs bite no burglars.

> If we are not allowed to speak truth boldly, we cannot save the church from teachers of error. Dumb dogs are not worth their bones. If they will not bite burglars, what is the good of them?

My dame fed her hens on thanks, but they laid no eggs.

And men who earn nothing but compliments are not likely to be very diligent in so unprofitable a service. "Pretty Pussy" and "Pretty Pussy" will not feed a cat. Fine speeches make poor suppers, and votes of thanks are notes of nothing.

My daughter-in-law tucked up her sleeves and upset the kettle into the fire.

She went at it with desperate zeal, as most newly-aroused people do, and, therefore, in her hurry she did more harm than good. Some stir the fire and poke it out; others make up such a fire that they set the chimney alight, and burn the house down. Too much zeal may be as harmful as too little.

My house is my castle, but "The Castle" is not my house.

My kingdom is what I do, not what I have.

A clear conscience is better than a golden crown.

My mind to me a kingdom is.

The man is more to himself than an empire could be. Mind that your mind is worth the having, for it is your only kingdom.

My son's mother—where's such another?

There is one good wife in the country, and many a man *thinks* that he hath her; but I know a man who *knows* that he is the man who hath the best wife in all the world.

> My own dear wife,
> Joy of my life.

My ugly dog is a beauty.

To me he is by no means a horribly ugly pug, but his black muzzle and red tongue are charming; for he loves his master, and rejoices at the sound of his coming home.

Sayings of a more Spiritual Sort.

Make a crutch of your cross.

Use it as a help on the road to heaven.

Make a saviour of nothing but the Saviour.

Make God your end, and your joy shall have no end.

"Man's chief end is to glorify God, and to enjoy him for ever."

"What is my being but for thee,
Its sure support, its noblest end?
Thy ever smiling face to see,
And serve the cause of such a friend?"

Make the Sabbath a delight from morning to night.

The poet *Coleridge* said to a friend, one Sunday morning, "I feel as if God had, by giving the Sabbath, given fifty-two Springs in every year."

Make Thou my spirit white and clear
As the first snowdrop of the year.

Man's extremity is God's opportunity.

Let the believer who is sorely tried remember this. The darkest part of the night is that which precedes the dawning of the day. When we are quite empty, the Lord will fill us.

Man's holiness is "Much-ado-about-nothing."

Man's life's a book of history,
The leaves thereof are days;
The letters, mercies closely joined;
The title is God's praise.

Man's merit is a madman's dream.

The legal path proud nature loves right well,
Though yet 'tis but the cleanest road to hell.

Many have gifts from God, but not "the gift of God."

They have the comforts of life, but not eternal life.

Many things may dim a Christian's view of Christ, but nothing can separate him from Christ.

Many wear God's livery, but are not his servants.

Many worlds would not be enough for *one carnal* man ; but one heaven shall be enough for *all Christian* men.

Mary was not praised for sitting still, but for sitting **at the** feet of Jesus.

Meditation fits a man for supplication.

It provides thought-fuel for the flame of prayer.

Meekness is the bridle of anger.

It is love put to school to the Man of Sorrows.

Men cannot practise unless they know, but they know in vain if they practise not.

Men lose their lives by accident, but not their souls.

No. It is their wilful fault, and not their misfortune, which **ruins** the souls of men.

Men may live fools, but fools they cannot die.

If they die in their senses, conscience usually drives out **their** foolish indifference.

Men may live in crowds, but they die one by one.

A saying which recalls *Faber's* pathetic lines :

"Alone to land upon that shore,
To begin alone, to live for evermore ;
To have no one to teach
The manners or the speech
Of that new life, or put us at our ease ;
Oh, that we might die in pairs or companies !

"Alone ? The God we know is on that shore ;
The God of whose attractions we know more
Than of those who may appear
Nearest and dearest here.
Oh, is he not the life-long Friend we know
More privately than any friend below ? "

Men who love much, will work much.

"The love of Christ constraineth us." It is the most powerful of the forces which work for good.

Mercy despised brings misery deserved.

Mercy is "*from* everlasting" to contrive thy salvation, and "*to* everlasting" to perfect it.

Mercy is without price, and beyond all price.

> 'Tis heaven, and yet it is given away :
> 'Tis all in all, and yet "nothing to pay."

Mercy's gate opens to those who knock.

Ministers can persuade, but God alone can prevail.

We can explain truth, but God must apply it.

Ministers should be stars to give light, not clouds to obscure.

In some cases the text is as clear as a mirror, till the preacher's breath bedims it. We ought to pick out all hard words from our speech : good cooks stone the plums.

Ministers should study as if all depended on study, and preach knowing that all depends on the Holy Spirit.

Miseries often drive men to their mercies.

Even as the black dog drives the stray sheep to the shepherd.

Most men forget God all day, and ask him to remember them at night.

Most people would sooner be told their fortunes than their faults.

Yet the first would be an idle lie, and the other a practical truth.

Mourners in Zion are more blessed than merry-makers in the world.

"Blessed are they that mourn : for they shall be comforted." Matt. v. 4.

Mourning only lasts till morning with the children of the morning.

My only plea—
Christ died for me.

AG, nag, nagging,
  Is very, very fagging.

This may come from either side of the house, and it is equally bad whoever is the first hand at it. It is a weariness to hear it as a visitor; but it must be horrible to bear it as a partaker in it. We know instances in which the husband is the more guilty of the two; but that makes it none the better.

What *she* proposes,
  Be it good or bad,
He still opposes,
  Till he drives her mad.

As married people grow old, the tendency to correct each other in every trifling mistake is often developed; and it is so trying that they will be wise to watch against it with the utmost care.

Nail your colours to the mast.

If you carry the flag of truth, never strike your colours, nor sail under false ones. Never be a turncoat or a traitor.

Be ready to die,
But never deny.

Nails unclinched are unsafe.

Make assurance doubly sure. Do not hang much on a nail which is not surely fastened. We are not saved by faith when dealing with our fellow-men.

Narrowness of waist shows narrowness of mind.

Nobody with a large mind would think of injuring all the delicate organs within the body by wickedly compressing them within unnatural limits. There is neither sense nor beauty in a figure shaped like a wasp or a half-quartern loaf.

Nature abhors a vacuum.

When a man's head is empty some nonsense or other is sure to get in, and when his stomach is empty it will not be comfortable till it is filled. Empty purses also are very restless things.

Nature needeth nurture, minds want minding.

Even as the vine needeth pruning,
And the harp still needeth tuning.

Nature, though driven out with a fork, will return.

So said the Latins: nature will assert itself, and have its way.

Near to church should not be late to service.

Yet is it often so. People who can run in so quickly wait till the last moment; till we half think that "the nearer the church the further from God."

Necessity cannot stand upon nicety.

It dispenses with decorum, and knows no law.

Necessity is a hard nurse, but she raises strong children.

Captain Butler, recounting his hardships in the Great Lone Land, says, "And yet how easy it all was, and how soundly one slept! *simply because one had to do it.* That one consideration is the greatest expounder of the possible." The sons of need are driven to exertion: their muscle is tried and strengthened, and we get a race of sturdy, independent men.

Hard work and harder fare
Breed men of vigour rare.

Necessity is the mother of invention.

When a want becomes pressing and common, somebody's mind is exercised to supply it, and a new discovery is the result. The necessity of the masses is great; how can we reach them? Now for a holy invention!

Necessity makes lame men run.

It would cure many a nervous lady if she had to work for her living, and many a dyspeptic man would be well if he lived upon sixpence a day, and earned it. We know not our force till we are forced to know it.

Necessity never made a good bargain.

Because the man wants money so badly that he cannot wait, but must take whatever he can get. This is the reason why poor manufacturers have so bad a market: they must sell, or be sold up.

Necessity sharpens industry.

The call for daily bread sets all the world to work, and rigorous climates tutor men to hardihood of labour. A man driven by distress will do as much as thirty, at least the Spaniards say so.

Adam delved and Eve span;
Need allowed no gentleman.

Necessity's budget is full of schemes.

> Kite-flying, speculation, day-dreaming, &c., make up the stock-in-trade of men who are hard up for hard cash.

Necks may be bent by the sword, but hearts will only bend to hearts.

> So say the Arabs; and they ought to know, for they once set up an empire by force, and they have seen it melt away.

Need is the frying-pan, but debt is the fire.

> Whatever trouble it may cause us to bear the want of comforts, we shall gain no comfort by running into debt.

Needles and pins, needles and pins;
When a man marries his trouble begins.

> A Quaker who married a couple said, "Now you are at the end of your troubles." Some time after, the afflicted husband reminded him of the saying, and charged him with misleading him. "Nay," said the friend, "I said ye were at the end of your troubles, but I did not say at which end."

Needles are not sharp at both ends.

> We ought not to be all sharpness; we must have an eye as well as a point—judgment as well as courage.

Ne'er let your tongue outrun your wit:
Wise men full oft in silence sit.

Neighbours are good when they are neighbourly.

> Some say, "No neighbour is best"; but another says, "No one is rich enough to do without his neighbour." Good neighbours make good neighbours. He that would have good neighbours must show himself neighbourly.

Neither break law nor go to law.

> Keep law, and keep from law.

Neither colour the truth nor the face.

> "When fair, no colour is required :
> When true, no colour is desired."

Neither crow nor croak.

> Neither of those sounds is becoming in men; leave them to fowls and frogs.

Neither give nor take offence.

> The world would be happy and peaceful indeed,
> If all men on this point were always agreed.

Neither seek a secret nor speak a secret.

> Don't want to be told it, and if told it, never tell it again. When any would tell thee a secret, be deaf; but once having heard it, be dumb. Secrets are useless and dangerous curiosities.

Neither shoot without aim, nor speak without thought.

> Or you may do as much mischief by a hasty speech as by a random shot.
>
> > Sometimes our words
> > Hurt more than swords.

Neither trust nor contend,
Nor lay wagers nor lend,
And you may depend,
You'll have peace to your end.

> That is to say, as much peace as this troublesome world allows of. Great worries arise out of the four things mentioned; but the old rhyme can only be accepted with a grain of salt.

Nettles are to be boldly dealt with.

> > Tender-handed stroke a nettle,
> > And it stings you for your pains;
> > Grasp it like a man of mettle,
> > And it soft as silk remains.
> >
> > 'Tis the same with vulgar natures,
> > Use them kindly, they rebel;
> > But be rough as nutmeg graters,
> > And the rogues obey you well.

Never argue for victory, but for verity.

> Controversy would wear a very different complexion if this were observed. We ought to fight for truth, not for party.

Never ask pardon before you're accused.

For those who excuse themselves accuse themselves. **To answer** an idle rumour is to confirm it in the minds of many. **Why go** into the dock when you have never been summoned?

Never bark up the wrong tree.

Don't accuse the wrong man, nor denounce a procedure mistakenly. Be quite sure before you open your mouth.

Never barter a pearl for a pippin.

You will do this if you lose modesty for pleasure, and still more if you lose your soul to gain the world's applause.

Never be a dog in a manger to friend or stranger.

Nor to anyone else. Surely, what you do not require should be cheerfully given up to others who can use it.

> The cur could never eat the hay,
> And yet he drove the ox away :
> So some who ne'er a penny made
> Yet do their best to spoil the trade.

Never bet even a gooseberry.

A friend of mine, who was a great enemy to gambling, once felt so sure of a matter that he incautiously said, "I'll bet a thousand pounds to a gooseberry that it is so." His companion cried, "I'll take you," and entered the bet in a book. The good man was in some trouble because of the bet, and would have given the thousand pounds to be out of it. As it happened he was right, and his friend in mirthfulness sent him a silver gooseberry as his winnings; but he never used the phrase again, nor ventured on such treacherous ground. In this matter excessive caution is justifiable excess.

Never bite a farthing in two.

Nor split a plum, nor dispute about a casual expression, nor make miserable debates over mere trifles.

Never bite back at back biters.

If you do so, they have caused you a serious injury of soul by bringing you down to their level. Leave them their miserable trade to themselves. "Bless them that curse you."

Never boil your rabbit till you've got him.

There are many such proverbs, and hence we gather that people are very prone to deal with mere hopes as if they were realities; like the milkmaid with her eggs.

Never bray at an ass.

Let a foolish person have the talk to himself. Do not imitate his folly. Your silence will be quite as melodious as his voice.

Never buy a pig in a poke.

Examine the article before you part with your money. If you do not so, and are taken in, you will have yourself to blame. If the pig in the poke should turn out to be very lean, it will be no wonder. If it had been fat, the seller would have allowed you to see it.

Never cackle till your egg is laid.

And you need not do much of it when the brave deed is done; leave cackling and crowing to feathered fowl.

Never challenge another to do wrong, lest he sin at thy bidding.

And in that case thou wilt have to share the sin; for thou wilt have acted the part of the tempter.

Never comb a bald head.

Don't criticize where there is nothing to work upon. Treat a poor helpless man with tenderness. If a man has no religion, don't dispute with him about its doctrines. When you meet with a person who has no money, don't ask him for a contribution.

Never commit what you would wish to conceal.

Do only that which will bear the light of day.

Never despise the day of small things.

Whether good or bad, things must begin as littles.
Out of small,
Cometh all.
Even the great eagle was once in an egg, and the terrible lion was a playful cub. The mother of mischief is a midge's egg.

Never dispute about the wool of a cat.

See if there is anything in a question before you discuss it, or you may make much ado about nothing.

Never fall out with your bread and butter.

To find fault with the way in which you earn your living is very absurd. Speak well of the ravens which bring you your bread and flesh, and don't find fault with the brook of which you drink.

Never find fault with the absent.

It is cowardly. Accuse a man when he can defend himself.

Never fish in troubled waters.

Or you may draw forth trouble for yourself. Yet some read the proverb the other way, and delight in a stir, because troubled waters are best for their sort of fishing.

Never flog the dead.

They cannot be improved by your remarks, neither can they meet your charges. Let them sleep on. When an error is clean dead, do not go on disproving it, lest, like the boy with his top, you set it going again by whipping it.

Never fry a fish till it's caught.

It will be a waste of fire and butter to attempt it. Yet angry folks threaten loudly what they will do when they get us in their power. *When?*

Never give up the ship.

Stand to your trust. As long as she is above water, never desert the ship; as long as hope remains, do not give up a good undertaking. Above all, never quit the glorious ship of the church, in which our Lord is captain: she will never go down.

Never grudge a penny for a pennyworth.

Pay a fair price cheerfully, and do not beat down the seller; for he in his turn will have to sweat the workman.

Never grumble nor mumble.

> Take things as they come,
> Eat crust as well as crumb.

As for mumbling, when men are making a complaining speech, they generally talk so fast that they eat one-half of their words, and whistle the rest. It would not matter much if they whistled all of them, for they are not worth much.

Never hang a man twice for one offence.

If he has borne his punishment, cease to persecute him. Some accusers can never have done; they would hang a man every morning for the offence of years ago.

Never have an idle hour, or an idle pound.

For these are buried talents, the Lord's goods wasted.

Never hold a candle to the devil.

Do not aid him in his work, nor pay deference to the powers of evil. "To hold a candle to the devil" is to abet an evil-doer out of fawning fear. The allusion is to the story of an old woman, who set one wax taper before the image of St. Michael, and another before the devil whom he was trampling under foot. Being reproved for paying such honour to Satan, she naïvely replied, "Ye see, your honour, it's quite uncertain which place I shall go to at last, and sure you'll not blame a poor woman for securing a friend in each." This policy is the sure way to ruin.

Never is a long day.

Therefore it is well not to vow so indefinitely, for we may change our mind. Moreover, it is wise never to despair, or say that we shall never be happy again; for after a while things will look brighter.

Never judge a horse by its harness, nor a man or a woman by outward appearances.

Very poor horses may be finely caparisoned, or decked with ribbons at a fair; and the same is true of two-legged creatures.

Never lean on a broken staff.

This you do whenever you trust in man; especially in yourself.

Never leave a certainty for an uncertainty.

Multitudes have quitted a small assured income for "the larger hope" of speculation. They have left rock for sand, and have been swallowed up. The same is specially true in religious matters.

Never leave till afternoon what can be done in the morning.

This the boy quoted as a reason for eating all the cheese for breakfast. In other directions it is a good rule of promptitude. We are informed that this proverb does not apply to lawyers, with whom "Procrastination is the hinge of business."

Never let plain-dealing die.

If all the world should twist and twine,
Still be thou straight as plummet line.

Never look for a knot in a bulrush.

Don't look for difficulties where there are none.

Never look for a ram with five feet.

Expect not the abnormal, the monstrous, the singular. Leave " the Derby ram " to those who are in love with penny shows.

Never look for pippins on a crab-tree.

Everything yields according to its nature. Sour yields sour, and it would be folly to look for sweet from it.

Never meet trouble half-way.

It will come soon enough, and then you will meet it where God meant you should meet it, and where he will help you to bear it.

Never mind who was your grandfather: what are you?

The man who has nothing to boast of but his good ancestors, is like a potato : all that is good of him is under ground. So said an author long since under ground himself.

Never mix mirth and malice.

It is a sort of treachery to do so : like Absalom inviting Amnon to a feast to kill him.

Never offer to teach fish to swim.

They know better than you do. It is absurd for young green-horns to set up to instruct experienced persons.

Never overdrive
The best horse alive.

He is just the horse you ought to take care of. If he be a weak horse it is cruel to overdrive him, and if he is a willing horse it is unfair to take advantage of him.

Never play with a mad dog.

Or you will soon have cause to repent of your play. Do not sport with sin, or speculate in false doctrine. Keep out of the way when a man is in a savage temper.

Never prophesy till you know.

And then it is too late to foretell. We had better not so despise prophesyings as to think ourselves capable of manufacturing them.

Never put your finger between the anvil and the hammer.

> Keep clear of violent opponents when they are in full action, or you may receive upon yourself the force of their blows.
>
> > Who interferes gets double blow :
> > It's not my business, off I go.

Never put your hand into a wasp's nest.

> It will be prudent to respect the quiet of that domestic circle. *Josh Billings* says, " When I see the tail of a rattlesnake sticking out of a hole, I say to myself, 'That hole belongs to that snake, and I am not going to try to take it from him. I believe in respecting the rights of property.'" Even if a man does not regard the rights of others, it may often be wise for him to consider his own peace before he commences to meddle.

Never raise
Your own praise.

> "Let another man praise thee, and not thine own mouth."—Prov. xxvii. 2.

Never ride a broken-kneed horse.

> Trust not the man who has failed you. Moreover, he who has been a bankrupt once is very apt to fail a second time : be cautious.
>
> > Thou didst deceive : the fault was thine.
> > A second time it will be mine.

Never roast so as to burn, nor sport so as to sin.

> Observe the bounds of righteousness, kindness, and truth.

Never say die !
Up, man, and try !

> Despondency does nothing ; perseverance works wonders.

Never say die till you're dead, and then it's no use.

> Bravely hold on, and do not give way to despondency under any circumstances whatever. (Easier said than done.)

Never say of another what you would not have him hear.

> This precept would put the extinguisher on many a tattler.

Never sell your customers by selling bad goods.

> It will be a rogue's action, and in the long run you will yourself, and be obliged to shut up shop.

Never shirk the hardest work.

Some do so habitually. If they can live on others they will not do a hand's turn. The age of chivalry is over, but the age of loafers lasts for ever. Let us be of another clan. Two negroes were loading goods into a cart. One of them was disposed to shirk; the other stopped, and looking sharply at the lazy one, said, "*Sam, do you expect to go to heaven?*" "*Yes.*" "*Then take hold and lift.*"

Never sigh, but send.

Do not long for a thing despondingly, but do your best to get it, if it is to be had, and is really desirable.

Never speak ill of those whose bread you eat.

Even a dog knows who feeds him. If he bites his keeper, he is likely to be hanged, and nobody will pity him.

Never stint soap and water.

The soap-makers seem, to judge by their advertisements, to be doing a thriving business; but we still know a few people who need to patronize them. We do not admire Pharisees, but we should like to see some persons become Pharisaical in one respect, namely, in their objection to eat with unwashen hands.

Never stint the cause of God.

Cut down expenses for self before you diminish offerings to God.

Never swap horses while crossing a stream.

While a difficult business is going on, make as few changes as possible. *Abraham Lincoln* quoted this with much effect.

Never tell in the parlour what you heard in the kitchen.

Servants' gossip, if repeated, may make mischief, and it cannot possibly do any good. Carry no slops into the parlour.
He that heareth much, and speaks not at all,
Shall be welcome both in kitchen and hall.

Never throw a hen's egg at a sparrow.

That will be an expensive throw. Do not spend a pound in the hope of getting a groat, nor waste great effort on an insignificant object.

Never too old to turn; never too late to learn.

If not too old to sin, we are not too old to repent.

Never trouble yourself with trouble till trouble troubles you.

Forestalling trouble is like burning yourself at a fire before it is lit. *Mr. S. C. Hall* tells of an underwriter at Lloyd's, an excellent and estimable gentleman, who had all his wealth in ventures on the sea, or thought he had. One night a terrific storm shook the house in which he lived. He awoke frightened, was haunted by a terror that all his ships were wrecked, and that he was ruined; and he was found in the morning under his garden hedge dead, having taken laudanum. It was afterwards ascertained that his losses were trifling.

Never trust a man who speaks ill of his mother.

He must be base at heart. If he turns on her that bore him, he will turn on you sooner or later.

Never trust a swearer, nor believe a boaster.

A friend once drove me out to a village to preach, and he put up his horse at an inn. When we stopped, the ostler used profane language at some one in the yard. I noticed that my friend did not come in to the service, and on asking him why, he replied: "I stopped in the stable to see my horse eat his feed of corn; for I felt sure that the ostler would steal it. He that will swear will steal." I admired his wisdom, and I doubt not that his horse profited thereby; for a swearing ostler is likely to be an oat-stealer.

Never trust a wolf with the care of lambs.

And least of all if he offers to do it for nothing. He will take it out in lamb.

Never try to prove what nobody doubts.

This is often done by preachers, and the result is that ever so many are made to doubt who never doubted before. It is like the minister who spent his time in harmonizing the four evangelists, and the old woman said, "Our minister is well set to work to try and make four men agree who never fell out." There is so much of this useless labour done, that the necessary work of preaching the gospel gets neglected. In *Carlyle's Reminiscences* we find an appropriate illustration: "Accidentally, one Sunday evening, I heard the famous Dr. Hall (of Leicester) preach; a flabby, puffy, but massy, earnest, forcible looking man, *homme alors célèbre!* Sermon extempore; text, 'God, who cannot lie.' He proved beyond shadow of doubt, in a really forcible but most superfluous way, that God never lied (had no need to do it, &c). 'As good prove that God never fought a duel,' sniffed Badams on my reporting at home."

Never use religion as a stalking-horse.

When a man endeavours to take you in by religious talk, he imitates the devil, of whom the French negroes say, that when he wants to get a man into his clutches he talks to him about God. Very hateful is this trying to make gain by the false pretence of superior godliness.

Never wake a sleeping lion.

Rouse not angry man or woman. Don't stir the fire of strife when it is dying out.

Never wash sheep in scalding water.

This is done when the faults of good men are rebuked in anger. They are Christ's sheep, and must be tended with gentleness akin to that of the Great Shepherd of souls. We have heard it said of certain hot-tempered church members, that they must have been baptized in boiling water. The fewer of such the better.

Never wear mourning before the dead man is in his coffin.

This is a Creole warning against anticipating evil for others. It may not come, and then malicious forecasts will prove wicked folly.

Never write what you dare not sign.

An anonymous letter-writer is a sort of assassin, who wears a mask, and stabs in the dark. Such a man is a fiend with a pen. If discovered, the wretch will be steeped in the blackest infamy.

New bread is a waster, but mouldy is worse; Day old suits the stomach, and also the purse.

Housekeepers will endorse this, and perhaps be glad to quote it to those who grumble for new bread.

New breeches shame an old coat.

Partial reformations only make old faults the more glaring. When we morally improve, we need a new suit from top to toe.

New churches and new taverns are seldom empty.

People rush to see the new place; like children who are eager to play with a new toy.

New corn grows in old fields.

There can be no need to run off to the fresh fields of new theology: the old land of promise bears food ever new.

New hearts are more needful than new hats.

> Those who are so particular about their go-to-meeting clothes should take good note of this.

New things are fine to look at.

> But whether they will be as fine in the using remains to be seen; or, quite as likely, not to be seen. Fine new rubbish is common.

Newspapers are the Bibles of worldlings.

> How diligently they read them! Here they find their law and profits, their judges and chronicles, their epistles and revelations.

Next to no wife a good wife is best.

> This must have been the grunt of some spiteful old bachelor, or of a bad husband who never deserved a wife. Solomon says, "He that findeth a wife findeth a good thing."

Nick-names are stick-names.

> There is no shaking them off. Therefore let us not be guilty of affixing them to anyone. Call every man by his proper name.

Nightingales will not sing in a cage.

> Liberty is essential to the full development of talent.

Nine tailors cannot make a man.

> Nor ninety of them. Yet some think so, and dote upon the fashions. One tailor can make a masher, but that is not a man.

No answer is also an answer.

> And it will be wise in many cases to accept it as such.

No Autumn fruit without Spring blossoms.

> There must be the hopeful beginning of repentance and faith, or there will be no enduring piety.

No bees, no honey;
No work, no money.

No carrion will poison a crow.

> It is used to the filthiness. So, no immorality disgusts a man of debauched habits, and no error will be too flagrant for one who has truth.

No cloth is too fine for moth to devour.

No estate is too honourable to be touched by decay; no man too great to die; no character too established to be injured.

No cross, no crown.

No conflict, no conquest.

No cure, no pay.

A fair principle, but it might be carried still further with advantage. Kien Long, Emperor of China, enquired of Sir G. Staunton the manner in which physicians were paid in England. When, with some difficulty, his majesty was made to comprehend the manner of paying physicians in England for the time that the patients were sick, he exclaimed: "Is any man well in England who can afford to be ill? Now I will inform you how I manage my physicians! I have four, to whom the care of my health is committed; a certain weekly salary is allowed them; but the moment I am ill, the salary stops till I am well again. I need not inform you that my illnesses are very short."

No fishing like fishing in the sea.

There you have plenty of room, and the largest sort of fish. A man naturally desires scope for his endeavours, whether he is engaged in business, in literary pursuits, or in religious work.

No fool was ever so foolish but some one thought him clever.

Let us hope that his wife and children think him a fine fellow: they will, if they love him; for love is blind.

No frost can freeze providence.

Despite all weathers, the river of God flows on. In the very worst of times God's providence is to the believer an ample heritage.

No gains without pains.

At least, none to be relied upon: windfalls are generally rotten apples; the sea of chance mostly washes up empty shells. In all labour there is profit; but labour withheld withholds the gains on which men live.

> " No gold is found beneath the ground
>   By idleness or shirking;
> The noblest brains have labour pains,
>   And live by honest working."

No gift on earth pure water can excel ;
Nature's the brewer, and she brews it well.

> "Not in the simmering still, over smoking fires, choked with poisonous gases, and surrounded with the stench of sickening odours and rank corruption, doth your Father in heaven prepare the precious essence of life, pure, cold water; but in the green glade and grassy dell, where the red deer wanders, and the child loves to play. There God himself brews it, and down, low down in the deepest valleys, where the fountains murmur and the rills sing ; and high upon the mountain-tops, where the naked granite glitters like gold in the sun; where the hurricane howls music; where big waves roar the chorus, 'sweeping the march of God'—there he brews it, that beverage of life, health-giving water !"

No grave-digger can bury the truth.

> Or if he did, it would have a resurrection.

No greater promisers than those who have nothing to give.

> They are lavish with a generosity which cannot cost them anything; but it is all wind. Here is another application of the proverb: "All this will I give thee," said Satan; but out of all the kingdoms of the world not one of them was really his to give. Satan owns nothing but sin ; and he is so great a liar that he will not own to that.

No horse so bold as the blind mare.

> She sees no danger, and therefore knows no fear. No men are more reckless than the utterly stupid, who have not sense enough to know the perils which surround them.

No house without mouse ; no throne without thorn.

> Both great and little people have their troubles. Thorns grow at Windsor as well as at Whitechapel.

No joy without alloy.

> No gain on earth without its loss ;
> No back of man without its cross ;
> No pleasure here without its pain :
> This earth and earthly things are vain.

No land without stones,
No meat without bones.

> Some measure of loss and discomfort attends all earthly affairs, and there is no use hoping to find perfection in an imperfect world.

4

No man can call again yesterday.

> He may call, but it will not come. It is "with the years beyond the flood." Take time in time.

No man can make a good coat with bad cloth;

> Nor fashion a pure life on bad principles, nor form a good government with bad men, nor a holy church with unregenerate persons.

No man hath a velvet cross.

> Neither hath he an iron one, though it may be painted with iron colours. Each man has a real burden to bear.

No man is always wise except a fool.

> The man who makes no mistakes usually makes nothing. The fool's abiding wisdom is the invention of his own folly. We have all blundered.
>
> > "If every one who's played the fool
> > Had died and turned to clay,
> > How many people would be left
> > Alive and well to-day?"

No man is bound to snuff the moon.

> We cannot alter the laws of nature, nor mend that which is of necessity beyond our reach.

No man is made top-heavy by a pull at the pump.

> He may empty the bucket, but he will not take a drop too much, so as to make him half-seas over.

No man is the worse for knowing the worst of himself.

> He will be the more humble and cautious. So far to know the worst helps towards the best. The celebrated Abernethy often gave this advice to the students of his hospital class: "Gentlemen, probe always to the bottom; find out the worst; and then act."

No man should live in this world who has nothing to do in it.

> > He who will not live by toil
> > Has no right on English soil.

No mill, no meal; no sweat, no sweet.

No need to be a cripple because crutches are cheap.

We must not be feeble in grace because help will come, nor fall into sin because repentance is accepted, nor limp with despondency because there are gracious consolations.

No news is good news;

For if there were an evil to tell, it would have been told you. It is the wisest course to hope that when no complaint reaches you, all is going well: it is generally so.

No one eats gold fish: riches yield small comfort.

In the life of the Rev. W. Harness it is said, "that when at Deepdene the tone of conversation amused him much, as when Rothschild observed to Hope that a man must be a poor scoundrel who could not afford to lose two millions, or replied to a nobleman who said he must be a supremely happy man: 'I happy! when only this morning I received a letter from a man to say, that if I did not send him £500, he would blow out my brains.'"

THE SENTENCES WHICH FOLLOW ARE THE SAYINGS OF CATWG THE WISE:—

No one is discreet but he that perceives himself to be simple:
No one is knowing but he that knows himself:
No one is mighty but he that conquers himself:
No one is sensible but he that is aware of his misconception:
No one is wise but he that understands his ignorance:
No one is watchful but he that watches over himself:
No one is wary but he that avoids what his desire craves for:
No one is blind but he that sees not his own fault:
No one is discerning but he that discerns his own failing:
No one is strong but he that overcomes his weakness.

No one is so poor as he was when he came into the world.

We brought nothing with us when we came hither. "Look," said one, "at that man: he is rich, and yet he is a nobody; for he came into this parish without a second shirt." "Well, well," said one who stood by, "you were born here, and so you came into the parish without even one shirt."

No one knows the weight of another's burden.

Hence the lack of sympathy. It is said that "other people's trials are easy to bear." Nay, some go the length of saying that "the misfortunes of our friends are not altogether painful to us." This last, it is to be hoped, is a calumny.

No one likes to bell the cat.

The mice all say, "Let a bell be fastened to the cat's neck," but no one mouse will accept the task himself. Here and there a brave soul cries, "I'll bell the cat." Bravo !

> In words to draw a pretty plan
> Is easy work for any man ;
> To execute the scheme designed,
> The proper man is hard to find.

No one man
All things can.

It would be a pity he should, for then there would be nothing for the rest of us to work at.

No one pays God, but all should praise God.

Praise is our peppercorn of rent to the great Owner of all things ; and it is such a joy to pay it, that he who robs God of praise robs himself of pleasure.

No pain, no palm.

We must endure the toil and the suffering, or we may not expect the reward. The winner must first be a runner.

No piper can please all ears.

Nor can any preacher do so. Two aged women of a village where John Foster preached gratuitously, were greatly divided in opinion respecting him—one setting him down for "a perfect fool," the other "longing to hear that good man all the winter."

No road is good if it leads to a bad end.

Pleasant it may seem, but not to those who see the dreadful end.

No Rome Rule for England or Ireland.
No sauce like appetite.

. This is the "Chef Sauce." This puts a flavour into dry bread.

No sense so uncommon as common sense.

> Old John Brown, of Haddington, used to address his students of the first year to this effect :—"Gentlemen, ye need three things to make ye good ministers; ye need learning, and grace, and common sense. As for the learning, I'll try to set ye in the way of it; as for the grace, ye must always pray for it; but if ye havena brought the common sense with ye, ye may go about your business."

No shine but hath its shade.

> "All sun," say the Arabs, "makes the desert."

No showers, no flowers, nor summer bowers.

> "God sendeth sun, He sendeth shower;
> Alike they're needful for the flower;
> And joys and tears alike are sent
> To give the soul fit nourishment:
> As comes to me or cloud or sun,
> Father, Thy will, not mine, be done."

No two things can agree much worse
Than notions high and beggar's purse.

> They irritate their owner. His tastes call for a large expenditure, but his purse forbids it, and so he is dragged to and fro by opposing forces. He must lower his notions, or he will be an unhappy man.

No whip cuts so sharply as the lash of conscience.

> Those under conviction of sin are in more pain than a felon at the whipping-post. Flesh-pain is terrible, but soul-pain drives the man to madness.

No wonder if he breaks his shins that walks in the dark.

> Of course he stumbles, for he cannot see his way. When we quit the light of God's Word we are on the way to many a blunder, stumble and fall.

No wool is so white that the dye cannot make it black.

> The best character will be injured by society. The cleanest reputation can be darkened by slander.

No word is ill spoken if it be not ill taken.

> Really unkind words have been made to lose their sting by being left unnoticed. If we won't be offended, nobody can offend us.

No work is worse than overwork.

Nobility without ability, is like a pudding without suet.

> A noble nobody is a poor peer, a barren baron, a benighted knight, a count of no account.

Nobody calls himself rogue.

> 'Tis not likely he would; and yet when he calls himself he calls a rogue.

Nobody can live longer in peace than his neighbour pleases.

> That neighbour can pick a quarrel if he pleases; and the less cause he has for it, the more fiercely will he contend.

Nobody can repeat it if it is not said.

Nobody may quarrel in my house except the cat and dog.

> And they are so friendly that to me a cat-and-dog life seems a most desirable one.

None are so credulous as the incredulous.

> No one is so readily duped as the sceptic. Nobody thinks he knows so much as the man who calls himself an agnostic, or knows nothing.

None are so well shod but they may slip.

> Therefore let no man presume that he can never fall.

None but fools and knaves lay wagers.

> When thou art sager,
> Thou'lt lay no wager.

None can tell what's in the husk until it's shelled.

> Many matters must be left for time to reveal.

None so blind as those who will not see.

> Prejudice makes a man resolve that he will not see, and he becomes blind indeed. No blinkers are like those of conceit. If a man will shut his eyes because he knows enough already, how can we make him see?

None so busy as those who do nothing.

None think the great unhappy but the great.

Nonsense is not sense.

Not a long day, but a good heart, gets through work.

> The longest day is not long enough for some to do their work in, for they are not in love with it. Of the slothful man Solomon says: "His hands refuse to work." We know the breed. An officer, seeing a man professedly employed in breaking stones for the road, doing his work as if he were half asleep, said, "Take care, my man, you will break that stone." "Oh, no, your honour," was the reply, "I knows too well for that."

Not all the strongest live the longest.

> It was said of Henry Jenkins, who was older than Old Parr:
>
>> He lived longer than men who were stronger,
>> And was too old to live any longer.

Not every light is the sun.

> Why praise up a farthing candle as if it were the orb of day? Some are greatly given to such laudations.

Not every parish priest can wear Martin Luther's shoes.

> Yet he probably thinks he can. If some men could but see themselves once they would never look again. Possibly a little conceit may help some poor souls to do more than they otherwise would have the courage to attempt.

Not everything which fair doth show,
When proof is made will turn out so.

Not race, nor place, but grace makes a man.

> Such was the argument of the young lady whom Philip Henry desired to marry. She belonged to an old and wealthy family, and her father opposed the match. Mr. Henry, he admitted, was a scholar and gentleman of no ordinary type, but, "we do not know where he comes from." "Perhaps so," replied his daughter; "but we know where he is going, and I should like to go with him."

Not that which is much is well, but that which is well is much.

> The apparent quantity vanishes when the quality is found to be inferior. There is not so much in a pound of copper as in an ounce of gold. Truth is the test. Nothing can be great which is not right. A little which is consistent with righteousness has more in it than the great thing which is questionable.

Not to break is better than to mend.

Prevention is better than cure. A dish well rivetted is not so good as one which was never cracked.

Not to wish to recover is a mortal symptom.

He who does not desire to reform gives evidence of desperate sinfulness.

Nothing comes amiss to a hungry man.

To him, even bitter things are sweet.

> Be it cold, or be it hot,
> Hungry man refuses not.

Nothing endeavoured, nothing discovered:

If we do not try we shall never find out the way. Without effort we shall stick in the mud, and never get further.

Nothing is a man's truly,
But what he came by duly.

That which we gain wrongfully can never be rightfully ours. Be ashamed to harbour stolen goods.

Nothing is cheap if you don't want it.

A great bargain is a pick-purse. If merely bought because the price was low, and not because we needed it, it is dear.

Nothing is clean to a carrion crow.

Its eye searches out rottenness, and sees nothing else; and thus men of vile character believe others to be vile, spy out all their faults, and shut their eyes to their virtues, and speak evil of the good.

Nothing is safe from fault-finders.

Even *Milton's* "Paradise Lost" was censured by a hard-headed Scotchman because, said he, "It proves nothing." Even proverbs come under the lash of *Chesterfield's* elegance. He says, "A man of fashion never has recourse to proverbs and vulgar aphorisms."

Nothing is so graceful in a woman as grace.

When she is full of grace she is graceful indeed, and all are compelled to see the beauty of her character, whether she has beauty of person or not. Moreover,

> Grace will last
> When beauty is past.

Nothing is so strong as gentleness; nothing so gentle as strength.

Nothing sharpens sight like envy.

> It spies out the smallest fault, but at the same time refuses to see anything which might excuse it. Was there ever one so holy that envy would not see evil in him?

Nothing should be done in haste except catching fleas.

Nothing stands in need of lying but a lie.

> Truth is always consistent with itself, and needs nothing to help it out; it is always near at hand, sits upon our lips, and is ready to drop out before we are aware; a lie is troublesome, and sets a man's invention upon the rack, and one trick needs a great many more to make it good. It is like building upon a false foundation, which continually stands in need of props to shore it up, and proves at last more chargeable than to have raised a substantial building at first upon a true and solid foundation.—*Addison.*

Nothing succeeds like success.

> Men are apt to aid that which is getting on; the very report of success helps to make itself true. Hence a crafty man recommends another to look like getting on, or he never will get on.

Nothing that is violent is permanent.

> The rushing torrent is soon over, and so is it with other things of the same impetuous character. Gently goes far.

Nothing venture, nothing win.

> Some measure of risk must attend all trading. We must also venture all, even to life itself for Christ's cause.

Novels contain little that is novel.

> But, alas! much that is unnatural, and many a time that which is polluting. The lives of many are rendered false by reading false lives. Truth is made sick by fiction.

Now that I have a hat, others take off theirs to me.

> The man has come to be what the world calls "respectable," and he is respected accordingly, but he ought not to be proud, for the respect is evidently paid to the hat rather than its wearer.

Now that I have got no gun,
Rabbits run about like fun.

> But why not have had a gun? Opportunities often come to men who are not ready for them. Why are they not ready?

Now the poet's starved and dead,
Raise a stone above his head.

'Tis the old story of *Homer*, begging in life, and honoured in death. The man needs bread, and they give him a stone; but not even that till he is gone. Alas, poor world! thy gratitude. is as late as it is worthless: after death a stone!

Now the thief is out of sight,
The police have come to light.

Hardly fair! In many cases the police have been singularly prompt and courageous.

Now that I have a sheep and a cow everyone bids me good morrow.

So much does even the courtesy of our fellow-men depend upon our possessions. A court of law decided that a man who keeps a gig is respectable, and three acres and a cow are the recognized limit of competence. What is that respect worth which depends on our owning cows and sheep?

Now that I no longer need
I can get full many a feed.

People run to grease the fat sow. Who will not give to a prince? Poverty craves in vain, where wealth asks and receives.

Now is now here, but to-morrow's nowhere.

Now is the only time we have; even when to-morrow comes, if it ever comes, it will also be "now." So *Doddridge* put it :—

" Strength for to-day is all we need,
For there never will be a to-morrow ;
For to-morrow will prove but another to-day,
With its measure of joy and of sorrow."

'Now" is the watchword of the wise.

"To-morrow" is the devil's great ally—the very Goliath in whom he trusts for victory : "Now" is the stripling sent forth against him. A great significance lies in that little word; it marks the point on which life's battle turns. That spot is the Hougomont of life's Waterloo; there the victory is lost or won.—*Arnot.*

Nuts are given us, but we must crack them ourselves.

Providence does not spare us the necessity for exertion, even when it is most favourable. Herein is wisdom.

Sayings of a more Spiritual Sort.

Natural men are spiritual monsters.

> The natural man's heart is where his feet should be, fixed upon earth; his heels are lifted up against heaven, which his heart should be set on. His face is towards hell: his back towards heaven. He loves what he should hate, and hates what he should love; joys in what he ought to mourn for, and mourns for what he ought to rejoice in; glories in his shame, and is ashamed of his glory; abhors what he should desire, and desires what he should abhor.—*Boston.*

Neither neglect the means nor rest in the means.

> Services and Sacraments are to be humbly used as channels for the water of life, but they are not that life in themselves.

**Never dare to despair
While God answers prayer.**

> There is a strange presumption in the wicked act of doubting the goodness of the Lord.

New sinnings call for new repentings.

"No answer required."

> This note often accompanies messages sent to man, but oftener those sent up in prayer to God.

No grace, no glory.

No happiness without holiness.

> There is no felicity in what the world adores. That wherein God himself is happy, the holy angels are happy, and in whose defect the devils are unhappy—that dare I call happiness.—*Sir Thomas Browne.*

No man is necessary.

> With this saying of Napoleon, we may compare the sentence on the monument to the two Wesleys, in Westminster Abbey—"God buries his workmen, but carries on his work."

No pillow so soft as God's promise.

**No skin, no hair;
No grace, no prayer.**

> There can be no hair where there is no skin where there is no grace. A prayerless soul is a

None can pray well but he who lives well.

> Prayer will make us leave off sinning, or sinning will make us leave off praying.—*Fuller.*

None should wear the name of saints but those who have the nature of saints.

> The Seventh General Council which met at Constantinople in 754 under the Iconoclast Emperor Constantine V., decreed, "If any one spend his labour in setting up figures of saints, or lifeless and deaf images, which cannot do any good; and has no care to represent in himself their virtues as he finds them on record in the Scriptures, let him be Anathema." Equally worthy of condemnation are they who profess to be saints, but have nothing saintly about their character and life.

Not a leaf moves on the trees,
Unless the Lord himself doth please.

> The wind shall not blow on the earth, nor on the sea, nor on any tree, till the permission of God be given.—Rev. vii. 1.

Not more *than* Christ, but more *of* Christ.

Not to love God is madness.

> It shows a mind disordered by the madness of sin.

Nothing is simpler than faith, and nothing more sublime.

> Faith is simple from the human side: it is a childlike trust. But it is sublime from the divine side, since it grasps the Invisible, and has power with the Omnipotent.

Nought can be gained
By a Sabbath profaned.

THOU Nazarite, go about, go about, and do not come near the vineyard!

The meaning is, that we should avoid the occasions of sin. The Nazarite was forbidden the use of wine; and it was therefore his wisest course to avoid all occasions of trespassing, by even keeping out of the vineyard. In matters of evil it is well to avoid the appearance of it, and the suggestion of it. He who dreads a spark will not play with fire.

Oaks fall when reeds stand.

To yield may sometimes be greater wisdom than to defy the storm; and it is always so when the hand of God goes out against us. Then we must either bow or break.

Obedience should be a child's first lesson.

And it will need to be repeated. If he learns it well as a child, it will be the foundation of his character as a man. Colts must be broken in, or they will be useless horses. All human beings need to be taught obedience; for as *Judge Halyburton* says—"Wherever there is authority there is a natural inclination to disobedience."

Obedience to his master is the wisdom of the disciple.

Thus he learns practically, and if he does not learn practically, he does not learn truly. The apprentice learns his trade by working at it; and even so we must learn Christianity by living like the Lord Jesus Christ. He who will *do* shall *know*.

Obedient wives lead their husbands.

Sensible men know when they have good wives, and they are glad to let them manage the house, and lead them on to prosperity. The author of the "Five Talents of Woman" tells the following story :— "As a clergyman was riding through a village in Fifeshire one day, a man came out and stopped him, addressing him in the following remarkable words: 'D'ye mind, sir, yon day, when ye married me, and when I wad insist upon vowing to obey my wife? Weel, ye may now see that I was in the right. Whether ye wad or no, I hae obeyed my wife; and behold, I am now the only man that has a twa-storey house in the hale town!'"

Obey orders if you break owners.

Meaning that the result of obeying orders is not for the mariner's consideration. He is a man under authority: . . . . . m why.

Obstinacy is absurdity.

There are people who, like pigs, always go the reverse way to that in which they are driven. One pig went all the way upstairs by having his tail pulled downwards. So *Swift* wrote of a woman :—

> "Lose no time to contradict her,
> Nor endeavour to convict her,
> Only take this rule along,
> Always to advise her wrong,
> And reprove her when she's right,
> She will then grow wise for spite."

We recommend no such method ; but with some it might be more successful than good advice. There are men also of this breed ; and indeed the English stock has a full share of obstinacy in it ; so that one said, "The crest of the southern English is a hog, and their motto is, ' We wun't be druv'."

Of a little spend a little and save a little.

Give a little, too, to consecrate the whole. What we give in alms will prevent covetousness.

> What is given
> Stops the leaven.

Of all cocks the worst is a weathercock.

From its turning with every wind. Men who are twisted about by every breeze, and are not to be depended upon, become the objects of supreme contempt.

Of all crafts honesty is the master craft.

He who is not crafty, but candid and open, will carry the day in the long run against all the cunning in the world. Cunning is folly wearing the mask of prudence, wisdom soured with falsehood. But plain honesty so puzzles the men of policy that they suspect it is working a scheme of more than ordinary depth, and so it baffles them.

Of all tame beasts I like sluts least.

Nobody can endure them : they make you feel sick. Dirty dishes, foul linen, filthy rooms, and so forth, cause nausea to clean people.

Of all things, men are most fond of their wrong notions.

Even as mothers love most their weakest children.

Of bowers and scrapers beware.

Too much politeness is suspicious. When men bow very often, they may be suspected of stooping because they think there is something to pick up.

Of dead and gone speak good or none.

De mortuis nil nisi bonum. Which one translates, "Concerning the dead nothing but *bones*"; another says, "Nothing but a *bonus.*"

Of hard striving comes sure thriving.

> He that would thrive,
> His work must drive.
> If work drives thee,
> Right poor thou'lt be.

Of honey eat not thou too fast
Lest it should make thee sick at last.

Human praise is sweet to our pride, but it should be accepted sparingly. The same is true of all earthly pleasures.

Of Lions white and red beware;
They always take the lion's share.

It is curious that these mythical animals should so often be selected as signs for houses of entertainment. Is it because the weary traveller will there find something to lie on? Or because, by means of wines, white and red, many are apt to make beasts of themselves? A lawyer's clerk in Manchester, being requested by his employer to show a gentleman the "lions," took him to all the public-houses designated by the titles of "The Red Lion," "The Black Lion," "The White Lion," &c.; and the gentleman, enjoying the joke, "stood Sam" at each place; the result being, that the clerk returned to the office anyhow but sober. The "lions" had proved too much for him.

Of little meddling comes great ease.

But even a little meddling may destroy all ease. "Hands off" is a good word. It is easier to keep out of a mess than to get out of one. Medlars are poor fruit, and so are meddlers.

Of pepper take none in thy nose,
However much thy friends oppose.

Friends mean well, even when they do not agree with us; therefore, let us not take offence at them.

Of saving cometh having.

Yet you must "have" first. Some save r~
sequently have nothing in the hour of need.
everything, and even rob themselves of ~
really have nothing. May we b~ ~
have what we have to the glor~

Of smoothsayers and soothsayers beware.

Those who prophesy smooth things, and those who prophesy future things at all apart from the Scriptures, are dangerous people. Modern prophets are unprofitable.

Of the dead say only what is good.

And if nothing good can be spoken, say nothing, but conclude—

> Seeing he is dead,
> No more shall be said.

Of wasting cometh wanting.

Some have wasted roast meat, and have come to long even for the smell of it. How gladly would they now eat the crusts they threw to the hogs! Waste first makes want, and then makes it bitter.

Of what use is a violin to a deaf man?

There must be a capacity for enjoying, or there will be no enjoyment. It is of no use casting pearls before swine. Here is an amusing instance of the usefulness of literature to the utterly ignorant. An agent for a new cyclopædia tells this incident :— " Among those to whom I have shown the volumes I found but one young man who did not need the work. He has a cyclopædia, a number of large volumes ; he did not know how many, nor did he know the name of the editor or publisher ; but they are very large, heavy volumes. Believing he did not frequently consult them, I asked if he ever used them. ' Certainly,' said he, ' I use them every day.' ' What can you possibly do with them?' ' Why, I press my trousers with them.' " There was some use in the encyclopædia ; but we wonder how the deaf man would use the fiddle.

Offenders never pardon.

It is strangely true that the man who wrongs you hates you far more surely and maliciously than the man whom you have injured.

> Forgiveness to the injured must belong ;
> For they ne'er pardon who have done the wrong.

Oil and truth will yet,
Tho uppermost get.

There is no keeping truth under. It is from above, and it tends towards its source.

> Despair not thou! Though truth be beaten oft,
> In God's own time she shall be set aloft.

Old age is honourable, but youthful pride is abominable.

> Yet there is far too much of the latter.
>> "Now every boy's the old man's teacher:
>> The father's a fool, the child a preacher."

Old age makes the head white, but not always wise.

> Yet "with the aged is wisdom." If years do not teach, what will?

Old birds are hard to pluck.

> Meddle not with others at all, but be sure not to take up the cudgels with those whose experience has taught them to take care of themselves. Lay not your hand on the mane of an old lion.

Old birds are seldom caught by chaff,
Old rats by wooden trap or gin;
And if you dig a pit, my friend,
The chances are you'll tumble in.

Old dogs are in no hurry to bark.

> Old hounds do not begin yelping the moment they are out of the kennel, but they only get into full cry when they see the fox. Practised preachers do not commence with a loud voice, but wait till they warm to their subject, and then give it tongue.

Old foxes are caught at last.

> And generally when they conclude that no one can catch such very sensible, wide-awake people.

Old foxes are not easily caught.

>> They are wary because of former mishaps;
>> And therefore they fight very shy of your traps.
> Experience makes men open their eyes and keep them open, and they are not readily imposed upon after a good drilling in the consequences of believing all they hear.

Old foxes want no tutors.

> They know too much already. One who has lived long in such a world as this knows a thing or two. "An old Parliamentary hand" knows his way about. Proverbs about foxes are very plentiful; the fact being that the creature so brings up the idea of sport that men like to talk about him. There is a love of animals innate in most people.
>> While the rich are hunting foxes,
>> Poor men mend their rabbit box—

Old gold, old hay, old bread,
Stand a man in good stead.

> He who is always taken with that which is new will soon be caught in a noose. Last year's stack of hay in the yard is a pretty sight to him who has horses to feed.

Old gold, old truth, and old friend,
These are treasures to the end.

> Satisfy yourself with the tried and proved, and let others have novelties if they choose.

Old head and young hand.

> A good combination : prudence and energy.

Old heads will not suit young shoulders.

> It would be hypocrisy for youths to speak with the certainty, caution, and experience of old men. It is neither natural nor desirable that grey heads should grow on green necks.

Old is the boat, but it still keeps afloat.

> It is pleasant to see the aged still trying to be useful. We say, "The old ferry-boat will carry us over the river yet once more"; and so the worn-out man may yet again serve his God.

Old Lawrence has got hold of you.

> Which means that the man is in the power of the demon of laziness, St. Lawrence being the patron of idleness. Surely that is not the Lawrence who was martyred on a gridiron! And yet perhaps it is; for lazy people will find things rather hot in these days, even if they do not go to the grill-room of utter bankruptcy.

Old men are as anxious to live as the young.

> Willingness to depart comes not with years ; in fact, the longer men live, the more they cling to life. The man has breakfasted, dined, and supped ; and yet he is in no hurry to go to bed.
>
> > The tree of deepest root is found
> > Unwilling most to quit the ground.

Old ovens are soon heated.

> Men long given to sin are soon excited to a repetition of their vicious practices.

Old oxen have stiff horns.

When a man of years makes up his mind, he is not easily prevented from carrying out his purpose.

Old reckonings breed new disputes.

Old accounts smell abominably. There is nothing like clearing up as you go.

> To-day and to-day we pay and we pay,
> And this from obstructions cleareth the way.

Old sacks want much patching.

Old bodies want nourishing and doctoring; old businesses need fresh methods to suit the times; old corporations need reforming.

Old shoes are easiest, and old friends are best.

We are used to them; they fit us; and we cannot bear to part with them. Bring me my old slippers when my feet ache, and fetch me my old friend when my heart aches.

Old sins breed new shame.

When they rise in the conscience, or when they are talked of in the world, they bring the blush to the cheek.

Old thanks do not suffice for new gifts.

Gratitude should spring up perpetually. Praises, though rendered a little ago, must be renewed as fresh benefits are received.

Old tunes are sweetest, and old friends surest.

Oh, for the old music, before the fly-away-jack tunes came in ! Oh, for the like of the grand old men who are now in heaven ! True as steel they were, though nowadays they call them narrow.

Old wounds soon bleed.

Well do I remember a grey horse falling, bleeding terribly, and cutting itself wofully. I could not understand why it was so grievously hurt till I learned that it had been down before, and was now injured in the same place. It is so with old sins. Men are apt to bleed in the old spot.

Omission of good is commission of evil.

In other words, " Omitted duty is committed sin." How this should humble us when making confession of sin ! Who can measure what he might have done and should have done ?

Omit ornament if it straitens strength.

A man had a plain strong bow with which he could shoot far and true. He loved his bow so well that he would needs have it curiously carved by a cunning workman. It was done; and at the first trial the bow snapped. We may make our style of speaking so fine that it loses its force. It is foolish to sacrifice strength to elegance.

Omittance is no quittance.

If your creditor does not call for the money, it is just as much his due. Pay it like an honest man ; and don't hint that "You thought he had given it to you."

> That is the brogue
> Of an old rogue.

On a good bargain think twice.

Or else leave it without a thought. It may not be all it looks ; and if you do not need the article, it may be folly to buy it at any price. Why should people sell you goods under cost price?

On a long journey even a straw is heavy.

Because of the length of time you will have to carry it. The less luggage the better, and the less care the happier you will be.

On his own saddle one rides safest.

Where a man is most at home, he has least fear, and least danger. In one's own line of things one is least apt to slip.

On Monday morning don't be looking for Saturday night.

It will be reached soon enough if you work your passage to its shores.

On some men's bread butter will not stick.

Ne'er-do-wells seldom remain in comfort long. If you were to put them into a river they would soon be high and dry in the bed of it. They attribute it to being born under a twopenny planet; but the fault, dear sillies, is not in your stars, but in yourselves.

On the heels of folly shame will surely tread.

Shame is the estate which is entailed on fools.

On the sea one hath not the sea in his hands.

You must put up with its changes, and manage your vessel accordingly. So in business, we cannot arrange circumstances. The storms of life we can neither raise nor lull.

On the sea sail, on the land settle.

Act as circumstances require, and utilize all opportunities.

On the spree still sober be.

But our London people can scarcely enjoy a holiday without a fiddle and a fuddle.

On their own merits modest men are dumb.

Praise of self from a man's own lips is loathsome.

Once bit twice shy.

Prudence forbids putting your hand a second time within reach of a dog. He who had his head bitten off by a lion had no chance of putting this proverb in action. A friend of mine had a little dog which had been bitten by a larger dog, and ever afterwards refused to go near the place where this happened. Another dog, which had been scratched by a cat, would not go within a couple of fields of the house where the cat lived. Are not dogs wiser than men?

Once cut the cheese, and the cheese will soon cut.

Householders find it so.

> Only change a pound,
> And it can't be found.

Once shot you cannot stop the arrow.

> "A word once spoken can return no more ;
> A wise man sets a watch before the door.
> The bird in hand we may at will restrain ;
> But being flown, we call her back in vain."—*Whitney.*

One action does not make a habit.

But it may be the beginning of it. We may not say, "Once is never," but we may hope it is not always. Yet there is fear that one sin may force on another, as *Dryden* says—

> "He that once sins, like him who slides on ice,
> Goes swiftly down the slippery paths of vice."

One always hits himself in a sore place.

Persons think that they are being alluded to, and even insulted in a discourse, when they are not even thought of. They have a sore place, and so they are always being touched upon it. Conscience makes cowards of men.

One barber shaves another.

An infidel critic generally practises his art by cutting up the man who followed the same craft before him.

One barking dog sets all the street a-barking.

"Lie down, sir!" We can't afford to have all dogdom pouring forth its howls in our ears.

One beats the bush, and another gets the birds.

It is often so with inventors, originators, authors, and other persons of genius, who cannot produce their work without outside help. They have the labour, and others take the profit. The hen lays the egg, but the man eats it.

One body may as well have two souls, as one soul two masters.

One broken wheel spoils the machine.

One grave fault may ruin a character, one weak point may prevent the success of a scheme, and one bad man may hinder the prosperity of a whole church.

One can go a long way after he is tired.

Pluck will keep a man going long after his strength is spent.

One can't hinder the wind from blowing.

Nor gossips from tattling, nor fashions from changing, nor troubles from coming, nor heresies from spreading.

One day may be better than a whole year.

At any rate, there is no time like time present. At certain seasons more can be done in a single day, than at other times in quite a long period. Let us use each passing day energetically, and with a large hopefulness.

One dog can drive a flock of sheep.

One brave man may face a multitude without fear. *Alexander* said, "One butcher does not fear a herd of cattle."

One chick keeps a hen busy.

It will need all our care to bring up even a single child.

One drop of ink
May make a million think.

>   Great is the power of the pen.   How carefully it should be used !

One enemy is many too many.

>   "The man who has a thousand friends
>   Has not a friend to spare,
>   But he who has one enemy,
>   Will meet him everywhere."

One expense leads to another.

>   The Sanscrit proverb says, "To protect his rags from the rats he got a cat, to get milk for the cat he bought a cow, to tend the cow he hired a servant, and to manage his servant he procured a wife." An insolvent said that he was ruined by a new sofa; and he thus explained the mode of his ruin :—"That sofa was the bad *beginning* —it was too fine for me.   It made my old chairs and table look mean, and I had to buy new ones.   Then the curtains had to be renewed.   Then the furniture in the other rooms had to be sold, and new articles bought to correspond with the parlour.   Soon we found the house was not good enough for the furniture, and we removed into a larger mansion.   And now, here I am, in the Insolvent Court."

One eye of the master sees more than four of the servants.

>   For he has greater influence and control.   Trusting to others is not one quarter so effective as looking after the matter yourself.   Where should the eye be but in the head?

One eye-witness is worth more than ten hearsays.

>   Seeing is good evidence, and carries conviction with it.

One fact is worth a ship-load of opinions.

>   We don't want to know how you think it ought to be; but tell us how it is.   Religious opinions are fickle as the wind; but the facts of Scripture are firm as a rock.

One false move may lose the game.

>   It is so in life, although it is no game.   Hence the need of great caution.   The Chinese have a proverb, which *Mr. Scarborough* has translated :—

>> For one bad move, if you're to blame,
>> Be sure that you will lose the game.

One father maintains ten children better than ten children will maintain one father.

For shame! Let us hope this is a calumny; yet have we seen sad instances of unkindness on the part of sons.

One fool in a house is enough in all conscience.

Say rather, "is one too many." Where is there a family without this piece of furniture? There is no need for us to increase the fraternity. The Ancient Order of Stupids is very large.

One fool makes many.

By his absurd actions he may win attention, and hold a gaping crowd. His folly may lead others into folly. Crazes are catching.

One foot is better than two crutches.

Better far to be independent and walk on your own legs, than depend on borrowed help. The power of extempore speech is infinitely to be preferred to the best notes.

One frog croaks to another, so doth sorrow to sorrow.

Troubles are many. "Deep calleth unto deep." Like the frogs of Egypt, they come into the kneading-trough and the bedchamber; but yet in the Lord's time they will all be swept away when their purpose is accomplished.

One good mother is worth a hundred schoolmasters.

The master's law *compels*, but the mother's love *impels*. He polishes, but she has the first hand in the fashioning. The man never forgets what he learnt at his mother's knee. When the conflict between Church and State in Piedmont was at its height, a deputation of noble ladies from Chambery waited on the king, imploring him to revoke the decree by which the nuns of the Sacred Heart were expelled from their city. They declared that they saw no prospect of having their daughters properly educated if the pious sisterhood should be removed. The king listened attentively, and at the close of their appeal most courteously replied: "I believe you are mistaken. I know that there are at this moment in the town of Chambery many ladies much better qualified to educate your children than the Sisters of the Sacred Heart." The ladies looked surprised, exchanged inquiring glances, and at length begged the king to point out the pious teachers of whose existence they were ignorant. "The pious teachers," replied Victor Emmanuel, bowing more courteously than before, "are yourselves; your daughters can have no persons better qualified to superintend their education than their own mothers."

One good stroke does not prove me a woodman.

One happy speech does not warrant a man in setting up as an orator. Balaam's ass spoke well once, but it never tried it again. Altogether it differed greatly from its brethren.

One good turn deserves another.

One good yawner makes two.

"The adage understates the case. I verily believe that one good yawner might make a hundred such, if he only had a fair field for his operations."—*C. J. Dunphie.*

One hair of a woman draws more than a team of horses.

Their tenderness subdues the stubborn heart, and for good or for evil has a mighty force within it. Who can resist its charms?

One half the world does not know how the other half lives.

But this is not the fault of Mrs. Tattle, for she has done her best to let them know. If without gossip we could know more of each other's trials it would promote sympathy and charity.

One hand washes another.

Many show kindness in expectation of getting similar help. "Sinners also lend to sinners that they may receive as much again." Yet it is surely nothing less than nature that those who are members of the one spiritual body should promote the holiness of others, and should be zealous to defend their character.

One hard word brings on another.

Do not open the ball. There is no credit in throwing the first stone, for you may be accountable for all that follow it.

One has need of much wit to deal with a fool.

Because he misunderstands you, and, if trusted, he will lead you into great blunders. It would seem that his folly is catching, for often if there is one fool in a business there is more than one.

One head cannot hold all wisdom.

Therefore we excuse mistakes in others, and do not dare to think ourselves perfectly wise. It is a marvel that some men know so much. Remember the schoolmaster and the peasants—

"And still they gazed, and still the wonder grew,
That one small head should carry all he knew."

One hour's sleep before midnight is worth two after.

This is often quoted to get young folks to bed; and we suppose there must be truth in it. One said, "One hour before midnight is worth two after." "Yes," said the other "that is why I sit up, for I don't like to be wasting the best of the hours in sleep."

One is never so rich as when one moves house.

Then you turn up such a collection of goods, which you had quite forgotten, that you wonder where you will put them all.

> Old spoons and old rings,
> And all sorts of things.

One keep-clean is better than ten make-cleans.

Frequent fouling leaves its mark, and the washing wears the material. It is with morals, as with linens.

One lie makes many.

One lie must be thatched with another, or it will soon rain through. Lies breed like fleas, or aphides.

One lie needs seven lies to wait on it.

And they will not be enough to keep its train off the ground.

> Oh, what a tangled web we weave,
> When once we venture to deceive!

One link broken, the whole chain is broken.

An illustration of the great truth, that he who breaks one commandment is guilty of the whole law.

> If from a chain a single link you strike,
> Tenth or ten thousandth, breaks the chain alike.

One log does not burn well by itself.

Fellowship in religion is a great stimulus to the heat of piety. Burning coals heaped together hold the fire, where separate portions die out. Union is force of fervour, as well as of strength.

One loss brings another.

In the Telugu we read, "First, he lost his horse, and then he had to pay for digging a pit in which to bury it." Merchants and traders know how one link of loss is part of a chain, and draws on other links. When one nine-pin falls it upsets others.

One man is worth a hundred, and a hundred is not worth one.

Many a time a solitary champion has won the victory, and far oftener a band of warriors has been scattered. The concentration of one may surpass the divided force of a hundred. One man with God on his side is more than a match for the whole world.

One man is no man.

Without followers the leader is nothing. One oar cannot win the boat race, even though it be the stroke oar. One man is invaluable as a captain, yet a captain can do nothing without his crew. It needs many men to man a ship, and many arms to make an army.

One man makes a chair, and another sits in it.

This is division of labour. He that sits in it may have less pleasure in it than he who made it, especially if he be the chairman of a noisy public meeting.

One man may better steal a horse, than another look over the hedge.

The first man has a character, and no one thinks that he will do wrong; the other is too well known to be trusted. No doubt also the world practises gross favouritism, and allows to one person liberties which it denies to another.

One man may lead a horse to the water, but twenty cannot make him drink.

We may preach the gospel, but only God's grace can lead a man to receive it into his heart. We may lead to the green pastures, but only the Good Shepherd can make the sheep to lie down therein.

One man may teach another to speak, but none can teach another to hold his peace.

The silent man must in this respect be self-made. He has mastered the greatest point of oratory. That is the true Chrysostom, or golden mouth, which can be kept closed at proper times.

> To use the tongue in speech is great,
> But greater to refrain:
> Thousands have taught the art to prate,
> Not one the tongue to rein.

One man with one eye sees more than twenty men without eyes.

Hence, one spiritually enlightened m
nation of worldlings.

One man's fault should be another man's lesson.

Instead of which it is too often another man's gossip. The right use of an observed fault is to talk to yourself about it, and to say nothing to anyone else.

One man's meat is another man's poison.

Certainly it is so, if the old saws were ever true which describe the health-giving food of our ancestors; for we should die on such diet. Take, for instance, the West-country rhyme:

> Eat leeks in March, and garlic in May,
> And all the year after physicians may play.

After such odorous and odious food one might well find doctors and everybody else keeping as far off as possible. Another proverb says:

> Eat an apple going to bed,
> Make the doctor beg his bread.

We should not like to try the prescription, unless the apple had been well roasted. We prefer the notion that "fruit is gold in the morning, silver at noon, and lead at night."

One master passion in the breast,
Like Aaron's serpent, swallows up the rest.

One may buy gold too dear.

If you part with princi le to procure it, or suffer spiritual loss to gain it. It is not of everp place that it could be said, "And the gold of that land is good."

One may have good eyes, and see nothing.

We have plenty of proofs of this, especially when people have no wish to see, or seeing do not care to perceive.

One may say too much even upon the best subject.

You may make a man sick with the honey which was intended to sweeten his mouth. You may keep on hammering at a nail till you first drive it in, and then drive it out again.

One may tire of eating tarts.

Monotony is wearisome. The repetition of the same thing is tiresome, whether it be in seeing, hearing, or tasting.

One may understand like an angel, and yet live like a devil.

> Sad fact. Light in the head may leave the heart in the dark. To know is little, but to practise is great. It involves a terrible responsibility when a man is forced to confess,—
>> " I see the right, and I approve it too,
>> Condemn the wrong, and yet the wrong pursue."

One mild answer quenches more than two buckets of water.

> Blessed are those firemen whose gentleness is as a fire engine to the flames of strife. Soft answers are hard to answer. A man cannot quarrel alone. Anger cares not to sing a solo.

One millstone alone,
Of meal makes none.

> A bachelor is that one alone. Some say he is like one of the legs of a pair of scissors, or a pair of compasses—of no use without the other.

One must never put a hawk into a hen-house.

> Nor introduce a bad fellow to your daughters.

One must plough with the horses one has.

> It is wisdom to do our best with what comes to hand. Men and women are not perfect, yet God uses them : if they are good enough for him, why should we refuse to work with them?

One of these days is none of these days.

> Business for which there is no fixed time seldom gets attended to.

One of his hands is unwilling to wash the other for nothing.

> This is the mercenary principle in an extreme degree, and doubtless it scarcely exaggerates the spirit of some who will do nothing unless they are to have a wage for it; and hardly then. It reminds me of an old man with a sluggish horse, who, as he struck it with the whip, would say, "Take that; you're just like a lawyer, you won't go an inch unless you are well paid."

One ploughs, another sows:
Who will reap no one knows.

> Yet it is ours to sow even if we do not live till harvest ; for others sowed, and we entered into their labours.

One pot of beer makes room for another.

Creates a craving for another. Till the first went down, the man was happy without the poison; but now he is not master of himself, and must have another pot to keep the first one company.

One potter loves not another potter.

Two of a trade will not agree. The above proverb is one of the very oldest on record; but we do not suppose that potters are any more cantankerous than other mortals. This is put into rhyme as follows:

> The potter hates another of the trade,
> If by his hands a finer dish is made;
> And thus his envy is betrayed.

One rotten egg will spoil a large pudding.

A grand life may be marred by a single evil deed.

One saddle is enough for one horse.

One office should satisfy one man; it is all that he can properly carry out. Some are saddled from head to tail, but carry little.

One seldom meets a lonely lie.

Lies go in droves. Truth can stand alone, but a lie needs a brother on the right, and another on the left, to keep it up.

One sheep follows another.

It is their sheepish nature; and men are even more sheepish than sheep.

> If one of them should go astray,
> Sure all the flock will tend that way.

Carlyle said that he would like to stop the stream of people in the Strand, and ask every man his history. On reflection he decided, " No, I will not stop them. If I did, I should find they were like a flock of sheep, following in the track of one another."

One sickly sheep infects the flock.

So spreading is an evil example.

One sin opens the door to another.

Satan puts a little sin in at the window to open the door for a bigger transgression.

One story is good till another is told.

If it be not a good story at all, but a bad one, it is fair to hear what may be said on the other side. It is wonderful in how different a light the same actions may be seen.

> Be slow to censure. Spare your blame;
> Rash speech may wound the fairest name.

One swallow makes not a summer.

Nor one woodcock a winter: but it prophesies the coming of it. One grasshopper makes many springs.

One thing at a time, if upward you'd climb.

> "A wag asked my lord, how it came to appear
> Such a great mass of work he got through in a year,
> Said Chesterfield promptly, 'You elderly dunce,'
> By never attempting, sir, two things at once.'"

One thread of kindness binds more surely than ten bonds of steel.

Yet men are afraid to try the bonds of love. How well will society be bound together when kindness shall bind man to man!

One to-day is worth a thousand to-morrows.

One tongue is enough for two women.

Are not women unfairly judged in this matter? Are there not many male chatterboxes? It is the men who say these hard things. One of them dares to write—

> "When man or woman dies, as poets sung,
> His heart's the last that stirs; of hers the tongue."

In our judgment there is little or no truth in the insinuation that the gentler sex talk more than the men. An old bachelor says—" A woman may be surprised, astonished, amazed, but never dumb-founded." But then he is a bachelor, and deserves to remain in that horrible condition during the term of his unnatural life.

One trick needs a great many more to make it good.

Thus from one act a man seems forced to become a trickster. By-and-by one of his tricks fails him, and where is he?

> Trick upon trick, like brick upon brick :
> All comes tumbling down right quick.

One wears white linen, but another did the washing.

The credit is not always, nor even generally, given where it is most deserved.

One would rather be bitten by wolves than by sheep.

Injuries inflicted by men whom we respect, are more keenly felt than those which come from bad men, of whom we expected evil.

One vice is more expensive than many virtues.

Think what lechery, gambling, drinking, and pride cost. All the virtues do not involve so much expense as one of these.

One volunteer is worth two pressed men.

It is certainly so in all holy service. Our God wants none in his armies who do not enter there with all their heart. Yet in another sense all the Lord's volunteers are conscripts by effectual calling, pressed into the Lord's service by his love.

One year of blow,
Makes three of hoe.

This appears to be an Essex proverb. If thistles and weeds are allowed to ripen, and their seed is blown about for one season, it will take three years to be rid of the mischief. If we allow bad habits to master us for a little while, it will cost us a long time to uproot them. Another form of the proverb is:
> One year's seeding:
> Seven years' weeding.

One's own hearth is gold's worth.

The lover of home is the wealthy man. God there gives us more of bliss than all the rest of the world could buy.

Only evil fears the light,
God will vindicate the right.

Open doors invite thieves.

Windows and doors badly fastened, or left open, practically say to a burglar, "Come in, and take what you please."

Open not your door when the devil knocks.

When he finds that he has no response he will go away. Alas! he hardly needs to knock twice in many cases, the door flies open at his first touch. It is not the prince of darkness, but the Lord of Love, who has to cry, "Behold, I stand at the door and knock."

Open thy mouth, and God will open his hand.

"We have not, because we ask not." A pleading heart on earth soon finds a yielding hand in heaven. The Lord is more ready to give than we are to receive.

Open thy mouth for the dumb.

Let every dumb animal find an eloquent advocate in every one of us. When men cannot speak for themselves, this proverb bids us act as their advocate.

Open thy mouth, that I may know thee.

Till then we can only see as far within a man as his teeth ; but speech lets us see further down his throat. We know no man till we have lived with him and heard his communications.

Opportunities do not wait.

We must seize them as they pass us. The tide remains not long at flood.

> The first occasion offer'd, quickly take,
> Lest thou repine at what thou didst forsake.

Orators without judgment are horses without bridles.

In such cases their tongues run away with them, and there is no telling where they will go, nor what mischief they will do.

Order well, that you may be well obeyed.

Be clear, thoughtful, and kind in your commands. When the master knows what he wants done, the servants are likely to do it.

Order your dog, but order not me;
For I was born before you could see.

A tart reply to one who takes too much upon himself, and would domineer over one older than he is, and independent of him.

Ornament an ass, but it does not make him a horse.

However fine the dress, the man is not altered thereby. An ass is still an ass even if you put on him a Mayor's chain, or cover him, ears and all, with stars and garters.

Our first breath is the beginning of death.

We have just that one breath the less to draw. "Our life is woven wind" and nothing more. "As a flower of the field, so he flourisheth."

> The sweetest flowers that scent the sky
> Are only born to blush and die.

Our greatest enemy is within ourselves.

With some especially it is so. We know a man of such ability that nobody hinders his usefulness except himself, but self stands in his way very sadly. Self-consciousness is a dreadful hindrance to a minister, missionary, or miss of any sort.

Our homes should be sweet, and airy, and light.

Our clothes should be clean, and never fit tight.

Our idle days are Satan's busy days.

> When our minds lie fallow, the wicked one sows them with weeds. "Beware of emptiness. Empty hours, empty hands, empty companions, empty words, empty hearts, draw in evil spirits, as a vacuum draws in air."—*Arnot.*

Our mercies are more than our miseries.

> Assuredly. God's deeds of kindness far exceed his acts of judgment. We can count the plagues of Egypt, but who can measure the manna which fell in the wilderness?

Our rust needs a rough file.

> Therefore we may expect many afflictions.
>
> > Till God hath wrought us to his will,
> > The hammer we must suffer still.

Ours is a duck of a climate—for a duck.

> And not always *that;* for one writes of a certain winter's day, "First it *blew*, and then it *snew*, and then it *driz*, and then it *friz*." We have no climate, but only weather.

Out of one quarrel will come a hundred sins.

> On all sides angry tempers will be engendered, falsehoods uttered, hard thoughts indulged, peace broken, and holiness grieved. Will it not be better to let it pass?

Out of the frying-pan into the fire is no gain.

> To rush from one form of evil to another and perhaps a worse, is of no avail to salvation. That was a true song of Bunyan's :—
>
> > "What danger is the pilgrim in!
> > How many are his foes!
> > How many ways there are to sin,
> > No living mortal knows.
> >
> > Some of the ditch shy are, yet can
> > Lie tumbling in the mire:
> > Some, though they shun the frying-pan,
> > Do leap into the fire."

Out of time and place even wisdom is folly.

Out of the path of duty into the path of danger.

Outside the precept is outside the promise.

When we quit the King's highway of holiness, the King's protection is no longer guaranteed us.

Overdone is worse than underdone.

You can always do more, but it is not easy to undo what is done. The following story is told of *Dean Swift:*—It happened one day that his cook had greatly over-roasted the only joint he had for dinner. "Cook," said the Dean in the blandest possible tones, "this leg of mutton is overdone, take it back into the kitchen and do it less." The cook replied that the thing was impossible. "But," said the Dean, "if it had been underdone you could have done it more." The cook assented. "Well then, cook" said he, "let this be a lesson to you. If you needs must commit a fault, at least take care it is one that will admit of a remedy."

Over-dressed is ill dressed.

When garments attract the eye they disfigure the figure upon which they are hung. Neatness and plainness bear the bell, and make the belle far more beautiful than if gaudily arrayed. A young Grecian painter was rebuked by his master for having decked his Helen with ornaments, because he had not the skill to make her beautiful. It is possible that some think to atone for the want of beauty by their gorgeous attire, but they make a great mistake. Ugliness bedizened advertises its deformity.

Over-reachers over-reach themselves.

Before long the biter is bitten : the grasper of all is left with nothing but a shadow. He makes a dirt-pie, and has the pleasure of eating it himself.

Over shoes over boots.

So the man plunges deeper into the mire. He is reckless of the worse, because already so used to the bad.

Owls hoot, but the sun shines on.

None of the mole-eyed critics have robbed the Bible of its power or blessing, or Christ of his crown, or God of his glory.

Own thyself foolish, that thou mayst be wise.

Confession of ignorance is the doorstep of knowledge.

Ox, keep to your grass.

Be satisfied with your daily fare. Covet not the luxuries which are not fit for you.

Sayings of a more Spiritual Sort.

Offer weekly to the Lord,
Even as thou canst afford.

> See Paul's rule of church finance. "On the first day of the
> week let every one of you lay by him in store, as God hath
> prospered him."—1 Cor. xvi. 2.   If this rule were followed,
> Christian people would be better off, and the cause of God would
> have no need of fancy fairs or other fancies.

On earth we roam,
Heaven is our home.

> May we keep our faces homeward, and, like horses, mend our pace
> as we see which way the road is going.

On Sinai we learn our duty, but on Calvary we find motives
    for doing it.

> The death of Jesus creates love in our heart, and so we come to
> obey the Lord.   That is not a bad verse:
>
> > Trust, for salvation comes by Faith alone—
> > But work, as though all Merit were thine own;
> > Live as though Gospel light the world ne'er saw
> > But die as one who is not under Law.

One day in seven is due to heaven.

> And when reserved for heaven, it becomes the best possession for
> ourselves.   The Sabbath which is made for God, is the day which,
> above all others, is said to have been "made for man."

One hour's cold will drive out seven years' heat.

> It will do so in the body, and assuredly it has this effect upon the
> soul.   A temporary declension robs us of the advantage of years of
> earnest spiritual life.   Some believers have to complain that holy
> heat is so soon gone.   They go to bed warm and wake up cold.
> This is a sad experience.

One in a house, of grace possessed,
May win for Jesus all the rest.

> Get one candle lighted, and all the candles in the house may be
> made to shine.   Grace is not contagious, but yet it is of a spreading
> character, and brings a blessing to a man's family.

One touch of grace makes the whole church kin.

> The saints in prayer, praise, and any other gracious services and acts appear as one in word, and deed, and mind.

Only those who follow the steps of Jesus are walking with God.

> For the way of obedience which Jesus followed is the path of fellowship, and he that wanders from it loses communion with God.

Ordinances without the Spirit are cisterns without water.

> We go to them in vain, and return from them bitterly disappointed when the Holy Ghost does not bless them. But when he works by them they are the appointed conduits of the water of life, and it flows fully and freely through them.

Our churches must not become chapels-of-ease.

> "Woe to them that are at ease in Zion."

Our conversation need not always be *about* grace, but it should always be *with* grace.

> We may add, that books upon religion are needed, but works upon common subjects, written in a religious spirit, are still more needed.

Our God we praise
For Sabbath days.

> The rest they bring, and the holy occupations they suggest, are matters for constant thankfulness. God must have loved the poor working-man, or he would not have taken such care to give him rest.

Our graces are the children of free grace.

> The law did not create them, but they are the outcome of the mighty grace of God which works all good in us.

Our Lord's last will and testament is fine reading for his heirs.

> A man was one day walking to church, reading the New Testament, when a friend who met him said, "Good morning, Mr. Price." "Good morning," replied he; "I am reading my Father's will as I walk along." "Well, what has he left you?" asked the friend. "Why, he has bequeathed me a hundredfold more in this life; and in the world to come, life everlasting." This beautiful reply was the means of comforting his Christian friend, who was at the time in sorrowful circumstances.

Our love to God arises out of our want: his love to us out of his fulness.

Our salvation begins with self-condemnation.

> We must plead "guilty," or mercy has no ground upon which to deal with us.

Our Saviour has a salve for every sore.

> *Herrick* wrote, in one of his better verses,
>
> > To all our wounds, how deep soe'er they be,
> > Christ is the one sufficient remedy.

Our sinful stains
Should cause us pains.

> Till they are washed out we ought not to give rest to our eyes, nor slumber to our eyelids.

Our sufficiency is in God's all-sufficiency.

> Self-sufficiency is mere self-deceit.

Over the bridge of sighs we pass to the palace of peace.

> Repentance is the road to rest. The way to heaven is round by Weeping Cross. Tears are the water in which we take Christ's healing medicines.

ADDLE your own canoe.

Join the Help-your-self Society. Don't be loafing on your father, or brother; much less upon your wife, as some worthless wretches are doing.

Paddy doesn't kill a deer every time he fires.

Great successes are occasional, and it would be idle to expect them every day. We don't find a sovereign every morning.

Pain past is pleasure.

When the shore is won at last,
We shall smile at billows past.

Pains are the payment for sinful pleasures.

What pains they are! Not a few have endured a hell upon earth in consequence of their wicked ways.

Paint not thy nose
At the sign of the Rose.

The paint is expensive, and the nose, despite its rubies, is by no means more of a jewel. "What are you doing there, Jane?" "Why, pa, I'm going to dye my doll's pinafore red." "But what have you to dye it with?" "Beer, pa." "Beer! Who on earth told you that beer would dye red?" "Why, ma said yesterday that it was beer that made your nose so red, and I thought that—" "Here, Susan, take this child to bed."

Pardon great, and pardon small;
But pardon not thyself at all.

One who felt the evil of his sin exclaimed: "God may forgive me, but I can never forgive myself." Yet in another sense we do forgive ourselves, for we enjoy a sense of peace when we are assured of pardon through the precious blood of the great sacrifice.

Parents' blessings can neither be drowned in water nor consumed in fire.

So say the Russians; and there is truth in the saying. The blessing invoked on us by godly parents is a rich endowment. The paternal blessing is a patrimony.

Partnerships with men in power
Can't be built on for an hour.

> Great ones are apt to look down upon you, and to think that your
> share of the profit is so much taken out of their pockets. Join in
> partnership with a man of your own size, or else keep yourself to
> yourself. You cannot well yoke an ox and a goat together.

Party is the madness of many for the gain of a few.

> One would think that each party man was going to make his own
> fortune, whereas he is only toiling to get into office a certain set
> of men who are hungering after place. These gentlemen w.ll do
> nothing whatever for the underlings whose sweet voices they now
> enlist in their favour. The outs and the ins are as like as two pins :
> they both want to stick in good places.

Party spirit is an evil spirit.

> It divides people who else might join together for the common
> good, and it makes men strive for power, rather than for the
> national benefit. Yet this spirit rules politics. Greed for office
> and its spoils is more potent than patriotism.

> > All their contentions are but these :
> > Which set of mice shall eat the cheese ?

Passion doth unman a man.

Passion is a fever that leaves us weaker than it finds us.

> > All in a heat it makes you run,
> > But how you tremble when it's done !

Past and future seem most fair
When with present we compare.

> But the comparison is not correctly made. We feel our present
> pains, and forget those which have come, and will yet come.

Past hope, past shame.

> Despair breeds a defiant spirit, and, as he has no prospect of
> mercy, the man cares not what becomes of him, and dashes into
> still greater infamy of sin.

Patches and darns are better than debts.

> By the right use of the needle some are half-clothed. Their
> mends and darns, as the ensigns of industry, are an honour to
> them. Better a thousand darns than a single debt.

Patience and cowardice are very different things.

The patient man is the bravest of the brave, and bears evil usage, not because he dares not resent it, but because he means to repay it in God's way—by giving good for evil.

Patience and water-gruel cure many diseases.

Of all prescriptions this is the most reliable, and practically this is the point to which doctors are coming. A little starving is very useful treatment. Grantham gruel is recommended: nine grits and a gallon of water will not overload the stomach.

Patience is a bitter plant, but it has sweet fruit.

It sweetens other bitter herbs. Those who let it have its perfect work will become perfect themselves. Like the anvil, it breaks many hammers simply by bearing their blows.

Patience is sister to meekness, and humility is its mother.

Patience is the cheapest law, as temperance is the safest physic.

Patience with poverty is all a poor man's remedy.

But it is a good remedy. Patience is a patent Poor-man's Plaster. It is wise to say, "If I cannot get it I will go without it." To be jolly under difficulties is the mark of a noble heart; but Mark Tapleys are not common persons. When *William Chambers* was young, he endured great hardships. But he says: "Over the door-way of an old house which I passed several times daily was the inscription, carved in stone,

'He that tholes overcomes.'

I made up my mind to *thole*—a pithy old Scottish word signifying to bear with patience; the whole inscription reminding us of a sentiment in Virgil: 'Whatever may happen, every kind of fortune is to be overcome by bearing it.'"

Patient waiters are no losers.

Everything comes to the man who is able to wait for it.

With patience I the storm sustain,
For sunshine still doth follow rain.

Paul Pry is on the spy.

The negroes say, "There are people who will help you to get your basket on your head, because they want to see what's in it." They would like to see how we pull on our stockings in the morning, and how we get between the blankets at night; and yet they hope they don't intrude.

Pay as you go,
And nothing you'll owe.

> And if you can't pay, don't go. Keep clear of debt, and then you will be like *Longfellow's* Village Blacksmith :
>
> > " He looks the whole world in the face,
> > For he owes not any man."
>
> *Gough* once said, "If one steal a penny, he is a thief. Is he not a thief who will '*do*' a creditor, shirk payment of an honest bill, or act the part of a mean trickster ? 'There goes a sculptor.' 'What do you mean ?' 'Only that he chisels tailors, bootmakers, and all who trust him.' "

Pay beforehand if you would have your work ill done.

> Men never like working for a dead horse, and that is the name they give to a job for which they have had the money, and spent it.

Pay down your rent
Ere cash is spent.

> Don't leave this matter till there is a man in possession, but keep yourself in possession by paying promptly.

Pay good wages, or your servants will pay themselves.

> By pilferings on a greater or less scale they will balance the account. When a man's wages are so small that he cannot live on them, he is apt to add to them by hook or by crook. Very dishonest ! True, but is it right to tempt men to such roguery ?

Pay the reckoning over-night, and you won't be troubled in the morning.

> Especially when leaving your hotel get all things settled soon, that there may be no delay in your going away.

Pay thy tithe, and be rich.

> So say the Rabbis. Nothing is gained by robbing God. It is my solemn belief that the dedication to the Lord of a portion of our substance, certainly not less than a tenth, would tend to prosperity. So have I found it.

Pay well when you are served well.

> A good horse that works hard requires and deserves a good measure of corn ; and a faithful servant deserves to be fully and even generously remunerated.

Pay without fail
Down on the nail.

This is the happiest and most economical way. If you wait, the
amount will not lessen. There may even be two nails to pay
upon instead of one. There are other debts which ought to be
paid. Give thy need, thine honour, thy friend, the church, and
the poor, their due. Be not in debt even to posterity. "There is
a significant entry in John Evelyn's diary of June 19, 1653: 'This
day I paid all my debts to a farthing. O blessed day!' One of
Shenstone's paragraph essays opens with the note of exclamation,
'What pleasure it is to pay one's debts!' Gay writes to Swift:
'I hate to be in debt, for I cannot bear to pawn £5 worth of my
liberty to a tailor or a butcher.'"—*Francis Jacox.*

Pay your share of the reckoning, like a true man,
Don't ever be scheming to shirk if you can.

Plenty are ready to feed or fuddle at other people's expense.

"They find a pleasure much more sweet
In being treated than to treat."

Very specially is this the case with the Lushington Club, who are
always ready to drink any *given* quantity, and to do their duty with
other folks' glasses. It is said of one of them—

"But though he likes his grog,
As all his friends do say,
He always likes it best
When other people pay."

Peace purchased by parting with principle is profanity.

There is plenty of it nowadays.

Peace is the price for which the Lord is sold,
And not for twenty pieces, as of old.

Pedigree won't sell a lame horse.

However famous the sire, people want speed in the steed him-
self. Many boast of their family connections, and conclude that
they must be great because their great grandfather was somebody.

Mules deliver thy discourses
Because their ancestors were horses.

Pelt all dogs that bark, and you will need many stones.

Answer all who slander you, and you will have a vocation for
life. Prosecute every slanderer, and you will need a court to
yourself.

But if all dogs upon this earth should bark,
It will not matter if you do not hark.

Pence well spent are better than pence ill-spared.

Pence were made to clear away expenses. Saving is sometimes a loss. When the time has come to spend, it is as injurious to withhold as it would be for the farmer to lock up the corn in the time of sowing. The street Arabs say, " Chuck out your mouldy coppers."

Penny goes after penny,
Till Peter hasn't any.

Little expenditures run away with a great deal of money ; in fact, more is lost by small leakages than by great overflows.

Penny is penny's brother, and likes his company.

If there were two pennies in a bag, they would get together. He that hath shall have. Shillings, like starlings, fly in flocks.

Penny laid on penny,
Very soon makes many.

Economy in small matters leads to savings which are little in themselves, but tell up before long. James Lackington, who began business as a bookseller, in 1774, with a few old books on a stall not worth £5, retired in 1792, when the profits of his business amounted to £5,000 a year. He said he had realized all his wealth by " small profits, bound by industry, and clasped by economy."

Penny wise is often pound foolish.

People count up the faults of those who keep them waiting.

If we are unfairly detaining people, we shall be the subject of a discourse which is not likely to be biased in our favour.

People never should sit talking till they don't know what to talk about.

Long before subjects are exhausted the tongue should be allowed a holiday. But so it is that, when all the yarn is gone, men spin the faster.

Men chew not when they have no bread,
Yet talk the more when nothing's said.

People take more pains to be lost than to be saved.

With resolute zeal some men go over hedge and ditch to hell ; while others, in going to heaven, are as slow in their movements as a boy going unwillingly to school.

People throw stones only at trees which have fruit on them.

So the French say. Certainly, the attacks made upon good men may be treated as a diploma of merit. If they had been what the world makes them out to be, they would not have been worth the powder and shot spent upon them. Wasps go after sweet fruit.

People who live in glass houses should never throw stones.

For some one else may do the same and break our windows. Indeed some of the stones we throw may do ourselves damage. When *Charles Dickens* heard an empty and pretentious young author declaiming against the follies and sins of the race, he remarked, "What a lucky thing it is that you and I don't belong to it!"

Perfect men and perfect horses nobody ever sees.

We have heard talk of them, but could never get either man or beast with any such warranty. We have not found perfect men quite quiet in harness; but we have remarked that they are generally a good deal touched in the wind, and not free from a nasty habit of carrying their heads high in the air. "I have never known but two women that were perfect," said one French lady to another. "Who was the other one?" asked her companion.

Perform all your work without uproar and din:
When wisdom goes out then clamour comes in.

Those who do nothing generally take to shouting. The best work in the world is done on the quiet.

"Perhaps" hinders folk from lying.

By using this, and other qualifying words, truthfulness is preserved. Those who talk as fast as express trains are ever known to run should always have buffers to their engine.

Perpetual chatterers are like crickets in the chimney-corner.

Oh, that we could silence their perpetual chirping!
On, on, on, on; for ever and a day:
Nothing but death will make their jawbones stay.

Perseverance wins.

"Hard pounding, gentlemen," said the Duke; but by steadily bearing this hard pounding Waterloo was won. Only hold on long enough, and the day will be yours.

Persevere and never fear.

"All things must yield to industry and tim
None cease to rise but those who cease t

Peter's in, Paul's out.

As much as to say, now that one person essential to the business is at home, another equally needful is away. We do not find all things working quite as we would like; but this is nothing new.

Petticoat government has proved good in England.

"God save our gracious Queen.   Long live our noble Queen."

"*A place under government,*
Was all that Paddy wanted:
He married soon a scolding wife,
When all he wished was granted."

Philosophers cover the pie of their ignorance with a Latin crust.

"Doctor," said an old lady the other day to her family physician, "kin you tell me how it is that some folks is born dumb?"   "Why, hem, certainly, madam," replied the doctor; "it is owing to the fact that they come into the world without the faculty of speech!" "La, me!" remarked the old lady; "Now just see what it is to have a physic edication! I've axed my old man more nor a hundred times that ar same thing, and all that I could get out of him was, '*Kase they is.*'"   Still, spiflication is no explanation.

Physicians are joked at only when we are well.

Hence, when *Voltaire* was well, he said, "A physician is a man who pours drugs of which he knows little, into a body of which he knows less."   But when he felt in a more respectful, because more sickly, condition, he said, "A physician is an unfortunate gentleman, who is every day called upon to perform a miracle, namely, to reconcile intemperance with health."   One thing is clear, doctors do not bleed us in the arm as much as they did; but they do bleed us in another place, and that without a lancet.

Piety is a greater honour than parentage.

It is of small use to have had a godly father if one is himself leading an evil life; yet those who are a disgrace to their ancestors are often the loudest in boasting of their descent. What a descent!

Those who on holy ancestry enlarge,
Produce their debt; but where is their discharge?

Pigs grow fat where lambs would starve.

Evil men can flourish where the honest would perish. The food of the wicked would be the poison of the gracious.

The talk which modern men adore
Would make me sick, and nothing more.

Pigs grunt about everything and nothing.

I think I must have heard some of these animals.

Pigs may whistle; but their mouths were not made for it.

Spoken of those who attempt performances for which they are evidently unfitted · a very common piece of uncommon folly.

Pigs when they fly go tail first.

They never do fly : but the old saying means that when men aspire to things of which they are not capable, they always go the wrong way to work. Whistling oysters are always out of tune.

Pills should be swallowed, not chewed.

Many disagreeable things had better be accepted in silence, and not much thought about, or their bitterness will be all the more perceptible. Accept the inevitable, and don't dwell upon it.

Pinch yourself, and learn how others feel when they are pinched.

It would do many an employer good to live for a week on the small wage he pays his men on Saturday.

Pity fair weather should do any harm.

Pity without relief is like mustard without beef.

Very tasty, but not very nourishing. A man who had been in good circumstances was reduced to selling cakes in the street. One who knew him in wealthier days commiserated him at great length, till, his patience being exhausted, he exclaimed, "Bother your pity ! Buy a bun." A pennyworth of help is worth a heap of pity.

Plain-dealing is a jewel, and he that useth it shall prosper.

Shall he? He ought to do so, but possibly he may not. But prosperity is not the greatest thing to desire. The plain-dealer will, at least, have a quiet conscience, and that is a pearl of great price. Diogenes would still need his lantern to find a plain-dealer.

Plant the crocus, but don't play the croaker.

It is said that crocus-growers in the olden time had a very precarious crop, and were called croakers, not from the frog, but from the saffron crocus which they cultivated, and which, for various reasons, tried them so much in its production. As farmers do not now grow saffron, they have of course left off being croakers (P).

Plaster thick,
And some will stick.

> A wicked piece of advice : belie a man's character very heavily, and some of the slander will be believed. Surely Satan himself is at the bottom of such a malicious precept. Speak evil of none.

Play, but do not play the fool.

> Be wise in your recreation as in all things else. Follow Rowland Hill's advice : "Keep up the distinction between pious cheerfulness and frothy levity." Play should be such as fits for work.

Play not with fire,
Nor with foul desire.

> For they are dangerous things, and must not be trifled with. It is an infinite folly to make gunpowder in a smith's shop, and then try to persuade people that there is no danger in it. Even when a man is not burned, he gets blackened if he meddles with hot coals.

Playful kittens make sober cats.

> May all our cheerful youth grow up to be earnest men and women.

Please ever, tease never.

> Unless it be the kind of teasing which is a form of pleasing, only flavoured with a little spice. Tease only as you would wish to be teased yourself.

> If you please,
> Do not tease.

Please yourself, and you'll please me.

> We cannot often say this ; but when people are worrying about mere trifles, we thus give them *carte blanche*, and hope we shall hear no more of their chatter.

Pleasures are like poppies spread ;
You seize the flower, its bloom is shed.

> So *Burns* found them ; but then he was too apt to snatch at pleasures of a kind which wisdom would forego.

Plough deep while sluggards sleep,
And you shall have corn to sell or to keep.

> Here we have *Franklin's* wisdom, as he put it into the mouth of Poor Richard. It suits England as well as America. Hard work is still the road to prosperity ; and there is no other.

Plough or not plough, you must pay your rent.

That will be demanded, and no mistake, for nothing is surer than death and quarter-day. Neither will landlords be content to go without their share because your share has been rusting in the furrow. If work does not pay, idleness will not.

Plough well if you plough slowly.

It will pay to take more time over it, rather than to do it in a slovenly manner. Do as little as you like, but do that little well.

Ploughmen on their legs are higher than gentlemen on their knees.

The independence of the working-man is more noble than the obsequiousness of the courtier or the tradesman who bows before others to get gain. Whatever you are, be a man.

Poach nothing but eggs.

Whatever we may think of the game laws, we don't intend to break them. Poached eggs are a family dish, but we don't get them from poachers. Stolen goods are too costly for honest purses.

Politeness is excellent, but it does not pay the bill.

Tradesmen would like more money even if they had less manners.

Poor, but honest.

"This reminds me of the reply of a wise man, whose son said to him, 'Father, I often hear people say, "Poor, but honest." Why don't they say, "Rich, but honest"?' 'Because, my son, no one would believe them.' But I was going to suggest whether we hadn't better make a change, and say, 'Poor, *because* honest.'"— *Dr. Philetus Dobbs.*

Poor folks are glad of porridge.

Therein they are rich, for their power to enjoy their food has a wider range than the taste of the epicure, who must have dainties, or he cannot make a satisfactory meal.

Poor folks must say, "Thank ye" for a litt

They must be grateful for small mer~~
waggon-load of homage for a ~~
a blanket it can hardly be ?
and a billion of bows.

Poor in the midst of wealth is poor indeed.

Such is the miser in his self-inflicted penury. Such again is the poor relation in a purse-proud family, and the man who is unhappy, on account of fear, where others rejoice in hope.

Poor men seek meat for their stomach ; rich men stomach for their meat.

Thus things are somewhat equalized. Which is the worst, appetite and no food, or food and no appetite ?

Poor men's tables are soon spread.

And very soon cleared again. *Charles Wesley's* Elegy on William Kingsbury, a man who lived and died in extreme poverty, is very touching :
> " Toiling hard for scanty bread,
>   Scanty bread he could not find."

Poor purse and dainty palate are ill met.

For you can't buy oysters with coppers, nor turtle-soup at a groat a quart. Beau Brummel, when asked if he took vegetables, replied, that he believed he had once tasted a pea. Poor Brummel ! Fancy this affected beau condemned to eat raw turnips.

Poor wages make poor work.

Of course no man will throw his heart into a task for which he is underpaid. If you are so unreasonable as to expect it, the workman will be reasonable enough to disappoint you. You may try to sweat a man, but he will not sweat for you.
> Give a fair day's wage for a fair day's work :
> Take a fair day's wages, and never shirk.

Positive men are oftenest in error.

Never are they more certain than when they are mistaken. No creature is more obstinate than a donkey ; no bird more dogmatic in his gibble-gabble than a turkey-cock.

Possession is nine points of the law.

And there is only one more point. Therefore, hold on like grim death, till lawful authority bids you be gone.

Possess your money, but let it not possess you.

" It is not the fact that a man *has* riches which keeps him from the kingdom of heaven, but the fact that riches *have* him."—*Dr. Caird.*

Poverty laughs at robbery.

The old story hath it: "There was a poor man, on a tyme, who said unto thieves who brake into his house at night, 'Sirs, I marvel that ye think to find anything here by night, for I assure you that I can find nothing here by day.'"

> By this tale plainly appeareth,
> That poverty little feareth.

Poverty tries friends and allies.

And too often in the trial they turn out to be base metal. Somewhat harshly a versifier puts it—

> If Fortune wrap thee warm,
> Then friends about thee swarm,
>   Like bees about a honey-pot.
> But if Dame Fortune frown,
> And cast thee fairly down,
>   Thy friends will let thee lie and rot.

Poverty wants some things, luxury many things, avarice all things.

So that the miser is the poorest man of all: you'll break your neck as soon as your fast in his house at his expense.

Practice makes perfect.

If that practice is careful, constant, and long continued.

Practise not your art,
And it will soon depart.

Out of work we lose the knack of working. After being in the marshes for a month the horse finds the collar galls him. He who would keep clever at his trade must keep ever at his work.

Practise thrift, or else you'll drift.

Whether you are rich or poor you will need management and economy. Go forward, or you will get backward.

> He that gets money before he gets wit,
> Will be but a short while master of it.

Praise a fool, and you water his folly.

And that folly will grow like willows by the water-courses. He will lift his head so high that it will go through the ceiling. His pride will rise over even a prophet's head, like the gourd which was the growth of a night. Let the green thing alone.

Praise from the worthless is worthless.

> Worse: it is suspicious. A philosopher, when a base fellow applauded him, asked, "What have I done that such a fellow should speak well of me?" Praise is worthy from the praiseworthy.

Praise God more, and blame neighbours less.

Praise invigorates the wise, but intoxicates the foolish.

> The sensible endeavour to do all the better because they are thought to have done well. Vain persons, by a little commendation, are first puffed up, and then puffed out. Few stomachs can digest the rich pastry of praise. Butter needs to be thinly spread.

Praise little, dispraise less.

> Let your expressions be well weighed, so that value may be attached to them. He who is constantly expressing his hasty opinions will find that little regard is paid to him. *Andrew Fuller* tells of one, who, being much edified by the discourse of a popular minister, met him at the pulpit stairs with, "I really must not say what I think of your sermon, it might do you harm." "Not at all, my friend," was the rejoinder, "speak out, for I do not attach much importance to your opinion." More frank than flattering.

Praise makes good men better and bad men worse.

> The unworthy grow proud, and the deserving become more humble. It is hard to live up to the good opinion of our friends.

Praise others far more than yourself.

> A hearty word of commendation to others is generous and good; but self-praise is no recommendation. Be not your own publisher.
>
> > If one hath serv'd thee, tell the deed to many:
> > Hast thou serv'd many?—tell it not to any.

Praise Peter, but don't find fault with Paul.

> Why should you run down one because you prefer another? This is a common and senseless habit. Praise John and Joan too.

Praise the hill, but keep below.

> If you desire easy travelling take the lower road, although you may admire the scenery of the mountain way. Admire wealth, rank and office; but do not hanker after them yourself.
>
> > There's wind on the hill, and the road is steep;
> > It's warm in the vale, so here I shall keep.

Praise the bridge which carries you over.

Honour the man who gave you an education. Love the country which gives you shelter. Speak well of the trade by which you get a living. Extol the truth which bears up your spirit.

Praise the horse which has brought you so far.

With a lively sense of favours to come, hoping that he will carry you safely the rest of the way.

Praise the sea, but keep on land.

So said *George Herbert*, and the wise men before him. They knew that Britannia ruled the waves, but wished that she ruled them straighter. It is all up with some when they go down to the sea.

Prate is prate : work is the duck which lays the eggs.

Sam Slick says :—Work ; earn your own pork, and see how sweet it will be. Work and see how well you will be. Work and see how cheerful you will be. Work and see how independent you will be. Work and see how religious you will be ; for before you know where you are, instead of repining at Providence, you will find yourself offering up thanks for all the numerous blessings you enjoy.

Pray and stay are words for every day.

Good words and wise. Practise both. Worship and wait. God's answers are not always immediate. His delays are not denials. *Erskine* rightly says :—

> " I'm heard when answered soon or late ;
> And heard when I no answer get :
> Yea, kindly answer'd when refused,
> And treated well when harshly us'd."

Pray brighten each day with domestic delight, And bring home the wages on Saturday night.

Pray, do hold your tongue a minute : What you say has nothing in it.

Cease your chatter and mind your platter. Your tongue runs on like a mill-wheel disconnected from the machinery : clatter, clatter, clatter, but grinding nothing whatever. The wonder is your teeth do not shake out of their sockets through the continual motion of your jaws ! Do be quiet for a change.

Pray for all, but prey on none.

How much difference one letter makes ! Let us not imitate the bankers who commenced business with supplication and ended in liquidation.

Pray to God, but keep the hammer going.

> He gives us our daily bread by enabling us to work and earn it.
> Throw not your tools away because you trust in God; on the con-
> trary, use them with braver heart.

Pray to God, sailor, but pull for the shore.

Prayer and pains
Bring best of gains.

> They should go together. Prayer without labour is hypocrisy,
> and labour without prayer is presumption.

Prayer and provender hinder no man's journey.

> Far rather do they speed
> Both the man and his steed.

Prayer is the key of the morning and the lock of the night.

> Let not your habitation be without it. It is ill living where this
> lock and key are unknown. As well have a house without a roof as
> a home without family prayer.

Praying without working is a bow without a string.

> There's nothing in it. If the man desired that which he pretends
> to pray for, he would be eager to labour for it.

Preach best in your own pulpit.

> The life at home should be even better than the conduct abroad.
> It is said that some would find it hard to stand on their own door-
> step and preach; they find it convenient to go where they are not
> known. From such preachers may the Lord deliver us!

Preach your own funeral sermon while living.

> Prepare the material of an honourable and instructive memorial
> by an earnest and useful life.

Precious ointments are put in small boxes.

> We cannot expect great quantity where we have high quality.
> Of otto of roses a drop is precious, and it needs only a very small
> bottle to hold as much as pounds can buy. Little people are rather
> proud of this proverb, and no one would wish to take it from them.
> There are many good little bodies. God bless them! Valuable
> articles are generally done up in small parcels.
>> Mark inward worth, and you shall find it then
>> That lesser bodies make not lesser men.

Peter's in, Paul's out.

As much as to say, now that one person essential to the business is at home, another equally needful is away. We do not find all things working quite as we would like; but this is nothing new.

Petticoat government has proved good in England.

"God save our gracious Queen.   Long live our noble Queen."

"*A place under government,*
Was all that Paddy wanted :
He married soon a scolding wife,
When all he wished was granted."

Philosophers cover the pie of their ignorance with a Latin crust.

"Doctor," said an old lady the other day to her family physician, "kin you tell me how it is that some folks is born dumb?"   "Why, hem, certainly, madam," replied the doctor; "it is owing to the fact that they come into the world without the faculty of speech!" "La, me!" remarked the old lady; "Now just see what it is to have a physic edication! I've axed my old man more nor a hundred times that ar same thing, and all that I could get out of him was, '*Kase they is.*'"   Still, spiflication is no explanation.

Physicians are joked at only when we are well.

Hence, when *Voltaire* was well, he said, "A physician is a man who pours drugs of which he knows little, into a body of which he knows less."   But when he felt in a more respectful, because more sickly, condition, he said, "A physician is an unfortunate gentleman, who is every day called upon to perform a miracle, namely, to reconcile intemperance with health."   One thing is clear, doctors do not bleed us in the arm as much as they did; but they do bleed us in another place, and that without a lancet.

Piety is a greater honour than parentage.

It is of small use to have had a godly father if one is himself leading an evil life; yet those who are a disgrace to their ancestors are often the loudest in boasting of their descent. What a descent!

Those who on holy ancestry enlarge,
Produce their debt; but where is their discharge?

Pigs grow fat where lambs would starve.

Evil men can flourish where the honest would perish. The food of the wicked would be the poison of the gracious.

The talk which modern men adore
                                        othing more.

Pretty children sing pretty songs.

Especially if they are our own children. "Music is the sound which one's own children make as they romp through the house. Noise is the sound which other people's children make under the same circumstances."

Pretty speeches will not sugar my gooseberries.

Yet they may be a spoon to hand out the sugar. For the sour things of life we need the loaf sugar of kindness, or the moist sugar of sympathy, or the saccharine of grace: when these come in the silver spoon of goodly words they are none the worse.

Prevention is better than cure.

The work of the Band of Hope, in keeping the children from ever touching the drink, is of even more value than temperance work for reclaiming those who have become drunkards.

Pride and poverty are ill met, yet often live together.

Pride only makes poverty more poor; yet some must seem "respectable" if they starve. They keep up show, and pinch for it. The Scotch wisely say : "A brass plate with a man's name on it is a pretty thing; but a dinner plate with meat on it is much better."

Pride and scorn are briar and thorn.

Tearing both the proud man and those around him. These are two fine things to look at, but they are the fruitful source of misery.

Pride breakfasted with plenty, dined with poverty, and supped with infamy.

Where it went to bed we may very easily guess.

Pride costs more than hunger, thirst, or cold.

Note the expense of money in dress, in cutting a dash, and in keeping up appearances: then note the loss of love, the loss of truth, and the loss of grace; and you will say that pride is a very expensive luxury. As it is worth nothing, it is indeed a costly thing. Pride will eat a man out of house and home.

Pride feels no cold.

Hence, ladies in the severest season will go out to parties less than half-dressed. Modesty should assist prudence, and make them dress decently; but pride has such sway that they will die to be in the fashion. As martyrs burn for Christ, so ladies freeze for fashion.

Peter's in, Paul's out.

As much as to say, now that one person essential to the business is at home, another equally needful is away. We do not find all things working quite as we would like; but this is nothing new.

Petticoat government has proved good in England.

"God save our gracious Queen. Long live our noble Queen."

> "*A place under government,*
> Was all that Paddy wanted:
> He married soon a scolding wife,
> When all he wished was granted."

Philosophers cover the pie of their ignorance with a Latin crust.

"Doctor," said an old lady the other day to her family physician, "kin you tell me how it is that some folks is born dumb?" "Why, hem, certainly, madam," replied the doctor; "it is owing to the fact that they come into the world without the faculty of speech!" "La, me!" remarked the old lady; "Now just see what it is to have a physic edication! I've axed my old man more nor a hundred times that ar same thing, and all that I could get out of him was, ' *Kase they is.*' " Still, spiflication is no explanation.

Physicians are joked at only when we are well.

Hence, when *Voltaire* was well, he said, "A physician is a man who pours drugs of which he knows little, into a body of which he knows less." But when he felt in a more respectful, because more sickly, condition, he said, "A physician is an unfortunate gentleman, who is every day called upon to perform a miracle, namely, to reconcile intemperance with health." One thing is clear, doctors do not bleed us in the arm as much as they did; but they do bleed us in another place, and that without a lancet.

Piety is a greater honour than parentage.

It is of small use to have had a godly father if one is himself leading an evil life; yet those who are a disgrace to their ancestors are often the loudest in boasting of their descent. What a descent!

> Those who on holy ancestry enlarge,
> Produce their debt; but where is their discharge?

Pigs grow fat where lambs would starve.

Evil men can flourish where the honest would perish. The food of the wicked would be the poison of the gracious.

> The talk which modern men adore
> othing more.

Pigs grunt about everything and nothing.

I think I must have heard some of these animals.

Pigs may whistle; but their mouths were not made for it.

Spoken of those who attempt performances for which they are evidently unfitted : a very common piece of uncommon folly.

Pigs when they fly go tail first.

They never do fly; but the old saying means that when men aspire to things of which they are not capable, they always go the wrong way to work. Whistling oysters are always out of tune.

Pills should be swallowed, not chewed.

Many disagreeable things had better be accepted in silence, and not much thought about, or their bitterness will be all the more perceptible. Accept the inevitable, and don't dwell upon it.

Pinch yourself, and learn how others feel when they are pinched.

It would do many an employer good to live for a week on the small wage he pays his men on Saturday.

Pity fair weather should do any harm.

Pity without relief is like mustard without beef.

Very tasty, but not very nourishing. A man who had been in good circumstances was reduced to selling cakes in the street. One who knew him in wealthier days commiserated him at great length, till, his patience being exhausted, he exclaimed, "Bother your pity! Buy a bun." A pennyworth of help is worth a heap of pity.

Plain-dealing is a jewel, and he that useth it shall prosper.

Shall he? He ought to do so, but possibly he may not. But prosperity is not the greatest thing to desire. The plain-dealer will, at least, have a quiet conscience, and that is a pearl of great price. Diogenes would still need his lantern to find a plain-dealer.

Plant the crocus, but don't play the croaker.

It is said that crocus-growers in the olden time had a very precarious crop, and were called croakers, not from the frog, but from the saffron crocus which they cultivated, and which, for various reasons, tried them so much in its production. As farmers do not now grow saffron, they have of course left off being croakers (?).

Plaster thick,
And some will stick.

> A wicked piece of advice : belie a man's character very heavily, and some of the slander will be believed. Surely Satan himself is at the bottom of such a malicious precept. Speak evil of none.

Play, but do not play the fool.

> Be wise in your recreation as in all things else. Follow Rowland Hill's advice : "Keep up the distinction between pious cheerfulness and frothy levity." Play should be such as fits for work.

Play not with fire,
Nor with foul desire.

> For they are dangerous things, and must not be trifled with. It is an infinite folly to make gunpowder in a smith's shop, and then try to persuade people that there is no danger in it. Even when a man is not burned, he gets blackened if he meddles with hot coals.

Playful kittens make sober cats.

> May all our cheerful youth grow up to be earnest men and women.

Please ever, tease never.

> Unless it be the kind of teasing which is a form of pleasing, only flavoured with a little spice. Tease only as you would wish to be teased yourself.

> **If you please,**
> **Do not tease.**

Please yourself, and you'll please me.

> We cannot often say this; but when people are worrying about mere trifles, we thus give them *carte blanche,* and hope we shall hear no more of their chatter.

Pleasures are like poppies spread ;
You seize the flower, its bloom is shed.

> So *Burns* found them ; but then he was too apt to snatch at pleasures of a kind which wisdom would forego.

Plough deep while sluggards sleep,
And you shall have corn to sell or to keep.

> Here we have *Franklin's* wisdom, as he put it into the mouth of Poor Richard. It suits England as well as America. Hard work *is still the road* to prosperity; and there is no other.

Prompt pay makes ready way.

You can go all over the world with a sovereign in your hand. Pay at once, and any one will deal with you.

Prosperity's right hand is industry, and her left hand is frugality.

The one produces, and the other preserves. A sensible writer gives the following rules for prospering in business :—

Early to bed, and early to rise ;
Wear the blue ribbon, and advertise.

Proud heart in poor breast :
Much fret and little rest.

Proud looks lose hearts, but courteous words win them. This was a favourite saying of Ferdinand of Spain, and it is undoubtedly true. A game cock has more fight than flesh.

Proud men hate pride in others.

Because it is a sort of defiance to their own pride. "I tread on the pride of Plato," said Diogenes as he walked over Plato's carpet. "Yes—and with more pride," said Plato.

Providence often puts a large potato in a little pig's way.

We marvel at the way in which some men get on, who do not appear to have any particular aptitude for business. In this strange world we meet with people who find the biggest possible potatoes, and yet are the very smallest of piggies.

Providence provides for the provident.

As for the lazy and drunken, providence soon provides for them rags and jags, and a place in the county gaol.

Prudence is good *before* the act, but courage *in* the act.

He saves the steed that keeps him under locks ;
Who looks may leap, nor fear his shins have knocks ;
Who tries may trust, nor flattering friends shall find ;
Who speaks with heed may boldly speak his mind.

Prudent youth is better than rash old age.

One occasionally meets with the latter. Certain men grow older, but not wiser. To have furrows on the brow, and folly in the heart, is a sad mixture. Grey heads are not always wise heads.

Publish a Revised Version of your life.

Correct the errata, add a supplement, and alter the type.

Pull down the nests and the rooks will fly.

Thus John Knox would demolish abbeys to get rid of monks; and there was common sense in the advice. If drink-shops were abolished, should we be rid of drunkards?

Pull the cat's tail, and she'll scratch without fail.

If you annoy people you must not wonder if they turn upon you.

Punctuality is only common honesty.

For it is due to others that we keep due time. What right have we to rob a man of his hours? Might we not as well steal his money as steal minutes in which he could be earning it?

Punctuality is the hinge of business.

Except with lawyers, who give this praise to procrastination. Punctuality may be a minor virtue, but the want of it produces some of the major evils. Keep Greenwich time.

Punish your enemies by doing them good.

Pure water is good within and without.

Certain drinkers have never tried cold water : they have no idea what a delicate taste it has, nor how refreshing it is when it comes in contact with the skin. Try *aqua pura!*

Purses shrink,
While workmen drink.

A prudent man advised his drunken servant to put by his money for a rainy day. In a few weeks his master inquired how much of his money he had saved. "Faith, none at all," said he; "it rained so hard yesterday, that it all went."

Put a key on your tongue.

Do not have lockjaw, but yet lock your jaw.

Put glasses to thine eyes, not to thy lips.

Wear spectacles, but do not make yourself a spectacle by taking too much liquor. You will not take too much if you take none.

Put in with the loaves, and taken out with the cakes.

> And so only half baked. Many are thus underdone as to common sense, and hence they remain for ever very soft and sappy.

Put not a ring of gold into the snout of a swine.

> Do not pay honour to the base. Do not tell the sacred mysteries of the inner life to the profane. Ask not an unworthy person to minister in holy things. Observe the propriety of things.

Put not all your crocks on one shelf.

> For if that shelf should fall, all your pottery would be smashed. Divide your ventures and risks. Trust not all your cash to one speculation. There is common sense in this proverb.

Put not milk into a leaky can.

> Don't tell your secrets to a blab, nor invest your cash in doubtful companies, and questionable speculations.

Put the saddle on the right horse.

> Adam blamed Eve; Eve blamed the Devil; they should have blamed themselves. This also applies to us.

Put the whip into the manger.

> Give corn instead of cord. Feed, but do not flog.

Put what you like into your mouth, but mind what comes out of it.

> If you like to eat dirt, that's your own concern; but if you speak dirt, others will be defiled.

Put your foot down where you mean to stand.

> Be firm. Resolve, and resolutely stand to your resolution.
>
> > If well thou hast begun, press on for right;
> > It is the end that crowns us, not the fight.

Put your hand quickly to your hat, and slowly to your purse, and you'll take no harm.

> Be liberal with your courtesy, but be economical in your expenditure. Civility costs nothing, but earns much.

Sayings of a more Spiritual Sort.

Pardon is not properly prized without a solemn sense of the fount, folly, filth, and fruit of sin.

See how David felt all this, and set it forth in the fifty-first Psalm. *Tennyson* wrote—

"He taught me all the mercy, for he show'd me all the sin."

Pardoned sin makes peace within.

It is the first in the catalogue of blessings, "Who forgiveth all thine iniquities."—Ps. ciii. 3. *Stillingfleet* asks: "How can we be at peace with ourselves till we have reason to believe that God is at peace with us?"

Partners in sin are justly made partners in punishment.

Therefore, both body and soul will suffer the future punishment of unrepented sin.

Patience is the livery of Christ's servants.

In it they are known to be of the household of the Crucified. It requires more grace to suffer patiently than to serve laboriously.

Peacemakers are the children of God : peace-breakers are the children of the devil.

John Trapp says : "Peace-making is as sure and as sweet a sign of a son of the God of Peace, as the parti-coloured clothes were anciently signs of a king's daughters.—2 Sam. xiii. 18."

Penitent sighs bring forth exulting songs.

"Sin, repentance, and pardon, are like to the three vernal months of the year, March, April, and May. Sin comes in like March, blustering, stormy, and full of bold violence. Repentance succeeds like April, showering, weeping, and full of tears. Pardon follows like May, springing, singing, full of joys and flowers. If our hands have been full of *March*, with the tempests of unrighteousness, our eyes must be full of *April*, with the sorrow of repentance ; and then our hearts shall be full of *May*, in the true joy of forgiveness."— *T. Adams.*

Perfect trust in a perfect Saviour brings perfect peace.

> " We may trust him solely, all for us to do :
> They who trust him wholly, find him wholly true."
> *R. F. Havergal.*

Pharisees and Publicans both pour out their hearts before God, the one in bragging, the other in begging.

Plead for Jesus, for he pleads for you.

Please God, and you will please good men.

Please God in all you do, and be pleased with all God does.

> This would be heaven on earth if we could fulfil it.

Poor are they that think themselves rich in grace : rich are they that see themselves poor.

> A clergyman once said to Mr. Newton, " Really, sir, what a beautiful tract that is of yours, ' The Progress of Grace ' ! I never saw so clearly that I was in the full ear." " Why," said Mr. Newton, " I put, or intended to put, as one mark of it, a humble opinion of ourselves."

Poor sinners have a rich gospel.

Poverty in the way of duty is to be chosen rather than plenty in the way of sin.

> When Philip Henry was fined for holding services, and his goods seized, he said, " Ah, well ! we may be losers *for* Christ, but we cannot in the end be losers *by* Christ : praise his name."

Poverty of spirit is the riches of the soul.

> " Humility is not only a precious grace, but the preserver of all other graces ; and without it (if that could be) they are but as a box of precious powder carried in the wind without a cover, in danger of being scattered and blown away."—*Leighton.*

Practical holiness is the seal of personal election.

Pray against sin, but don't sin against prayer.

> We sin against prayer when we ask for what we will not
> pray one thing and act another. To forget our own ʋ
> refuse their answers when they come, is an
> mercy-seat. So also to pray holiness and
> crime against the throne of grace.

Pray David's prayer if you would sing David's song.

Pray for a blessing, and your prayer will be a blessing.

> In the very seeking of a benediction grace is put into action, and is strengthened by the exercise.

Pray for those who do not pray for themselves.

> Some one prayed for you when you were yet unsaved : return that effectual prayer to the treasury of the church by pleading for others. Plead hard for the hard heart which never pleads.

Pray for your minister, and you will be praying for yourself.

> Whatever blessing he obtains will appear in his ministry, and you will be a partaker of it.

Prayer breathes in the air of heaven, and praise breathes it out again.

> Thus we have heavenly respiration, and by it we live unto God.
>
>> Prayer and praise, with sins forgiven,
>> Bring down to earth the bliss of heaven.

Prayer bringeth heaven down to man, and carrieth man up to heaven.

Prayer is God's rod which fetches forth streams of blessing from the Rock of affliction.

Prayer knocks till the door opens.

> Open it will, for so runs the promise of our faithful God, "To him that knocketh it shall be opened." "If the angel opened the door of the prison to let Peter out, it was prayer that opened the door of heaven to let the angel out."

Prayer moves the hand that moves the world.

> "Prayer is a creature's strength, his very breath and being;
> Prayer is the golden key that can open the wicket of Mercy.
> Prayer is the magic sound that saith to Fate, 'So be it';
> Prayer is the slender nerve that moveth the muscles of Omnipotence."—*Martin Tupper.*

Prayer must not come from the roof of the mouth, but from the root of the heart.

Prayer oils the wheels of the waggon of life.

Try the effect of it when the wheel begins to creak. A missionary in a heathen land had grown sadly weary and discouraged. He was going forth to his work with a joyless face, when his young wife called him back, went to him, put her hands on his shoulders, and, with tears in her eyes, said, "O Willie, Willie! much work and little prayer is hard work." Then she led him to a private room, and there, kneeling down, prayed with him as only one who loved with a true heavenly love could pray. From that room he went forth strong in the strength which never failed him; never again was he tempted to sever work and prayer.

Prayer rightly offered is richly answered.

"Prayer, like Jonathan's bow, returns not empty; never was faithful prayer lost. No tradesman trades with such certainty as the praying saint. Some prayers, indeed, have a longer voyage than others, but then they return with richer lading at last; the praying soul is a gainer by waiting for an answer."—*Gurnall.*

Prayer should be pillared on promises, and pinnacled with praises.

Prayer without words can win :
Words without heart are sin.

"She also prayed who touched Christ's garment's hem with reverent faith; ay, and was answered too, although no word escaped her."—*Partridge.*

Preach Christ to sinners if you would preach sinners to Christ.

Daniel Wilson suggested to a friend, as a text for a sermon, the word "Christ." "Begin with Christ, go on with Christ, and end with Christ, and I am sure your hearers will never be tired, for his name is as ointment poured forth."

Preachers are apt to think more of their own credit as God's messengers, than of the credit given to God's messages.

Faithful preachers will get little credit from men of the world, or from worldly Christians; for the religion of to-day leans to unfaithfulness :

"It calls for pleasing pulpiteers,
Modern, and brilliant, and fast;
Who will show how men may live as they list,
And go to heaven at last."

Preachers often draw the bow at a venture, but the Spirit of God takes sure aim.

Preaching in pride is doing God's work in the devil's livery.

Precious promises are the provender of faith.

> *Dr. Gordon* says, "We would commend a faith that even seems audacious, like that of the sturdy covenanter Robert Bruce, who requested, as he was dying, that his finger might be placed on one of God's strong promises, as though to challenge the Judge of all with it as he should enter his presence. As we stand face to face with the Word we cannot be too bold."

Pride climbs up, not as Zacchæus to see Jesus, but to be seen itself.

Prize the doctrine of grace and the grace of the doctrine.

> Take care that these go together, for so hath God appointed.

Providence may change, but the promise must stand.

> The wheel of providence revolves, but the axle of divine faithfulness remains in its place. "He cannot deny himself."

Punishment usually bears upon it the image of the sin.

> Jacob deceived his brother, and his sons deceived him; David took another man's wife, and his own bed was defiled by Absalom. These are two instances out of thousands. The Lord makes his children see their sin in the smart which it brings upon them.

UACKERY has no friend like gullibility.

> If none would swallow, none would make the pill. Persons invite deception by the eager way in which they snap at the bait. Advertise enough, and you may sell liquorice water at a guinea a gill.

Quality is better than quantity.

> They do not often go together. Prefer to do a little well rather than a great deal in a poor style.

Quarrel only at twelve o'clock, and get it over at noon.

> Which is much the same as—Never quarrel at all.

Quarrellers seldom grow fat.

> They worry the flesh off their bones by agitation, waste their substance in litigation, and weary their minds in disputation.

Quarrelling dogs come limping home.

> They give and receive hurts; and many a painful footstep they cause themselves by their fighting propensities.
>> Since dogs delight to bark and bite,
>> When they get hurt it serves them right.

Quarter on the enemy.

> It is a wise thing to make missions and other good works as nearly as possible self-supporting. It has been done in several cases; and in the process many good purposes have been answered, for the people have been trained to independence and generosity.

"Queen Elizabeth is dead."

> A sarcastic remark when stale news is reported.

Queries from queer quarters may be left to answer themselves.

> If we are to answer all questions, we have our work cut out for the next thousand years. We are bound to tell the truth if we tell anything; but we are not bound to tell anything at all. Here is a neat answer which says nothing :—
>> Said a mortgagee to a mortgagor,
>> What do you want my money for?
>> Said the mortgagor to the mortgagee,
>> Lend me the money, and then you'll see.

Quick and well seldom go together.

"Hurry and Cunning are the two apprentices of Dispatch and Skill; but neither of them ever learns his master's trade."—*Colton.*

Quick believers need broad shoulders.

To support the burden of all which they accept as gospel.

Quick believers will need wide swallows.

To take in all that is told them. Better be a little inhospitable when the story looks like a traveller; for if you take it in, it may take you in. The foolish believeth every word, but the wise man enquireth.

Quick removals are slow prosperings.

Two removals are as bad as a fire. He who shifts his place often, is like a tree frequently transplanted, whose fruit is very small.

"Change for spite and rue it,
And wish you could undo it."

Quick steps are best over miry ground.

When you come into a dangerous place, and must needs pass through it, use all speed, and be away as soon as possible. If in the course of your calling you must needs speak with bad men, have done with them as soon as ever you can, and be on your guard all the while. A person caught in a shower puts up his umbrella, and mends his pace; so should we protect ourselves, and hurry on.

Quick to borrow is always slow to pay.

Those, on the other hand, who will never borrow till they are driven to it, are the people who are eager to get out of debt.

Quickly come is often quickly go.

Easy gainings make easy spendings. Is this why a spendthrift is said to be *fast?* He came by his money on a sudden, and as suddenly he makes it vanish.

Quiet is sweet when riot is over.

Nobody values peace more than he who knows the evil of contention. "Then are they glad, because they be quiet."—Ps. cvii. 30.

Quiet sleep feels no foul weather.

Once off into the land of Nod, we are to the east of Eden, and care not whether it rains or snows. *Bed*ford is a quiet place.

Quiet sleep is the best patent medicine.

> What a blessing to be able to enjoy it ! *Hood* calls bed—
>> " That heaven upon earth to the weary head ;
>> But a place that to name would be ill-bred
>>> To the head with a wakeful trouble—
>> 'Tis held by such a different lease !
>> To one, a place of comfort and peace,
>> All stuffed with the down of stubble geese,
>>> To another with only the stubble ! "

Quit not certainty for hope.

> Better a sure shilling than a sovereign in the clouds, to come or not to come. Never trust promising appearances so as to give up what you have realized.

Quit your pots, and your potations ;
Yield to wisdom's exhortations.

> " Will you take something ? " said a teetotaler to a friend standing near a tavern. " I don't care if I do," was the reply. " Well," said the teetotaler, " let's take a walk."

Quizzing is pleasant, but it is a game which two can play at.

> This is a bit of Judge Halyburton's humour, and he practically illustrated it in his own way. For a very clever fellow to be quietly taken in while he thinks he is showing his superiority to others, is a merited chastisement which is likely to do him good.

Quoth the dog to the Bishop, "Every man to his trade."

> A capital specimen of impudence, cool as a cucumber. We have met with observations quite as cheeky from very small puppies.

Sayings of a more Spiritual Sort.

Quick, quick, in holy things ;
For flying time has lightning wings.

>> Choose, O youth, the narrow way,
>>> Flee at once from sin and sorrow ;
>> Say not, 'tis too soon to-day,
>>> Lest it be too late to-morrow.

Quickened by grace, quicken your pace.

AGGED colts may make handsome horses.

> But they will need breaking in, and a good deal of curry-comb. Never despair of a boy because he has high spirits. This will sober down into quiet energy.

Rags are the livery of laziness.

> They may come of blameless poverty, but they seldom do; for the industrious poor patch and mend.
>
> > Thou barefooted lout!
> > Why not cobble and clout?

Rainbow at night is the shepherd's delight,
Rainbow in the morning gives the shepherd warning.

> These weather signs vary according to the place, and do not apply universally. Other weather prophets foresee rain when—
>
> > "Last night the sun went pale to bed,
> > The moon in halos hid her head;
> > The boding shepherd heaves a sigh,
> > For see, a rainbow spans the sky!"

Rainy days will come; prepare for them.

> Just as bees store honey against the coming of winter.
>
> > Wise saving is not mean: the best of men may see
> > That rainy day which surely comes to man and bee.

Rainy days will surely come;
Take your friend's umbrella home.

> We see in the shops "*Umbrellas Recovered.*" We should like to recover those we have lent; but to return an umbrella is a lost art. A plain-spoken preacher delivered the following from his desk: "I would announce to the congregation that, probably by mistake, there was left at the meeting-house this morning a small cotton umbrella, much damaged by time and wear, and of an exceeding pale blue colour, in place whereof was taken a very large black silk umbrella of great beauty. Blunders of this sort, my brethren, are getting a little too common." There is nothing so rigidly Catholic as an umbrella, it keeps Lent the year round.

Raise no more devils than you can lay.

> Do not provoke animosities which you cannot pacify, nor set in motion elements of disorder which you will be unable to control. It is easy to open the cages of wild beasts and let them loose; but who will coax tigers back again?

Rake not the bottom of an old canal.

> Old quarrels and old charges are best left alone. Raise no unsavoury odours. If evil will die, let it die.

Rank folly is a weed which often grows in the ranks of fashion.

> And elsewhere too. Whether the grass be long or short, this green-stuff is sure to grow. There is a rather rude verse which brings this matter very closely home :—
>
> > Of fools the world is full,
> > Whom if you would not see,
> > Follow one simple rule,
> > Effectual it will be.
> > Alone you must remain,
> > And, as you hate an ass,
> > Excuse my being plain,
> > Quick! Smash your looking-glass.

Rare birds are sure to be noticed.

> More was at first made of a black swan than of all the royal birds on the Thames. Something eccentric and out of the common soon commands attention; yet wise men value not things by their rarity, but by their real worth.

Rash presumption is a ladder, which will break the mounter's neck.

> > Who climbs too high may break his neck:
> > Let this thy pert presumption check.

Rashness is not valour.

> It has for a while led to the same sort of action as that which comes of true courage, but it will not bear the test of time.

Rather look on the good of evil men than on the evil of good men.

> It is a great thing to have an eye for goodness everywhere; but it is a disease to be always spying out the faults of the truly excellent. See most of the least, and least of the worst in your fellows.

Rather the egg to-day than the hen to-morrow.

> Present advantage is thus set above future gain. This proverb is true, or not true, according to its application.

Rats play a rare game
When cats are too tame.

If authority does not show its power, the lovers of disorder will play their pranks. Why have we cats if they are afraid of rats?

Raw leather will stretch.

There's a good deal of it in use for making consciences just now.

Awkward corners of truth away they will whittle;
If their creed does not suit, they will stretch it a little.

Read men as well as books.

Or else the most interesting records will be unknown to you. Read man as well as manuscripts. Be not mere book-worms. "The proper study of mankind is man." There is wisdom in that sentence of *Hobbes*, "If I had read as much as other men, I should have been as ignorant."

Reading maketh a full man, conversation a ready man, and writing an exact man.

Ready money has the pick of the market.

Those whose pay is questionable will have questionable wares sent to them. Nobody is eager to press the best of his goods upon long-winded purchasers.

Ready money gets the first;
Doubtful credit takes the worst.

Ready money is a wonderful medicine.

To the estate it is a balm, to the temper a calm, to no wise man a harm. Go thou with money in thy palm, it worketh like a charm. Another proverb is: Ready money works great cures.

Ready money is sweet as honey.

So says the tradesman: it enables him to replenish his stock, and turn over his capital. Credit is not creditable to those who have cash. Everybody is glad to get his money; he calls it sugar.

Ready money is the secret of economy.

For people who pay know where they are, and are able to regulate their expenses by knowing how the money goes. Besides, they buy better. Yet true is the old proverb, "Ready money will away." Even on cash principles money evaporates very fast.

Reason governs the wise man, and cudgels the fool.

> The wise obey reason, and so are rightly led; but the fool refuses
> obedience to common sense, and therefore before long he endures
> remorse, which is repentance armed with a scourge of thorns and
> briars. Reason binds the man; but he is never more free than
> when he yields to its constraint.

Reason is most reasonable when it leaves off reasoning
  on things above reason.

> This saying of *Sir Philip Sydney* deserves such frequent quotation
> as to make it proverbial, if it be not already so. The mysteries of
> faith are not contrary to reason, but they are so much above and
> beyond it that they can only be received by faith.

Reason lies between bridle and spur.

> The medium between reserve and resolve, between restraint and
> energy, is hard to hit; but it is the golden mean.
>
> > Between the bridle and the spur
> > How very apt we are to err!

Reason not with the great :
'Tis a perilous gait.

> It requires much courage to argue with those on whom you are
> dependent : you may be proving away your bread and butter. Still,
> if truth requires it, we dare face a parliament of kings.

Reasoning often banishes reason.

> Argument confuses where men are not anxious after truth. It is
> easy for reason to throw dust into its own eyes.

Rebukes ought to have a grain more of sugar than of salt.

> Or else they may be rejected and resented. Yet it is not easy to
> sugar the pill of reproof. Let us try to do so, for rebuke is sharp
> enough in itself without the addition of needless severity. Rebuke
> with soft words and hard arguments.

Reckless youth makes rueful eld.

> When the sins of youth lie in a man's bones in his later year
> has bitter cause to mourn his folly ; but his mourning cannot
> the consequences of his early faults. Wild oats sown in o
> days make an awful harvest in the autumn of life.

Recklessness soon wrecks an estate.

> Let us therefore act with thoughtfulness, be our estate little or great, for we don't want it wrecked.
>
>> Though some men do as do they would,
>> Let the thrifty do as do they should.

Red Lane needs watching.

> That is to say, we must be careful of what goes down our throat. "Doctor," said a patient to one of the great hydropathic lights of Malvern, whom ill-health had obliged him to consult, "Do you think that a little spirits, now and then, would hurt me very much?" "Why, no, sir," said the doctor, deliberately, "I do not know that a little, now and then, would hurt very much; but, sir, if you don't take any, you won't be hurt at all."

Reform your wife's husband.

> I mean your children's father. Try your level best to make your own roof-tree "the Reformer's Tree in the Home Park."

Regard the world with open eye,
For sure the blind eat many a fly.

> This is not the world to be blind in. We need all our wits about us, or we shall be killed, cooked, and eaten before we know it. If we escape so dire a fate, still the clouds of flies will half choke us if we do not see them and brush them off.

Rejoice in little, shun what is extreme :
A boat floats safest in a little stream.

Relatives are best with a wall between them.

> Else they take sundry liberties; these liberties are resented, and the fat gets into the fire. Family quarrels arise out of freedoms which are very naturally taken, but are not quite so naturally liked by those upon whom they encroach.

Religion is the best of armour, and the worst of cloaks.

> As a defence it wards off ten thousand ills; but as a pretence it is the worst form of deceit.

Religion lies more in *walk* than in *talk*.

> People should prefer the "w" to the "t." Words are all very fine, but character has far more weight in it.

Remove an old tree, and it will wither and die.

> It is not well to make great changes in old age.

Remove not the ancient land-marks which thy fathers have
set up.

> A curse was solemnly pronounced by the law of Moses on those
> who did so. (See Deut. xxvii. 17.) Neither openly nor secretly
> were the boundary stones to be shifted. The old land-marks of
> truthful doctrine, holy practice, and lawful custom, should be kept
> in their appointed places. Mark the men who move land-marks,
> and move yourself away from them.

Renewed spirits can forego ardent spirits.

> Raised from the dead I quit my *beer;*
> My joys from canted *w(h)ines* are clear;
> Made free, I am no *brand(i)ed* slave;
> No *spirit* vault's my spirit's grave.

Rent and taxes never sleep;
Up and earn them, lest you weep.

> No three letters are so remunerative to a tradesman as N.R.G.
> He must use them or run short of L.S.D.

Repair the gutter, or you'll have to repair the whole house.

> The wet will run down the walls, or get through the roof, and
> the damage will be most serious. Remember the stitch in time in
> connection with every form of business.

Repentance costs dear.

> That is to say, it is far better to avoid a wrong action than to do
> it, and have to repent of it. It is a great waste of time and labour
> to go the wrong road, even if you are happy enough to return from
> it into the right path. Do not buy repentance at a high rate by
> rushing into sin.

Repentance is never too soon.

> It is a blessing that it is never too late, if it be but true. It is
> the heart's medicine, and the sooner it deals with the disease of
> sin the better. To delay repentance is sinful and dangerous.
> Repent, or God will break the thread
> By which thy doom hangs o'er thy head.

Report makes crows blacker than they are.

> No doubt an ill story grows, and the worst are made out worse
> than they really are. They say that even the devil is not so bad as
> he is painted; but of *that* we have great doubt.

Report makes the wolf bigger than he is.

Thus men are needlessly frightened, and the wolf has all the more chance to worry the sheep. No good comes of exaggeration. Yet the wolves of the present day are able, by their sheeps' coats, to make themselves out to be no wolves at all; and our great danger is not from undue alarm, but from deadly indifference.

Reputation is commonly measured by the acre.

The multitude judge of a man's worth by what he is worth, and if he has a great estate he must needs be a great man. It is not always for what he has done, but for how much he owns, that a man is considered a man of mark. According to this, the best judge of character is a land-surveyor. Squire Broadacres shall be asked to take the chair at our next public meeting, though he is mute as a mackerel; for he speaks guineas.

Resist the devil, but flee from lust.

Fénelon makes Mentor say to his young disciple, in the island of Calypso, "Fly, Télémaque, fly! There remains no way of conflict, but by flight." By this means Joseph conquered. It is the only mode of conquest in this most seductive of conflicts.

Respect a man, that you may make him respect himself.

In this way some may be raised out of the gutter. Your generous treatment will make them feel their manhood. Treat them like men, and they will try to live up to your idea of them.

Respect yourself, or no one else will respect you.

Play the fool on your own account, and others will play the fool with you. Paul said to Timothy, "Let no man despise thy youth." Despise it they will if the young man despises it.

Rest and let rest; bless and be blest.
Rest, but do not rust.

Rest in order to future work; and so time and manage the vacation that it shall not make you vacant. When you are called to do nothing, do it heartily. Rest as hard as you can, that you may the sooner get to your work again, and do it better than ever.

Rest comes from unrest, and unrest from rest.

When the heart has been troubled for sin, it is driven to repose in Jesus; and, on the other hand, when the soul has for a while rejoiced in peace, it is too apt to grow carnally secure, and then it falls *into distress* almost as bitter as at the first.

Rest is honest when work is finished.

Then rest is deserved, and so it may be freely enjoyed.

> " Toiling—rejoicing—sorrowing,
>   Onward through life he goes ;
> Each morning sees some task begun,
>   Each evening sees it close ;
> Something attempted, something done,
>   Has earned a night's repose."
>   *Longfellow's* " Village Blacksmith."

Rest is won only by work.

The lazy man idles away his time, but does not rest: even if he has a holiday, he is restless. The science of rest is quite beyond the reach of the non-worker.

Rest on the Sabbath, or you will be worse than a slave.

> "A Sabbath well spent
>   Brings a week of content,
> With rest for the toils of the morrow ;
>   But a Sabbath profaned,
>   Whate'er may be gained,
> Is sure to be followed by sorrow."

Revenge is sweet when it avenges injury with love.

Any other form of revenge is bitter. Revenge of a wrong only makes another wrong. To heap kindness on an enemy is after the manner of God.

> The sandal-tree, most sacred tree of all,
> Perfumes the very axe which works its fall.

Rich enough is he who does not want.

> " A man contented's greatly rich,
>   Possessed of e'er so small ;
> But not contented, though most rich,
>   He poorest is of all."

Rich men have no faults.

Say, rather, they have no friend kind enough to tell them of their faults. Their spots are covered by their money, in the judgment of those who wish to get something out of them. Yet riches at times cause arrogance, and a man with a big purse is apt to purse-proud. This sort of bumptiousness is a fault of the contemptible kind.

Riches adorn the house, but virtue adorns the man.

It enters into the very being of the man, and is a beauty of the highest order. Yet *Herrick* very properly complains—

How rich a man is, all desire to know,
But none enquire if good he be or no.

Riches and cares are inseparable.

The care to get, to keep, to increase, to invest, to transmit : these and innumerable other worms gnaw at the heart which is the slave of wealth. Riches are the shell, and the kernel is care. High stations have heavy duties. Why long to be burdened with a lump of clay, and a load of care? *Isaac Walton* says : "Cares that are the keys that keep those riches hang often so heavily at the rich man's girdle that they clog him with weary days and restless nights, even when others sleep quietly."

Riches are not his who gathers them, but his who uses them.

Why starve yourself to feast an unknown heir?

Riches are often abused, but never refused.

Sages decry them and desire them. They say, "Riches rule the roost"; yet all men wish them to roost on their tree. *Colton* says, "Many speak the truth when they say that they despise riches and preferment; but they mean the riches and preferment possessed by *other men.*"

Riches are unstable ;
Beauty will decay ;
But faithful love will ever last
Till death drive it away.

Brooks says, "Riches are like bad servants, whose shoes are made of running leather, and will never tarry long with one master. Love, however, suffereth long, and is kind; and where it fixes its abode it remains till death." A Scotch proverb says, "Riches are got with pain, kept with care, and lost with grief."

Riches have made more men covetous than covetousness hath made men rich.

Riches, like manure, do no good till they are spread.

One wonders how men can find such pleasure in hoarding. Surely it must be as one says, "They are manured to it." Riches must be spread abroad. Fork them out. Dispurse and disperse. What heaps now lie reeking up offensively to heaven! If generosity does not use them, death will diffuse them.

Riches take to themselves wings and fly away.

Do not let yours thus depart. Clip their wings, and send the feathers to the Stockwell Orphanage, to feather the nest of the five hundred orphans. Address, C. H. Spurgeon, "Westwood," Upper Norwood.

It is a sweet thought, that while riches may take wings and fly *from* us, grace takes wings and flies *with* us to heaven.

Hugh Stowell Brown remarks most wisely: "Riches do often make to themselves wings and fly away; and they are not the wings of a goose, that can hardly fly over a hedge; nor the wings of a pigeon, that will return to its dovecote; nor the wings of any common or weakly bird, that might not fly fast, or might drop the prey from its bill; no, they are the wings of an eagle, a rapacious bird, a strong bird, a bird of swift and lofty and untiring flight, a bird not easily shot when flying, not easily reached when in its aerie; there is little hope of recovering what the eagle carries away; and thus riches lost are, as a rule, lost for ever."

Riches will ourselves abuse,
Unless we rightly learn to use.

If we hoard them for ourselves, they are like waters collected in a stagnant pool, breeding all manner of evils; but if by generosity we let them flow abroad they become a fountain of fertility. Wisdom is needed with wealth. The Greeks of old said—

"Abundance is a blessing to the wise:
The use of riches in discretion lies.
Learn this, ye men of wealth! A heavy purse
In a fool's pocket is a heavy curse."

Ride on, but look before you.

Go ahead, but know which way you are going, lest you rush to ruin. Keep your eyes in advance of your nose.

Right, if pulled too tight, turns to wrong.

Sometimes it is right to waive a right; especially when it would involve hardship to push your claim to an extreme. Rights should fit like bracelets, and not grip like handcuffs.

Right mixture makes good mortar.

Due proportion and thorough blending of various graces make up a good character. Also in forming a partnership a wise arrangement and a good spirit will secure lasting unity. In marriage a fit blend is almost everything.

Right wrongs no man.

He that is the gainer by right makes no man a loser, for no man can lose what is not rightfully his own. Right is right all round.

Rivers need a spring.

That they may begin they must have a source: that they may continue they must be supplied from flowing springs. A worthy course of life must have a holy motive to sustain it.

Rogues reckon all men rascals.

They know themselves, and they suppose none to be better than they themselves are. The dog who runs away with stolen meat thinks that every other dog would rob him of it. Men see themselves in other men's eyes. Innocence is not suspicious; but guilt is always ready to turn informer.

Rome was not built in a day, but many are building it in the night.

Yet nobody seems to care. Protestants enter very faint protests, and Rome everywhere finds room enough for growth.

Roses fade away:
Thorns for ever stay.

This is a hard saying, and by no means true. Our sorrows pass away even as our joys. There is a Rose which never fades, and this takes away the sharpness of the thorns, both in life and death.

Rotten apples abide no handling.

When a matter is far gone in the wrong direction, people cannot bear you to mention it. "Let ill alone" is the motto of very many. The state of affairs is very bad, therefore you must not stir in it, nor even look at it. Remember who it was in the gospel that said, "Let us alone."

Rough nets are not the best bird-catchers.

And in the case of birds of the human order, the less of roughness the better. He that would win a soul must have a tender heart and a gentle tongue.

> Who scares the linnet
> Shall not win it.

Rub your sore eye with your elbow.

That is to say, don't rub it at all. So my father used to say to me at the dinner table, "Pick your teeth with your elbow"; that is, let them alone when in the company of others.

Rubs and snubs and drubs make the man.

They develop the hardier qualities, and prepare the man to bear prosperity should God be pleased to send it. As *Kingsley*, in his "Ode to the North-East Wind," says:

"'Tis the hard gray winter
Breeds hard Englishmen."

Rue and balm grow in the same garden.

The sorrow and the succour, the cross and the comfort, are generally joined together.

Our dangers and delights are near allies:
From the same stem the rose and prickle rise.

Rule your children, or you'll ruin them.

Unruly children are not happy even as children, and when they grow up they prove a curse to all around. Break them in, or they will break out, and in the end break your hearts. An aged woman, speaking of the days when her children were all young and all around her, said, "*I let them be happy, but I aye keepit the crown on my head.*" In contrast to this it has been said that this is "the age of obedient parents."

Rule your temper, or it will ruin you.

No danger is greater than that which may come from an ungoverned temper. Better sleep on a bed of dynamite. This is harder for some than for others. "A grove of cactus in the tropics is almost sure to swarm with serpents; and there are natures in which bad passions breed and multiply as if that were the law of their being. It is easy for a man who is free naturally from such pests to look down on the unfortunates, and scourge them with rebukes. 'I wish,' said a certain cool, phlegmatic old gentleman to his neighbour, 'that you would govern your temper.' 'My dear sir,' was the answer, 'I control more temper in five minutes than you do in five years.'"—*Dr. Willcox.*

Run! run! Here's a cockney with a gun.

You are likely to be shot if you get within range; unless you can keep near the game, so as to be aimed at, in which case you are as safe as the Bank of England.

Rust consumes more than use wears.

Leave a knife outdoors sticking in the earth, and it will be eaten up a hundred to one more than if it had been in constant use.

Sayings of a more Spiritual Sort.

Reason makes us men, grace makes us saints.

Unaided reason never rises to saintship; and yet there is the highest reason for being saintly.

Religion without Christ is a lamp without oil.

"The foolish took their lamps, but took no oil with them." Jesus says, "Without me ye can do nothing."

Religion without head is fire without wood.

It runs to superstition and fanaticism; and after blazing with fury, it dies down into ashes, which the wind carries away.

Religion without heart is a dead formality.

The heart is the life, the essence, the joy of it; and that gone, all is gone but the mere shell. "The puffing system is an advertisement of hollowness. He whose religion is ever on his lips, has seldom any of that valuable treasure in his heart; it keeps watch, like a liveried porter at his door, but there is nobody at home, and there is nothing to steal; if it were well lodged in his soul, he would not be so afraid of its escape."

Remember the shame of sin when tempted by the sweet of sin.

Repentance looks upon the past with a weeping eye, and upon the future with a watchful eye.

Repentance must be universal to be effectual.

Every sin is to be bewailed, and forsaken: one sin reserved will ruin all our hope. One leak will sink a ship; one bullet in the heart will kill a man; one sin delighted in will ruin a soul. *Brooks* says, "He that turns not from every sin, turns not aright from any one sin."

Resignation is putting God between one's self and one's grief.

Thus one is shielded in the best possible manner. Accept affliction, and the sharpness of it is gone.

Rest not till you rest in Christ.

> For any rest, short of Christ, is like the deadly pause of Lot's wife, which sealed her destruction.

Rest the body and feast the soul,
And keep for God the Sabbath whole.

> *Chateaubriand* says that during the time of the Revolution, when an attempt was made to substitute decades for Sabbaths, the peasants of France were in the habit of saying, "Our oxen know when Sunday comes, and will not work on that day."

"Retire, and read thy Bible to be gay."

Righteous men believe themselves to be sinners, and sinners believe themselves to be righteous.

> So says *Pascal,* in his "Pensées"; and his saying is true. The late Dr. —— did not satisfy, by his preaching, the Calvinistic portion of his flock. "Why, sir," said they, "we think you dinna tell us enough about renouncing our ain righteousness." "Renouncing your ain righteousness!" vociferated the doctor, "I never saw any ye had to renounce."

ADNESS and gladness take turn about.
> Sunshine and shower
> Make up life's hour.

Safe bind, safe find.

Have everything legally correct, and so be free from anxiety and dispute. But specially make things sure for eternity; for a flaw in your title to a mansion in the skies will be serious indeed.

> Deeds for your lands you prove and keep with care,
> Oh, that for heaven you but as careful were!

Safer on shore in an old cart than at sea in a new ship.

Yet our brave sailors don't think so. When they are out at sea they glory that they are safe from falling tiles and chimney-pots, and the horse does not run away with the cart, or fall down.

Saint Francis shaved himself before he shaved his brethren.

Reform should begin with the reformer himself. Yet personal reformation is often most distasteful. *Charles Kingsley* said, "I don't deny, my friends, that it is much cheaper and pleasanter to be reformed by the devil than by God, for God will only reform society on condition of our reforming every man his own self; while the devil is quite ready to help us to mend the laws and the parliament, earth and heaven, without ever starting such an impertinent and 'personal' request as that a man should mend himself."

Saint Monday is one of the devil's saints.

Truly "Saint Monday maketh many sinners."

Saint Swithin's day, if it doth rain,
For forty days it will remain.

Sheer superstition; yet so commonly repeated when July 15th comes round, that we must needs mention it. In *Poor Robin's Almanack* for 1697, this silly prognostication is given at length:

> "In this month is St. Swithin's day,
> On which, if that it rain, they say,
> Full forty days after it will,
> Or more or less some rain distil.
> This Swithin was a saint, I trow,
> And Winchester's bishop also,
> Who in his time did many a feat,
> As popish legends do repeat."

Salt never cries out that it is salty.

> So say the Creoles. True virtue never boasts. Fire never cries out "I burn." Goodness has no need to proclaim its own qualities.

Salt spilt is never all gathered.

> When wrong is done, you cannot undo it all; and when anger is excited, and ill words spoken, it is hard to clear it all up, and put a complete end to the scandal.
>
> > When out of bag the cat is let
> > Its tail inside you cannot get.

Salute, and be saluted.

> All the world over this is the rule. As you do to others, others will do to you; at least, in matters of courtesy. Bow and be bowed.

Same clothes every day
Make clouts for Sunday.

> It is a sad lack of economy to go on all the week without change of garments, and have no "Sunday go-to-meeting coat"; but it would seem that in the olden times there were wasters of this sort.

Samson was a strong man, but even he could not pay money before he had it.

> Yet he took care, when he fell into debt to those who found out his riddle, that they were not long without the reward which he had promised them. It is true we cannot pay money before we have it, but we ought not to come under obligation to pay unless we see the means of doing so.

Sands form the mountains, moments make the year.

> *Dr. Stoughton* says, "As in money, so in time, we are to look chiefly to the smallest portions. Take care of the pence, and the pounds will take care of themselves. Take care of the minutes, and the hours and years will take care of themselves. Gold is not found in California for the most part in great masses, but in little grains. It is sifted out of the sand in minute particles, which, melted together, produce the rich ingots that excite the world's cupidity. So the spare pieces of time, the shreds, the odds and ends of time put together, may form a very great and beautiful work."

Sanguine men are seldom safe men.

> They reckon as assets all that they hope to get. They are all very well as acquaintances for a little cheering up; but, if you follow their advice they will soon let you down. They may be cheerful travelling companions, but they will never do for bankers.

Satan is a lion to those that fly him, and a fly to those
  that face him.

Submit, and he roars ; resist, and he flees.

Satan is wiser than in days of yore,
And tempts by making rich, not making poor.

Assuredly there are more perils to most men in wealth than in
poverty. It is easier to keep your footing in the low dungeon than
on the lofty tower.

Satan keeps school for neglected children.

The schools and schoolmasters of the devil are very many : a
book might be written about the Satanic method of instruction.
When a lady once told Archbishop Sharpe that she would not
communicate religious instruction to her children until they had
attained to years of discretion, the shrewd prelate replied, "Madam,
if you do not teach them, the devil will ! "

Satan promises the best, and pays the worst.

He is a liar from the beginning. The foolish are deceived by
him. "I have read of King Canute," says an excellent minister,
"that he promised to make him the highest man in England who
should kill King Edmund, his rival ; which, when one had per-
formed, and expected his reward, he commanded him to be hung
on the highest tower in London. So Satan promises great things
to people in pursuit of their lusts, but he puts them off with great
mischief in the end. The promised crown turns to a halter ; the
promised comfort to a torment ; the promised honour into shame ;
the promised consolation into desolation ; and the promised heaven
into a hell."

Satan shows the bait, but hides the hook.

He is far too crafty to let men see the naked sin, or the unveiled
punishment. He covers the hook with the bait of pleasure, or
profit, or philosophy, or progress, or even piety.

Satan's palace—the gin palace.

Doubtless he is the real king of the place where evil spirits are
retailed. His is the blue ruin, his the fire-water, his the reeling
brain, and the delirium tremens. A pamphlet having been written
to prove that temperance and other societies were the seven last
plagues predicted by John, a tavern-keeper in America got a
supply, and in front of his bar posted a bill bearing this inscription—
"*The Seven Last Plagues sold here.*" Some of his customers took
the hint, and bought no more of them.

" Saturday night is my delight,
    And so is Sunday morning ;
But Sunday noon comes round too soon,
    And so does Monday morning."

Either this is the song of the lazy man who loves to escape from work, or of the truly devout man, to whom even the eve of the Sabbath is precious. The Lord's day should begin on the previous evening if possible, for the blessing on the seventh day has never been withdrawn. Never is the Sabbath too long : we would like to clip the wings of time to cause the holy hours to linger. We dread to go back into the cold world again.

Sauce for the goose is sauce for the gander.

What is fair for women is fair for men. Our laws should be equal, though they are not. In social life we should deal evenly with both sexes. Women and men are very much alike in goodness, especially women. Let us hope that men and women are not both geese, as the proverb insinuates.

Save a thief from prison, and he'll pick your pocket.

He is incapable of gratitude from his very nature, and will prey upon his benefactor as soon as upon anyone else. Warm a viper in your bosom, and its first act is to sting you.

Save me from a boar, a boor, and a bore.

Three dreadful creatures, alike in name, and equally objects of dread to those who know them.

Save me from my friends.

These are often more injurious than enemies. Some through their flattery, others by implicating us in their imprudence, and others by what they call their candour—a smiling cruelty which reminds one of threading a worm on a hook tenderly, as if you loved it.

" But of all plagues that heaven in wrath can send,
    Save, save, oh, save me from the candid friend ! "

Save sixpence, and lay the foundation of a fortune.

Most great fortunes have been commenced by littles, and have grown by slow degrees.

Come to London with half-a-crown ;
And by-and-by you'll own a town.

Save something for the sore foot.

For yourself, when you cannot move in so lively a way as you now do; and for others, that you may help those who are incapable of work. In order to achieve a fair measure of saving, old writers warn men against the three B's:—Back, Belly, and Building. Fine clothes, fine tables, and fine houses cause heavy expenses. Wastefulness is a sin against that providence of which thrift is a humble imitation.

Save while you have, and give while you live.

It is too late to begin saving when all is gone, or to become a generous giver after you are dead. Be your own executor; for very frequently, if money is left for a good purpose, the purpose gets no good from it.

Save yourself pains by taking pains.

To do a thing thoroughly well is the easiest plan after all; for if you have to do it over again, you will wish you had done it well at first. Take trouble that you may be saved trouble.

Saved pence make men rich, but saved minutes make them wise.

It is more needful to be economical of time than of money. We may get more money, but we cannot buy more time: it is not in the market. Goldsmiths save even the sweepings of their shops: utilize the fragments of your time. Great things can be accomplished by the persevering use of odd minutes.

Saving is a greater art than getting.

Professor Bluntschli, the famous jurist, celebrated his seventieth birthday by sending a present of seven hundred francs to Zurich, his native city, which was to be expended in buying money-boxes for the children of the working-classes in the schools, "in order to train them," as he says, "by the regular laying by of their little savings, to begin the collection of a small capital early in life."

Say "God help me"; but don't lie on your back.

Remember how Hercules advised the rustic to put his own shoulder to the wheel, and get the cart out of the slough.

Say less in thy promise than thou dost intend;
Surprise with thy bounty, and gladden thy friend.

This is much better than promising acres, and giving only the scrapings from your muddy boots. He who is better than his word, is better than the man whose words end in words.

Say little, write less, print least.

Or better, print none at all. It would be a great relief to this press-ridden nation if this advice could be enforced. The following motto for a "waste basket" appeared in the *Atlantic's* "Contributors' Club":—

> " If all the trees in all the woods were men,
> And each and every blade of grass a pen ;
> If every leaf on every shrub and tree
> Turned to a sheet of foolscap ; every sea
> Were changed to ink, and all earth's living tribes
> Had nothing else to do but act as scribes,
> And for ten thousand ages, day and night,
> The human race should write, and write, and write,
> Till all the pens and paper were used up,
> And each great inkstand was an empty cup,
> Still would the scribblers clustered round its brink
> Call for more pens, more paper, and more ink."

Say " No," before you know it to your cost.

Little by little men are drawn on by seductive arts, till they are seriously involved. If they had but manliness enough to say " No," they would not be drawn in by schemers.

"Nay," *John*, "Nay," *John*, that's what you must say, *John*,
Whenever you are asked to drink, or you'll be led astray, *John*.
> Say that though you are not old,
> Nor yet so very wise, *John*,
> Yet what is right, and good, and true,
> You're old enough to prize, *John*.
> Let the people drink who will,
> But when they come to you, *John*,
> Boldly say, " I've signed the pledge,
> And mean to keep it too," *John*.

**Say not all the say ;
Let others share the day.**

Do not imitate Dr. Johnson, who would have all the talk for two hours, then rub his hands and say, " What a splendid conversation we've had ! " Treat your friends in conversation as you would at table, when you are carving :—

> " Give no more to every guest,
> Than he's able to digest :
> And that you may have your due,
> Let your neighbour carve for you."

If they listen to you, take your turn in listening to them. Most people like the sound of their own voices better than that of others ; at least, let them have a sandwich of your meat and their bread.

Say not all you know ; do not all you can.

Keep a reserve. Always have a shot in the locker. If you fire all your cartridges, you will be out of the battle. Never talk yourself dry, nor run yourself lame.

Say, say ; but you cannot unsay.

Therefore do not "say, say," without a good deal of consideration. Think twice before you speak once; and once having spoken, stand to your word as a brave soldier stands to his guns.

Say well when you may, but do well all the day.

Say-well and Do-well end with one letter:
Say-well is good, but Do-well is better.

**Saying and unsaying
Are truth's decaying.**

A sort of playing fast and loose with truth is the ruin of the mind's honesty. Say what you believe, and believe what you say.

Saying is one thing, doing is another.

Alas ! with many there are miles of distance between their tongue and their hand. They promise you fairly, but they act foully, for never a word do they carry out as you understood it.

Scalded cats dread cold water.

Having felt the power of water when it is boiling, they are afraid of it in all conditions. A dog that burned his mouth with a hot pancake, was henceforth terrified at the sight of the frying pan, even when cold. Men would be more safe if they learned caution as readily as cats and dogs learn it.

Scandal is a serpent with wings.

It grovels, it stings, yet it flies as with wings.

"There is a lust in man no charm can tame,
Of loudly publishing his neighbour's shame ;
On eagle's wings immortal scandals fly,
While virtuous actions are but born and die."—*Harvey.*

Scandal will rub out like dirt when it's dry.

Let it alone, and never try to answer it. The more you meddle with it, the more will the wet mud be spread. Wait till you can use the clothes-brush with real effect.

Scorn no man's love,
'Tis from above.

> Whatever the degree of the person who loves you, value the love itself as a true jewel. A dog kindly fawned on a person, but he did not notice him; and when another day the dog bit him, it was no great wonder. Kindness despised curdles into ill will. The lion may yet need the mouse; let him value his little friend.

Sea and air are common to all men.

> So said *Queen Elizabeth.* But without something more, men would only have a flood to drown in, and a place to starve in.

Search in a hurry, and you'll have to search again.

> It is wasted time to scamp the search. Examine drawers and boxes with care. To do your work thoroughly at once is the easiest and the cheapest method in the end.
>
> > Yet 'tis a truth well-known to most,
> > That whatsoever thing is lost,
> > We search it, ere it come to light,
> > In every corner but the right.

Search the Scriptures, and let them search you.

> In the Word of God you have a search-warrant for the whole Bible : "Search the Scriptures." From the Court of Conscience let us issue a warrant for the sacred Scripture to search our inmost souls.

Search thy friend for his virtues : thyself for thy faults.

> The first is generosity, the other is faithfulness : both are justice.

Season should weigh with reason.

> The occasion has much to do with the fitness of things. That which is good to-day may not be so good to-morrow. There is a time for every purpose under heaven, and, out of the proper time, the purpose may be improper. Marriage in old age is like spring flowers in autumn.
>
> > Fruit out of season,
> > Gripes out of reason.

Season thy tongue with salt, not with pepper.

> With cool truth, and not with hot wrath. Be sincere and sensible; but not fierce and sarcastic. Too many use cayenne. A leading member of a church was talking with his pastor about an excellent, but somewhat aggressive lady of the parish. After descanting at length on her virtues, he concluded by saying : "In fact, she may be called the salt of the earth." "Yes," responded the clergyman, quickly, "and the pepper too."

Seat yourself in your place, and you will not be made to quit it.

> Right will be on your side ; but if you seat yourself too high, you may be forced with shame to take the lowest room.

Second thoughts are best.

> This is not always true. Generous impulses, which are often the first thoughts, are much to be preferred to the hard second, and second-class thoughts of selfish prudence, which smother the man's better self. The first thoughts of the generous are best; but, in the case of the rash, we would prefer the second and revised edition.

Secrets had better remain secrets.

> The countryman in *Plutarch* was asked, by an inquisitive person, what he carried so closely covered in his basket. To this he wisely answered, "If I wished you to know what it is, I should not so carefully have covered it up." Why wish to see what thy neighbour desires to conceal ?

See, hear, consider, and say nothing.

> Then you may hope to live in peace ; but is this the only thing worth considering ?

See to the carrying out of your dying will while you have a living will.

> Be your own executor, and save both duties and disputes.
>
> > Silver from the living
> > Is gold in the giving ;
> > Gold from the dying
> > Is but silver a-flying.
> > Gold and silver from the dead,
> > Turn too often into lead.
>
> So said old *Fuller*, and he spake the truth. What infinite trouble has been made through wills which looked well enough, but turned out ill enough ! Mortmain is a mortifying foe to charitable legacies. Better give a thousand than bequeath a hundred.

See with your eyelids as well as with your eyes.

> "Let thine eyes look right on, and let thine eyelids look straight before thee."—Prov. iv. 25. Sometimes see, and do not see. God has given you eyelids as well as eyes.

See what you see, and know what you know.

> Don't be in doubt. Make sure, and be sure. Arouse your five wits to be undeniable witnesses for the truth.

See yourself in other men.

Especially in other men's faults and failures.

Seeing is believing.

But it is not those who stare most who see best. Eye-witness is the best of witness. In the Scriptural use of terms seeing is *not* believing, but believing is seeing.

Seed must be sown,
If crops are grown.

We shall get nothing without using the proper means.

> Don't expect to gather corn,
> If from sowing you've forborne.

Seek not a physician for every qualm.

He who must be physicked for every pain will soon be ill indeed. He that must see a doctor every time his stomach aches, will have a consumption in his purse, and in his body something worse.

Seek not a náme, but have an aim.

Have a noble aim in life, but let it not be merely to get thyself renown among men. "What's in a name?"

Seek that first which is first.

That which is real substance should have the preference of the shadows of time.

> Some there be that shadows kiss:
> Such have but a shadow's bliss.

Seek the love that hath no wings;
Follow pleasures without stings.

Sensual pleasures are like to those locusts mentioned in the Revelation ix. 7, the crowns upon whose heads are said to be only "as it were crowns like gold." In everything they were but as this, and as that, till we come to verse ten, and then we read, "there were stings in their tails." These were not "as it were," but they were killing facts. There is nothing real about the pleasure of sin, the reality lies in the punishment of it.

Seek till you find, and you'll not lose your labour.

If the search is worth beginning it is worth continuing. Perseverance is the practical way of expressing our conviction that we have been acting wisely. To give over is to lose what we have wrought. Stick-to-it finds the hidden treasure.

Seen or unseen
Always be clean.

> A dirty child of God ! How can it be ?

Seethe stones in butter the broth will be good.

> That's all : the stones will be hard as ever. Surround bad men with wealth and honour, and their possessions and glories will be desirable; et the men themselves will contribute nothing to the goodness of their surroundings, but remain base and ignoble.

Seldom at church, he'd such a busy life ;
But duly sent his family and wife.

> A common practice. The man is self-condemned: he owns that the worship is good by sending his family ; but for staying away himself he is without excuse.

Seldom poke another's fire,
Or you may rouse his burning ire.

> One must be very much at home indeed before he may venture to use the poker in another's house. Unwise persons who rush in where their betters fear to tread, deserve to overhear the remarks made by the housewife when they are gone.

Seldom seen, soon forgotten.

> One must keep himself in evidence if he desires to be favourably remembered. If you advertise, do it on a liberal scale.
>
> > If ou would boil your business pot,
> > Advertisements must keep it hot.

Self is always at home.

> Yes, a man is always alive to his own interest. You can always get his attention to this important point. One minds number one.

Self loves itself best.

> " What must I do to get a picture of the one whom I love best ? " said a mean man to a friend who knew him only too well. " The easiest way," was the reply, " is to sit for your own portrait."

Self-conceit is self-deceit.

> He who thinks much of himself thinks too much of himself : he mistakes his new farthing for a sovereign ; but it is worth none the more for his silly opinion.

Self-preservation is the first law of nature.

This makes men bear the ills of life. Alas! this law sours into selfishness, and makes men careless how they tread down others so that they can take care of themselves.

Self-seekers are self-losers.

"Whosoever will save his life shall lose it."—Matt. xvi. 25.

Self-will cannot please itself.

A man who is doggedly determined to do whatever he likes, does not even like to bow to his own will, but hesitates for fear that, in having his own way, he should be forfeiting his liberty to take twenty other ways. It reminds us of the verse about the Englishman's dress: he is represented as saying;

> " I'm an Englishman, and I stand here,
> And I don't know what clothes I will wear;
> Now I will have this, now I will have that,
> Now I will have I don't know what."

Sell honestly, but never sell honesty.

If a profit can be made, never mind what you deal in ; but never part with a grain of principle, even if the world could be gained by it.

Sell not your fowls on a rainy day.

Then they look wretched and draggled. One may as well present one's goods at their best; and when they are undergoing a necessary process which injures their appearance we had better wait a while.

Sell your wheat at market price,
And keep it not for rats and mice.

Hoarding of wheat is senseless ; and is sure to bring a bad name with it. " He that withholdeth corn, the people shall curse him." The Africans say, " Mice eat the miser's corn." Mice are the miser's misery.

Selling at a great sacrifice usually means sacrificing the customers.

There may be genuine sales of goods greatly at a loss, but it do not look very likely, and the probability is that the buyers wir sold as well as the goods. On the other hand, it is har right thing to be looking out to get articles at less than their Is it not a sort of stealing ? Are not under-price buyers sweaters who have to supply their greed?

Send a portion to the needy,
Lest through wealth thy soul grow greedy.

Men cannot safely and healthily possess large properties unless they habitually give away considerable amounts to the poor and to the cause of God.

Send hearers away, not loathing, but longing.

Long sermons only make people long for the end of them; the best discourses are those which leave us longing for more of the same matter. Hear what a sermon should be:

> " It should be brief : if lengthy, it will steep
> Our hearts in apathy, our eyes in sleep.
> The dull will yawn, the chapel lounger doze,
> Attention flag, and memory's portals close."

Send not for a hatchet to break an egg.

Don't deal with trifles in the grandiose style. Don't alarm yourself and summon an army to attack a maggot. Adapt means to an end, and let not the labour be worth ten times more than the result.

Send you to the sea, and you'll not find salt water.

You are so utterly blind and stupid, that you cannot discover that which is all around you. If you were surrounded by reasoning, you would not see an argument. If you had your Bible before you, you would not see the Lord Jesus Christ in it.

Separation is hard; but every two must come in two.

Happy are they who live together in perfect harmony through a long life : but even these must be divided.

> One in purpose, one in heart,
> Yet the mortal stroke must part.

September blow soft
Till the fruit's in the loft.

Lest the fruit should be blown off from the trees, and in falling be bruised so that it cannot be stored for winter use.

Seriousness should not be a covering for foolishness.

Some people are as solemn as owls, and about as stupid. *Cowper* wrote of one in his day :—

> " A shallow brain behind a serious mask :
> An oracle within an empty cask."

Service unrequested is generally unrequited.

> For proffered service stinks. Men begin to inquire why it is thus presented ; and, not perceiving a reasonable motive, they imagine evil. Yet I, for one, have not found the proverb true ; but, on the contrary, having gratefully accepted spontaneous help, have felt very thankful for it, and have been justified in my gratitude.

Set a beggar on a horse, and he'll ride it to death.

> Some say to a worse place still. No doubt those who are the least acquainted with luxury go in for it with a vengeance whenever they have a chance. Nobody is so extravagant as a pauper when he once gets a little money to lay out.

Set a frog on a golden stool,
Away it hops to reach the pool.

> It is out of its element, and returns to its proper condition as soon as it can. Official etiquette is terribly irksome to certain humans as well as to froggies, and persons with simple tastes, and natural habits, are glad enough to get off their golden stools.

Set a stout heart to a steep hill.

> Say, I mean to climb it, by the help of God. It is wonderful how little hill is left when faith has resolved to reach the top. Everything gives way before a steadfast purpose.
>
> > Pluck made the gap,
> >   Push got through it ;
> > Plod had good hap,
> >   Pith stuck to it.

Set a thief to catch a thief.

> He knows where to look, and when to expect the rascal. Yet one does not like this sort of thief-catching : it is too much like taking the devil into one's pay.

Set hard heart against hard hap.

> There is nothing so hard but it may be cut by something harder. A resolution like a diamond would bore through a mountain, even if it were all of granite.

Set not thy foot to cause the blind to fall ;
Nor daub the dead with slander's bitter gall.

> These are two inexcusable offences. We are to protect the blind, and guard the reputation of the departed.

Shall goslings teach the goose to swim?

Often enough they try it. Just out of the egg, with bits of shell on their heads, they open school for the old birds, and talk of modern natation and the progress of aquatic locomotion. The Africans say, "Every monkey's grandmother was a fool," and no doubt most young monkeys think so; but their grandmothers see that the folly is pretty plain further down in the family.

Shall the devil have the wine, and God the lees?

'Tis often so: the best part of life is wasted in sin, and only the declining years are spent for the Lord.

Shallow streams make most din.

The less there is in a man the more noise he makes about it. Perhaps he is afraid that no one will think anything of him unless he calls attention to himself. Bang! Bang! It's only powder.

Shame comes to no man unless he himself help it on the way.

Nobody can be truly put to shame unless he has done something shameful. The innocent man may hold his head up and defy all the abuse that can be heaped on him.

Shame take him that shame thinks.

Honi soit qui mal y pense.

> He that smells evil where there's none,
> Will smell himself before he's done.

Share alike to-day, and share again to-morrow.

This is the leveller's motto. If we were all equal at this moment, one would spend all, and another would labour to increase his stock, and so the demand would arise for sharing again. Very just that!

> What is a Communist? One who hath yearnings
> For equal division of unequal earnings.
> Idler or bungler, he's one who is willing
> To fork out his penny and pocket your shilling.

Sharp appetites make clean tables.

None of your picking over the food, and cutting out little bits of fat and gristle when a fellow is hungry. It is a pleasure to see fellows eat who are sharp set: there's no nonsense about them.

She hath goods enough if she is good enough.

Property is not the main thing in a wife, but a good and amiable character. Neither is beauty the main consideration, for another saying is—"She is fair enough if she is good enough." Happy is the man who has found that measure of goodness in his partner of life which will secure blessedness to him and to his family.

> If fair of face be scant of grace,
> I find no grace in that fair face ;
> But if the grace of God be there,
> Though plain the face, to me 'tis fair.

She that marries secretly is defamed openly.

People will have it that there was a reason for the concealment, and you need not wonder that they think so. When wedded people fear to have their marriage known they have concealed their own honour, and people doubt if all is right.

She would not have the walkers, and the riders have gone by.

The poorer sort of admirers were not good enough for her, and she was not good enough for the richer ones, and so she remains without a husband. She waited for Mr. Right, and she remains Miss Left, and will probably join the Woman's Rights Society.

She's better than she's bonny.

It is well when the character is more beautiful than the face. "She's black," said one, "but she has a sweet smack." If a woman cannot be said to be good-looking, yet it is better if we may say that she looks good. The Highlander blundered over our proverb, and said that his wife was bonnier than she was better.

Sheathing the sword does not heal the wound.

Or in another form, "Shutting up the knife does not cure the cut." To cease from slander is well ; but this does not undo the harm which has been done. Who is to restore what has been burned ? Even if you put the fire out, that question remains.

Sheep may fall into the mire ; swine wallow in it.

Herein is a great difference between a fallen believer and a sinner acting according to his evil nature. The swallow may touch the stagnant pond with his wing, but he is soon up in the air : the duck revels in the foul element, for he is another sort of bird.

Shine like a light, but do not flash like lightning.

Be not ambitious to dazzle. A steady light is far more valued than the brilliant flash which startles and astounds, but goes out as soon as it comes out.

Ships fear fire more than water.

Water bears them up, but fire burns them up. It seems strange that a vessel should burn in the middle of the sea. It is sadly singular that men should perish with salvation all around them.

Ships leak: some amidships, some in the bows, some in the hold.

Men have faults of different orders; but a man quite without failing you have not yet met with.

Shirt sleeves are a noble uniform.

Industry bears for its coat of arms, a coat without arms.

Shoot me sooner than put me in a damp bed.

To put a man in a damp bed is little short of murder: nay, in some respects it would be better to kill a man outright than to injure him for life. Those who are itinerant preachers endure, among other imminent perils, "perils of damp beds."

Short cuts are often the longest way.

Especially short cuts to wealth: they usually end in the mire.

Short hair is soon brushed.

A little property is soon looked over; a small wage is soon laid out. Slender knowledge is speedily arranged, and a short speech is soon delivered.

Short pleasure may cost long sorrow.

And if we are delivered from the sins themselves, yet they often involve long and bitter repentances. Sinful pleasures are always dearly bought. Short the sin, but long the shame.

Short reckonings make long friends.

Towards men it will be wise to settle up at brief intervals, for then we shall feel free and independent. Towards our God it is needful to make frequent confession, and exercise constant faith. Daily we incur guilt, daily let us seek cleansing.

Short tempers often go with long tongues.

> Then both the short and the long of it are hard to bear. "Double up your whip," said one to an angry talker. The tongue goes nineteen to the dozen when a man's monkey is up.

Show me a liar, and I will show you a thief.

> The same evil of heart which makes a man false with his tongue, makes him false with his hand.
>
> > He that to a lie will stick
> > With pleasure would a pocket pick.

Show me a man without a spot,
I'll show a maid without a fault.

> But not till then. In man, and maid, of human kind, no perfection we shall find.

Showers of repentance breed flowers of rejoicing.

> Blessed drops which fall from the eye of penitence! Sweet flowers which spring in the garden of faith!

Shrouds have no pockets.

> We brought nothing with us into the world, and it is certain that we can carry nothing out.

Shut up your mouth, or it will shut you up.

> In certain cases it is sadly so. If some people could be gagged, they would get on, for silence catches the mouse; but with so much jaw they must ruin themselves, for open doors let out prosperity. Talk takes the value out of a servant. Who cares to hire a horse which keeps on neighing throughout the journey?

Sickness tells us what we are.

> Then the very good-tempered man becomes touchy; patience, which was so assured, gives way to complaining; and courage yields to depression. See a man when he is ill to know how little a man he is. Great Cæsar cries for drink like a sick girl.

Sift him grain by grain, and you will find him all chaff.

> Poor creature! There are some such, no doubt; but it is rather hard judgment. Is there no grain of hopefulness even in the worst we have ever met? Don't let the chaff blind our eyes.

Sighs fill no sails;
But prayer prevails.

> Fretting and stewing do no real good, but prayer does wonders.

Sign nothing without reading,
Or else you'll soon be bleeding.

> You may, without knowing it, sign away your estate, or become surety and have to pay, or you may slander a friend. Read carefully, and sign cautiously. Don't swallow the pudding while it is tied up in a bag.

Silence and reflection,
With circumspection,
Save from dejection.

Silence cannot be put in the papers.

> Nor can it even be written down for private circulation. To say nothing, is to tease the slanderer, and baffle the gossip.

Silence is a fine ornament for a woman.

> Or for a man either. He that can hold his tongue can hold his peace; and nothing is more worth holding than peace. A quiet spirit is said by the apostle to be of great price. "Do you love her still?" asked a judge of a fellow who applied to be divorced from his wife. "Yes, sir, I do; but the trouble is that she is never still for a moment." Query: Would he let her be still?

Silence is consent.

> Not from a dumb man; nor of a surety from any man. Many a man is silent, not because he consents or dissents, but because he treats the whole question with utter contempt.

Silence is not golden when it is guilty.

> He who stood speechless did not therefore escape. If a man is silent because he knows he is guilty, his silence is not commendable. Well may he be silent who has nothing to say. "We must give an account of idle silence, as well as of idle speech."

Silence scandal by silence.

> It is the surest way. "Where no wood is, the fire goeth out." If you make no defence there is the less for the assailant to work upon. Dr. Henry Rink, the learned Dane, who has written the best book about the Eskimo, says that they show annoyance at an offence by silence. Let this Eskimo fashion prevail everywhere.
>
> > Should envious tongues some malice frame,
> > To soil and tarnish your good name,
> > > Live it down!
> >
> > Rail not in answer, but be calm;
> > For silence yields a rapid balm,
> > > Live it down!

Silent sense is better than fluent folly.

A quiet man is worth a dozen chattering monkeys.

> Silence seldom causes harm :
> Gossip raises great alarm.

Silken cords are fast binders.

The cords of love outlast the bonds of force, the chains of interest, the ties of party, and the fetters of fear.

Silken tongue and hempen heart often go together.

That is to say, in hypocrites, who would both hug you and hang you, butter you and eat you.

> They give a kiss,
> But mean a curse.

Silly birds eat the seed, but see not the net.

So are the foolish beguiled by the pleasure of sin, and see not the deadly consequences which will surely follow.

Silly lasses linger long at looking-glasses.

When there is nothing whatever to be seen but their own silliness, why should they be so long in seeing so little?

Silver keys open iron locks.

Simple must always serve.

He is fit for nothing else, and, though he may be a fair servant, he will fail as a master.

> From wit and wisdom wholly free,
> Dog to another thou must be.

Sin begets sloth, and sloth begets sin.

Thus they take turns in the parentage of each other. Vice leads to idleness, and idleness leads to vice.

Sin has many tools, but a lie is a handle which fits them all.

By this it works its devices. Virtue and truth fit well, and so do vice and falsehood. Because there is a lie in his right hand, a man becomes dexterous in evil.

Sin is learned without going to school.

It is the natural behaviour of the natural mind, the mother-tongue of the sons of Adam.

Sin is sin even if it be not seen.

Secrecy does not screen, nor even diminish its wickedness. Yet many are sorry for being found out, who were never sorry for the sin which was found out.

Sin kisses, but kills.

It is a sweet poison. Like a glittering sword, it is brightness to the eye, and death to the heart.

Sin, which drowned the old world, will burn this.

Sipping sour milk with a fork is the height of nonsense.

Punch awards the palm of folly to the man who spends his very last shilling in buying a purse. There are others quite as bad, and one is for a dying man to live as if he were immortal.

Sir Hobbard de Hoy, be no longer a boy!

Prove yourself a man, by manly deeds; put away childish things. Get wisdom within now the down's on your chin.

Sir John Barleycorn is not the working-man's friend.

He professes to give the man strength, but makes him so that he can neither walk nor stand. He drains the man's purse, by making him say, "Let us have a drain." Sir John very often makes work for the surgeon.

Sit still rather than rise and fall down.

Be quiet sooner than talk to your own confusion : keep in a small way of business rather than launch out and come to bankruptcy.

"Six days shalt thou labour" :
Mind that, lazy neighbour!

This is as much a part of the commandment as resting on the seventh day. Many an idler forgets this. A missionary from the Congo says of the natives, "Six days' labour, and one day's rest, is not exactly the proportion to their minds ; more the other way round. The only piece of higher criticism in which they indulge is to say that one day's rest, and six days' labour, is manifestly not the Word of God."

Six feet of earth make all men equal.

> Death is the great leveller. The worm has no respect for knighthood or nobility.
>> The mighty monarch and the slave,
>> Find common bed within the grave.

Skin-flints and split-plums would rob a workhouse child of his breakfast.

> "Bless you, man!" said a woman, concerning a certain tanner, "He'd flay two devils to get one skin." To this I had no objection, for those evil spirits are too plentiful. I knew the style of man, and abhorred him: he lived at Greediton, the abode of those very respectable families, the Pinchpoors, the Closefists, the Hoarders, the Graspalls, the Squeezers, and the Grinders. Nice people to work for—any one of them!

Slake your thirst with Adam's ale.

> There is not a headache in a hogshead of it.
>> Pure water for me! Pure water for me!
>> 'Tis the drink of the wise; 'tis the wine of the free.

Slander is a coward's revenge.

> He dares not strike with his fist, and so he stabs with his tongue. He has nothing to say that is true, and so he lies like a Cretan. He loses his revenge if no notice whatever is taken.

Slander is the devil's daughter, and speaks her father's language.

> Yes, and speaks it with a more diabolical accent than her sire The devil is Abaddon, but slander is fifty bad ones.

Slander is tongue-murder.

>> A poison, neither mineral nor herbal,
>> But a much deadlier—a poison verbal.

Slanderers are best let alone.

> It is so difficult to deal with the creatures:—
>> "However thou the viper take,
>> A dangerous hazard thou dost make."

Slanderers are the devil's bellows to blow up strife.

> And what a fire they can make! What a vice is this habit of backbiting! One has truly said, "A foul breath is a calamity; but a foul mouth is a criminality."

Sleep not too little nor too much.

Our old proverbs prescribe too little sleep : they are more suitable for the strong than for the weak. All time is not lost which is spent in bed : sometimes it is true economy to be well rested before getting to work. The stern discipline of our fathers said concerning the hours of sleep :—

> " Nature requires five, custom takes seven,
> Laziness takes nine, and wickedness eleven."

Sleep over it, or you may weep over it.

Sleep upon it, and pray before you sleep.

> " A good night's rest
> Will counsel best."

Sleeping cats make saucy mice.

When masters and magistrates tolerate evil, evil ones take great liberties, and iniquity abounds.

Sleeping dogs catch no hares.

In another form we have it : Sleeping foxes catch no chickens. One had need be wide awake nowadays to catch anything unless it be the measles.

Sleepy hearers make sleepy preachers.

Preachers and people act and react upon each other. The pulpit can mesmerize the pew, and the pew can electrify the pulpit, or *vice versâ*. In England all places are liable to rates and taxes if anybody sleeps on the premises. Query : Should not many churches and chapels be called upon to pay ? A clergyman remarked that none could sleep in his church, for he had instructed the sexton to wake them up. He was wisely asked if it would not be better for the sexton to wake *him* up. Wakeful preachers have wakeful hearers. Some preachers are great mesmerizers.

Slippery is the stone at the rich man's door.

He is apt to trip who goes there begging and cringing, and the owner himself is apt to slip when he comes out with his head up.

Sloth begat poverty, and poverty begat fraud.

So runs the genealogy of many another sin : idleness is usually the grandfather of the crime, whatever the father might be.

Sloth is the key of poverty.

> If thou wouldst know where want doth dwell,
> Sloth will conduct thee to its cell.

Sloth makes all things difficult, industry all things easy.

The least exertion fatigues an idle man, and he is glad of the excuse of difficulty, that he may shirk work. The difficulty lies in his own lazy bones. He is loth to carry his meat to his mouth. Diligence does not *take* things easy, but it does *make* them easy.

Sloth shortens life and lengthens sin.

> " Fly sloth, which body tires and mind benumbs:
> It is a taste of death before death comes."—*Sir R. Baker.*

Slothful men never have time.

You would fancy that they were working like niggers, while they are just throwing time away in doing nothing. That was a smart old lady, who, to a man's complaint that he had "no time," replied, "You have all the time there is."

Slow and sure.

On one occasion, at a council of war, during a siege, General Wolfe complained greatly of the slowness of the approaches. "My maxim," said the engineer, "is slow and sure." "And mine," replied Wolfe, "is quick and sure—a much better maxim."

Slow and sure will long endure.

The offspring of an hour dies in the next hour; but that which comes of thought and plodding stands firm as the hills. Better an oak of ages than a mushroom of minutes.

Slow fires make sweet malt.

Quiet, thoughtful action is best. Thoroughly good work comes out of deliberation. Good temper promotes a loving, amiable conversation. Steady, patient perseverance makes happy life.

Slow in choosing, slow in changing.

Apply this especially to friendship, and even more emphatically to courtship; for once married, it is for better or worse. True love neither ranges nor changes. Among old ring-posies we find:

> " Let love abide till death divide."
> " God did decree our unity."

Sluggards grow busy when the hours grow late.

They wake up when it is time to go to sleep. It is their nature to run contrary to nature.

> Ever is it sluggard's guise :
> Loth to bed, and loth to rise.

Small bags hold large diamonds.

Little bodies often contain great souls. Five feet of sense is better than six of folly. Wilberforce was a very small man. *Boswell* says of his appearance at the election for York county : " I saw what seemed a mere shrimp mount on the table ; but as I listened, he grew and grew, until the shrimp became a whale."

Small beginnings may have great endings.

Sparks set the prairie on flame. Little springs begin the mighty Thames. Two or three praying men may bring down a great revival for a whole nation.

Small birds must have meat.

The least must be fed as well as the greatest. Should not the big birds leave a little more room for the sparrows and the finches ? Should not great monopolists think of the hundreds whose livings they absorb ? Live, and let the little folk live.

Small differences make great discords.

It is wonderful how little a thing will cause grievous quarrels. Outsiders can hardly see the point. It looks like the division of the Lilliputians into Big-endians, and Little-endians, all arising out of their views as to how an egg should be eaten. We may say, as another did on another subject :—

> Strange that such difference should be
> 'Twixt tweedle-dum and tweedle-dee.

Sma' fish are better than nae fish.

Quite true, Scotch friend ! Better to keep on earning pence than lose your place, and be without a penny to bless yourself with.

Small habits, well pursued betimes,
May reach the dignity of crimes.

Bad habits soon grow to something worse, and these corrupt into villainies, and make the man too bad to be tolerated in society.

Small profits are sweet.

Especially if often repeated, and long continued. Those who reach after rapid riches miss many pleasures, and run ruinous risks.

Small should be content with small.

So *Herrick* sings :—

> "A little seed best fits a little soil,
> A little trade best fits a little toil;
> As my small jar best fits my little oil.
>
> A little bin best fits a little bread,
> A little garland fits a little head;
> As my small stuff best fits my little shed."

Small rain lays great dust.

Gentle words end great quarrels. Loving tenderness removes irritation. Many like kicking up a dust; let us try to lay it.

Smooth bullets fly farthest.

Kind words, and arguments courteously advanced, have greater currency than uncouth denunciations.

Smooth words make smooth ways.

An atmosphere of gentleness is created, and roughness and unkindness are banished where all have learned to speak tenderly.

Snakes may have fine colours, and yet have deadly stings.

So many lusts, so many lords.

For every evil passion strives for the mastery, and holds the mind in subjection. He that would be free from bondage must wear the yoke of Christ, and deny his own passions.

So many skulls, so many schemes.

Every man has his own plan, and each one believes that his method is preferable to every other. Specially is this true in medicine: so many skulls, twice as many pills. Liniments are as varied as the lineaments of the doctors' faces.

So much meal cannot all have come from your own sack.

You must have borrowed some of that discourse : it is too full, too deep to be all your own. Thus men overdo their borrowings, and are found out. The excellence of what they steal is the plague of plagiarists.

So rejoice that you can rejoice over your rejoicing.

Wine that you can drink when you have made it, and think of with pleasure after you have drunk it, is alone worth making and drinking. A joy fit to be looked back upon is alone a real joy.

" So to the dust
    Return we must."

For out of it we were taken, and our dust longs to be back with its brother.

Soap and water, soap and water!
Wash yourself, and wash your daughter.

A lady in Utica took a child to a physician to consult him about its health. Among other things, she inquired if he did not think the springs would be useful. "Certainly, madam," replied the doctor, as he looked at the child. "I advise you to try the springs at once." "You really think it would be good for the poor little thing?" "Decidedly I do." "What springs would you recommend, doctor?" "Any will do, madam, where you can get plenty of soap and water."

Sobriety is the door of prosperity.

Not only in the health it brings, and in the sin it prevents; but in the saving it involves, the thrift it promotes, and the industry it encourages. A prosperous drunkard is a rare bird.

Soft and fair goes long journeys.

A staying pace is what is desirable. Begin as you hope to go on; and mind you do go on. Rush and dash make headway for a short time, and then there comes a fall or a stop.

An early start and a steady pace
Take the slowest through the race.

Soft words scald not the mouth.

You may talk any quantity of them without needing to regret their use. Ugly expressions are like boiling water, as well to those who use them as to those who hear them.

Soft words win hard hearts.

Many a man yields to loving entreaty who cannot be touched by threatening. Soft words break no bones, but they break hard hearts. Kindness wins where roughness fails.

"Softly! softly!" caught the monkey.

> So say the negroes; and these darkies know a thing or two. Sambo very sensible! Gently gets the game.

Solid arguments are lost on shallow minds.

> Yet what else are we to use? We are bound to give them reasons; but we are not called upon to give them understandings.

Solitude is often the best society.

> Yet the Italians say, "One would not wish to be alone even in Paradise." If it were to last always there would be no charms in solitude, but an occasional interval of it is the joy of good men. To be alone with God is to be in the best company.

Solomon made a book of proverbs; but a book of proverbs never made a Solomon.

> Even the present book may fail with here and there a reader. Friend, it may be you are a Solomon already; and in that case, there remains no hope for our book of proverbs.

Some are always doing, and never do anything.

> Like a dog in a fair, they are in and out everywhere, and they do no more than a dog would do, who seems to be always busy, but what his business is no man knoweth.

Some are made ill by trying to be cured.

> So we have read an epitaph, which we look upon as a sheer invention—
>
> > Here lie I and my two daughters
> > All through drinking mineral waters;
> > If we'd been contented with Epsom salts,
> > We shouldn't have been lying in these here vaults.

Some are mated who are not matched.

> > Every couple's not a pair;
> > Wife a mule, her man a bear.
>
> For such a couple the following epitaph might be appropriate: "Here lies the body of James Robinson, and Ruth his wife"; and underneath is this text, "Their warfare is accomplished."

Some are too ignorant to be humble.

> It needs a measure of self-knowledge to take down pride. Many carry their heads high because there is nothing in them.

Some are wise, and some are otherwise.

Some are wise, and others are like-wise by associating with them; but the otherwise people grow without watering in anywise.

Some boys have too much rope, and too little rope's end.

They are allowed to take great liberties, and are never corrected for their faults. Abstinence from correction is a patent method for growing bad men.

Some chop at every tree and fell none.

They attempt many things, and, therefore, succeed in nothing.

Some dangers are avoided by facing them at once.

It is only timidity which makes them dangers. Go straight on, and they vanish like the mere shadows which they are.

Some defy the devil with their lips, but deify him in their lives.

In fact, those who talk most flippantly about the arch-enemy are generally his friends. Those who have really fought with him have a salutary horror of his very name.

Some do not bite because they have no teeth;
Some give a kiss, but hate is underneath.

Hatred has been often veiled where it still prevailed. In other cases it is held back by inability, and not by amiability.

Some dog or other will be barking to-day.

Expect to be spoken against, and when it comes it will not surprise you. Who can stop all mouths? A dog may as well bark at you as at anyone else. Bitter bark is a good tonic.

Some drink healths till they drink away their own health.

An Irishman used often to come home drunk; and once, when he was watering his horse, his wife said to him, "Now, Paddy, isn't the baste an example to ye? Don't ye see he leaves off when he has had enough! the craythur, he's the most sensible baste of the two." "Oh, it's very well to discourse like that, Biddy," cried Paddy, "but if there was another baste at the other side of the trough to say, 'Here's your health me ould boy!' would he stop till he drank the whole trough, think ye?"

Some earn a farthing, and get two pennyworth of thirst.

> So that with their parched throats, they are forced to hurry to the drink. Pity the sorrows of such little-working and much-thirsting men! They hardly earn enough to keep their throats oiled.

Some ears are left after the cleanest gleaners.

> Still is there truth unnoticed in a text. Still are persons overlooked in the best visited district. Still is a living to be picked up, though many have traded in the place.

Some go to church to take a walk ;
Some go there to laugh and talk ;
Some go there to meet a friend ;
Some go there their time to spend ;
Some go there to meet a lover ;
Some go there a fault to cover ;
Some go there for speculation ;
Some go there for observation ;
Some go there to doze and nod ;
The wise go there to worship God.

Some have milk in their mouths, and gall in their hearts.

> Dreadful is it to have to deal with these double-distilled wretches. Happily we are able to discover their false-heartedness, and then we despise them, and give them a wide berth.

Some men die before they begin to live.

> " He lives who lives to God alone,
> And all are dead beside ;
> For other source than God is none
> Whence life can be supplied."—*Cowper*.

Some men follow their consciences as navvies follow the wheelbarrows which they push before them.

> It is all very fine to be pleading "conscience," but we are responsible *for* conscience, as well as responsible *to* it. If we keep conscience in the dark, or render it morbid, it will not excuse us in wrong-doing. If a captain falsifies his compass, and then steers by it, his shipwreck will be his own fault.

Some men go through a forest and see no firewood.

> They are unobservant. That which is everywhere for others is nowhere for them. In the holiest church some see no virtue, and in the Bible no divine utterances.

Some men have no heads, but every man has a heart.

For this reason intellectual preaching can only impress a few; but warm, loving discourse will have power with everybody.

Some men have rats in their mouths, and mice in their heads.

Their talk is larger than their real intent: the brag is bigger than the brain. They thunder with their tongues, but squeak in their thoughts.

Some men would skin a grindstone if they could.

Nothing is too bare for them to get something out of it. They would shave an egg, and make soup of a stone.

Some men's principles follow their interests.

Interest should arise out of principle; principle must never be subordinate to interest. There is a pun here, but a truth also.

Some people are little and loud.

There is not much of them, but they make much more noise for their size than you might expect.

Some people's words go many to a pound.

They seem resolved to make up for the quality by the quantity. Though their words are light as air, it is heavy work to hear them, for they heap them on in such superabundance. When we suspect a man's truthfulness his words are wind. He who looks one way and walks another, may talk a horse's hind leg off, but his chatter is of small account.

Some stumble at a straw, and jump over a stack.

They "strain out a gnat, but swallow a camel."

Some swim in wealth, yet sink in tears;
Some rise in state, yet fall in fears.

Rich men have often described themselves as specially miserable. There is nothing in rank and station which can ensure happiness to the mind. It is very cold on the high Alps. Not where we are, but what we are, determines our happiness.

Some take so much time in getting advice, that no time is left in which to carry it out.

Delaying and delaying, they break while learning how to prosper, and die learning how to live.

Some women conceal only what they do not know.

Mrs. Blab, for instance, tells all her secrets over a cup or two of tea. You can only be sure that she will never say what she does not know, and cannot make up.

Some would eat a house, and still be hungry.

Their greed is so great that the world itself would not content them. An old gentleman once asked a lad—When was a covetous man rich enough ? "When he has a thousand pounds," was the reply. "No." "Two thousand." "No." "Twenty thousand." "No." "A hundred thousand," said the lad at last, in desperation ; and still being told "No," he confessed that he could not say. His questioner then informed him—"When he has a little more than he has, and that is never."

Some would play a tune before you could tune your fiddle.

Like the Welsh preacher, who sets the world on fire while the Englishman is looking for a match.

Some would see faults if their eyes were out.

Their minds are made up to carp and cavil ; and in the dark, with their eyes out, they can see what never existed.

Somebody will grumble at the weather to-day.

Probably you will yourself. Englishmen are always criticizing the weather ; but the weather takes no notice of their remarks.

Something is better than nothing.

Therefore, hold on to your employment, however poor the pay, and don't plunge into utter poverty because you are dissatisfied. This proverb sometimes runs, "Something *tastes* better than nothing." Dry bread is sweeter than fried nothing.

"Something short"—a drunkard's sense.

If this were not true he would never ask for this "something short;" which is apt to make him short of money, short of health, and short of character before very long.

Sometimes the best gain is to lose.

Young men beginning to gamble, or to speculate, have been saved by making an ugly loss at the very beginning. Had they gained a pound or two they would have been lured on, and would have been utterly, and perhaps, eternally ruined.

Sometimes 'tis wise
To shut one's eyes.

>   When you can do no good by seeing, it is well to remember that
>   an unseeing eye leaves us an unruing heart.

Soon ripe, soon rotten.

>   Precocious children often make silly men. Those who soon come
>   to perfection are soon past their prime. He who is a man when
>   a child, is in danger of being a child when a man; but it is by no
>   means always so. If the rule were invariable some of our friends
>   would be able to tell us very startling stories of their own early
>   wisdom.

Sorrow and trouble break many a bubble.

>   Airy notions in religion are soon destroyed by the rough hand of
>   real trouble. If adversity should once get hold of some of our
>   cultured bodies it would shake them like a rat, or say, as a child
>   shakes all the inside out of a bran doll.

Sorrow and worry wear us more than hard work.

>   Assuredly this is very true. These turn the hair grey, and plough
>   the forehead with furrows.
>
>   Sorrow and strife
>   Soon age a wife.

Sorrow is fit sauce for sin.

>   Many have had to dip their sin into it; and if they had not done
>   so, evil would have poisoned them. Take heed that you do not have
>   to taste these bitters to all eternity.

Sorrow is the cloud; tears are the rain.

Sorrow rode in my cart.

>   Yes. We unwittingly bring home grief in our own waggon. We
>   pick up a trouble on the road, and give it a seat in our cart, and
>   thus bring it home. Trade brings trial, pleasure leads to pain,
>   friendship breeds grief, and wedlock has its woes. Never mind.
>   Let us be glad we have a cart to ride in.

Sorrow will pay no debt.

>   "I'm very sorry," said the lady when a dog had bitten a man
>   in the leg. "Sorry won't heal my wound," said he. Nor would it.

Sounding professions are seldom sound.

>   They are often all sound, and there is nothing solid about them.

Sour grapes, as the fox said when he could not reach them.

Sour grapes can ne'er make sweet wine.

> Unless they are left to ripen. In their sour state they cannot yield sweetness. Neither can bad motives, and bad principles, bring us peace and happiness.

Sow an act, reap a habit ;
Sow a habit, reap a character ;
Sow a character, reap a destiny.

> Thus an act may decide destiny. "There was an abbot of this land who desired a piece of ground that lay conveniently for him. The owner refused to sell it, yet, with much persuasion, was contented to let it. The abbot hired it for his rent, and covenanted only to farm it for one crop. He had his bargain, and sowed it with acorns—a crop that lasted three hundred years. Thus, Satan begs but for the first crop ; let him sow thy youth with acorns, they will grow up with thy years to sturdy oaks, so big-bulked and deep-rooted, that they shall last all thy life."

Sow beans in the mud, and they'll grow like wood.

> So our gardening forefathers thought. Do the moderns find it so ?

Sow cockle, and it will not yield corn.

> What folly to sow it ! How many work hard at this bad sowing !

Sow ill, reap ill.

Sow the seeds of heart's-ease.

> Get a packet of kindly actions, a handful of old honesty, a bag of peace, and a selection of sweet herbs, and you will find that heart's-ease will spring up naturally among them.

Spare dinner, spare doctor.

> Sparingly feed,
> No doctor you'll need.

Spare when you're young, and spend when you're old.

> Often the reverse is done : the youth squanders, and the old man hoards. This is folly writ in capitals.

Spare your bait, and lose your fish.

> Economy in advertising is no economy. Want of preparation before preaching is extreme folly in one who would hold the attention.

Sparrows fight for corn which is none of their own.

> So do the rank and file engage in battle for that which does not concern them an atom. Men will discuss doctrines in which they have really no personal concern. Why dispute about a heaven to which I am not likely to go?

Speak as wisely as you list,
Some will still your language twist.

> It is the nature of the beast. The twister makes a man an offender for a word which he did not utter.

Speak as you find, says Old Suffolk.

> And he was by no means "Silly Suffolk" when he made the observation. Go not by common report, but by your own actual experience.
> > What others are saying never you mind,
> > Do me the justice to speak as you find.

Speak fitly, and then you may speak freely.

Speak of a man, and his shadow falls on you.

> So does it often happen according to the chapter of accidents.

Speak of the wolf, and you'll see his tail.

> And speak of the devil, and one of his imps will be near. Often have we noticed that just as we were talking about a matter the individual concerned in it put in an appearance.

Speak only that which is worth speaking.

> It will be well to make a selection rather than a collection of themes for conversation. It is well in helping others to our thoughts, to remember the rule in carving for a guest:—
> > "Give him always of the prime,
> > And but little at a time.
> > Carve to all but just enough,
> > Let him rather starve than stuff."

Speak up for the absent.

> Alas! few do this: the absent are set in the stocks. The Arabs say, "Fellows rail at the Sultan himself when he is not there."

Speak well of your friend; of your enemy speak neither well nor ill.

Speak plain English.

> *Dr. Taylor* says, "Never say 'hebdomadal' when you mean 'weekly'; and do not lament that men have 'perverse proclivities to prevarication,' when you might express the same thought in Falstaff's words, 'How this world is given to lying!'" Don't go roundabout to conceal your meaning. If you want to be forcible use pure Saxon. It will take a man a lifetime to speak our language correctly, and that advice is not bad which is given in the rhyme :
>
> > Leave all the foreign tongues alone,
> > Till you can spell and read your own.

Speak when ye're spoken to,
Do what ye're bidden,
Come when ye're called,
And ye'll not be chidden.

> Good advice for children. It will be well for families if the youngsters will heed it.

Speak your mind,
But still be kind.

> In being frank some are rough, and this is by no means needful. Speak the truth in love.

Speaking silence is better than senseless speech.

> "Some feel it a cross to speak, and others feel it a cross not to speak; I would advise both to take up their cross," was the remark of a shrewd writer quoted by *J. B. Gough.*

Spears are not made of bulrushes.

> Strength is wanted in those who have stern work to do. Poor, vacillating mortals are out of place when a fight is on.

Speculation is jumping out of the window to get upon the housetop.

> The man takes a desperate leap, and, in the vain hope of rising, he plunges into the abyss.

Speculation leads to peculation.

> Not always, but often it is so. He who would grasp a fortune all at once seldom waits to see whether it can come honestly. When a man goes up in a balloon, there is generally foul gas about.
>
> > Gambling's grown to such a pitch
> > In all quarters of the nation,
> > Some get poor and others rich
> > By mere daily speculation.

Speech is silver, but silence is gold.

> It is an old saying that few words are best,
> And he that says little shall live most at rest.

Spend not all, or want may befall.

> Seldom live up to the full height of your income, and never over-run the constable. Let not all the roast meat of thy wealth run away in the dripping of little wastes, and let none of it burn in wantonness. Be a good steward, and act with thy substance as one who has to give in an account to his lord.

Spend not when you ought to spare, and spare not when you ought to spend.

> They said of a certain poor economist that he never tapped his beer till it was sour, nor cut his cheese till it was mouldy, nor ate his meat till it was putrid. This is the reverse of thrift. One refused to pay for a pane of glass in a window, took cold from the draught, and had to pay the doctor, and lose a fortnight's work.

> Spend with great glee
> When the time be :
> Save with firm hand
> When times demand.

Spend not your money before it be got:
Speak not your mind before you have thought.

> A stock-broker's rule was also wise : " Never sell what you have not got, and never buy what you cannot pay for." On the last line of our old saw, we would say, Do not take down the shutters till there is something in the shop. There can be no need to display the nakedness of the land.

Spend nothing on silk
Till you've paid for your milk.

> It is a sort of thieving to buy luxuries while bills are running. To let small sums accumulate to great ones by long delay is a cruel wrong to the little dealer who is standing out of his money. No wonder the milk looks blue when it has not been paid for week after week.

Spend your evening at the sign of " The Teakettle."

> Sing as the kettle does, " Hum, hum, sweet hum."

Spending your money with many a guest,
Empties the larder, the cellar, and chest.

Spin not too fine a thread, lest it break in the weaving.

If the discourse is too fine people will not understand it, and if the theory is too subtle it will go to pieces in the discussing. Many sermons are too grand: they will be of no more use to common hearers than the Requiem of Mozart to a field of cabbages.

Splitting plums is a beggarly business.

The tin-pot economy habit in trade does not pay. People grow disgusted with the farthings and mites, and half-inches; and deal with a more liberal shop-keeper. It seems silly to lose a large profit because you will not lower your price a very little. Some men might have been rich if they had not been so mean-spirited.

Squeaking will not get the pig out of the ditch.

Complaining will not alter the trial into which providence has brought us. No hog ever grunted the ring out of his nose.

Stability is ability.

He that can put his foot down and stand firm has force with which to lift the load of life. To be unstable is to be unable; but to be well established is to possess influence.

Stake your dahlias, but don't bet.

Leave betting to fools and knaves: it is the peculiar delight of these two sorts of gentlemen. They know where the active pea is hiding, and you do not; therefore, bet nothing whatever.

Stand fast, but do not stand still.

Stand fast, stand firm, stand sure.

> Still for the good old cause stand buff,
> 'Gainst many a bitter kick and cuff.

Stand on your head, and the world will be upside down.

Your own position affects your view of things. If you will turn yourself upside down, everything around you will appear to have done the same.

Standing pools do quickly putrefy.

Stay a little, that you may make an end the sooner.

This was a favourite saying with a statesman when he found people in a great hurry to decide a question.

Stay a while, sir!   Stay a while!
Help a lame dog o'er a stile.

> Be not in such haste that you cannot help the needy.   You will
> make all the greater headway for lending a hand to the distressed.

Stay not at a friend's house too long, lest thou overstay thy
welcome.

> Go before they want you gone.   Why should you become stale
> where once you were so much desired ?   Yet there are exceptions.
> Dr. Watts was invited by Sir Thomas Abney to stay a week at his
> house ; and though this week extended to thirty-six years, it was
> none too long.   The old distich says :—
>
> > " Fish, and the friend who comes and stays,
> >   Don't do to keep beyond three days."

Steady toil and earnest prayer
Often prove a cure for care.

Steal eels and they'll turn to snakes.

> Reckon that a fishy transaction will turn out badly.

Steal not from the closet to pay the kitchen.

> Do not neglect prayer because of household duties.   Domestic and
> secret claims should both be met.

Steel whets steel.

> Or, as Solomon saith, " Iron sharpeneth iron."

Step by step the hill will be climbed.

> Don't dream of doing all at once ; but divide the labour and
> conquer the difficulty bit by bit.

Step by step one goes far.

> The Burmese say, " A wise man takes a step at a time : he fixes
> one foot firmly before he moves the other."   An old place is not to
> be left till another is secured.
>
> > " One step, and then another,
> > And the longest walk is ended ;
> >   One stitch, and then another,
> > And the longest rent is mended ;
> >   One brick upon another,
> > And the highest wall is made ;
> >   One flake upon another,
> > And the deepest snow is laid."

Step not on a sleeping serpent.

Do not arouse hostility. If the bad man is quiet let him keep so. Never stir up a hornet's nest, nor wake a kennel of hounds.

Stick well to your trade,
Or profits will fade.

These are not times for sloth or sudden changes. If a man does not look after his business while he has it, it will run away, and then he may look after it in vain. Where? Where? And O where is the bonnie business gone?

Sticks and stones may break my bones, but names will never hurt me.

Therefore let us take patiently the nicknames which ridicule may append to us, which usually, before long, mellow into titles of honour.

Stolen grapes give woful gripes.

Tom Fuller says:—" Upon the question, What is the worst bread that is eaten? one answered, in respect of the coarseness thereof, Bread made of beans. Another said, Bread made of acorns; but the third hit the truth, and said, Bread taken out of other men's mouths who are the proprietors thereof. Such bread may be sweet in the mouth to taste, but it is not wholesome in the stomach to digest."

Stoop to conquer. He who yields wins.

It is so in Christian life. We are to be anvils, and overcome the hammers, not by striking again, but by patiently bearing the blows. Non-resistance and self-sacrifice will conquer all the world.

Stories grow as they flow.

De Quincey says, "All anecdotes are false"; and this comes of their shape being altered as they pass from mouth to mouth. They not only grow as they flow, but change as they range.

Storms make oaks take deeper root.

Stout makes many men lean.

But the leaning is against the lamp-post. A quaint versifier says :—

" Leave stout alone if you should ail,
And ale if you are stout;
A drinking bout won't make you well,
Mind well what you're about !
Be doctored, if you please, with stout,
The stout is *doctored* too."

Straightforward is the nearest way.

Go to the man himself if you have anything to complain of, or to ask from him. A straight line is the shortest distance ; and plain, personal speaking is the wisest method. Don't be always sneaking up the back-stairs. Leave crooked ways to crooked men.

Straightforward makes the best runner.

Run at once to the Lord with your wants instead of going round about to friends and neighbours. He must help, even if it be by human agency ; and if we go to him first of all, we shall be going in a sure way and a short way, thus saving both time and honour.

Straws show which way the wind blows.

Straying shepherd makes straying sheep.

The people follow the pastor, and his going aside is therefore all the more lamentable. If a private man's watch does not keep time he will himself be misled ; but if the church clock is wrong, the whole parish will be unpunctual.

Strike while the iron's hot.

But don't keep on striking till it's cold. Don't preach the people into a good state of mind, and then preach them out of it. Speak while people delight to listen, and there and then endeavour to work them to decision.

Strip not before you reach the water.

Some give up their property before death ; but as it is unwise to take off your clothes till you go to bed, or to undress for the bath when you are a mile off it, so is it foolish to part with property which you may yet need. While you keep on living keep something to live on.

Strong drink is the devil's way to man, and man's way to the devil.

Both portions of this saying are equally true, and so we have a double reason for leaving strong drink alone. If we will put evil spirits into our bodies we may not marvel if we go where evil spirits dwell. Those who have a strong weakness for strong drink are making a short journey to their long home.

Strong is the vinegar of sweet wine.

When good-tempered men grow angry, it *is* anger. When mercy kindles into wrath, it is terrible indeed. When persons, who were very loving, disagree, the quarrel is often very sharp. "Spoons before marriage may become knives and forks afterwards."

Strong reasons make strong actions.

> Sure that he is right
> Man puts forth his might.

Study yourself to death, and pray yourself alive again.

> *Adam Clarke's* advice to students. Let them carry it out.

Subtlety set a trap, and was caught itself.

Success is the blessing of God on a good cause, and his curse on a bad one.

> Thoughtless people consider that success always proves that their course is right. The true man, when defeated in a right cause, is by no means daunted, but fights on expecting victory in some form or other. Success in evil is a terrible calamity.

Such as ye give, such shall ye get.

> Your chickens come home to roost. The echo repeats your own words. As you have measured, it will be meted back to you.

Such mistress, such Nan;
Such master, such man.

> Like strangely calls its like to itself. Difference in rank does not prevent similarity in character. The head of a household gives a tone to all in it down to the scullery-maid.

Such the mind, and such the man.

> Not his bodily condition, but the state of his mind, makes the man's happiness or woe.

> > The mind, by its own force, as by a spell,
> > Could make a hell of heaven, a heaven of hell.

Sudden friendship, sure repentance.

> At least, it is often so :—

> > We give our love without a test
> > To those whom we shall soon detest.

Sugared words generally prove bitter.

> A French priest praising the soft word that turns away wrath said, "It is with honey that we catch flies." A listener replied, "Yes, to kill them !" Beware of men made of molasses.

Sunday newspapers are Satan's sermons.

In London they command enormous congregations. It is sad to see religious people supporting such things. It was not always so.

Sunday oils the wheels of the week.

Its bodily rest is useful, but its spiritual anointing is far more so. Let us go on the Sabbath where there is oil in the ministry.

Sunday profits in trade
Are the worst ever made.

They come out of the life-blood of the Sabbath-breaker's soul. What can it profit him? His Sunday gains are cankered money which will defile all the takings of the week.

Surety for his borrowing friend,
Sure tied to trouble without end.

When a young man cannot afford to give his needy friend the money, it is not honest to become security for the amount. Never promise to give what you have not got. The surety will be sure to be called upon to pay; and what then? He that is surety shall smart for it. Yes, and his wife and family with him.

Surgeons should have an eagle's eye, a lion's heart, and a lady's hand.

They should be quick to see, brave to operate, and tender in every touch. Not one of these points may be absent in a skilful surgeon.

Suspect suspicion, and trust trustfulness.

Suspicion is ruinous to peace. Those who are most quick to excite it, are generally persons who deserve no confidence. Better far to see a thing through to the end, than to be tortured with continual suspicion. In the darkness of ignorance the vampires of suspicion fly abroad. Let in the light upon them, and they will no longer be seen. Better trust too much, and suffer the consequences, than pine under the withering blast of perpetual mistrust.

Swearers use oaths because they know their words will not be taken.

But if a man is not to be believed upon his word, we shall be very unwise to trust him when his profane expressions declare the rottenness of his heart. He that will blaspheme God will cheat me.

Sweeping judgments are unjust judgments.

For thus are the innocent condemned with the guilty. There are exceptions to general iniquity, and those exceptions deserve our sympathy all the more because of the difficulty which surrounds them. Confound not the righteous with the wicked.

Sweet May, how short thy stay !

Like every other pleasure, it is short and sweet. We no sooner reach the merry month than it is gone.

Sweets to the sweet.

This is an appropriate distribution. How much will the reader get? I hope a lapful. Let him take home much to his wife, if he has one ; and if he lives in single wretchedness, let him carry home the sweets to his mother, or his sister.

Sweetest nuts have hardest shells.

As if to bring forth and reward our diligence everything worth the having requires of us pains and strains.

Sayings of a more Spiritual Sort.

Sabbath-breakers are their own enemies.

They rob themselves of earthly rest, and of the sweet hope of rest in heaven. No enemy could do them a worse turn. A traveller in Pennsylvania says, that passing a coal mine he saw a small field full of mules. The boy who was with him said, "These are the mules that work all the week down in the mine, but Sunday they have to come up into the light, or else in a little while they would go blind." Are not many men blinded by never quitting the darkness of worldly care?

Saints are blessed when they are cursed.

It is with them as with Israel when Balaam sought to curse them : "Howbeit our God turned the curse into a blessing."

Saints are never far from home.

In the remotest places they are in the dominions of their Father, and on the borders of heaven.

" The earth is God's, and in his hands
Are all the corners of the lands."

Saints cannot fall without hurt, nor rise without help.

Saints may feel the stroke of death, but not the sting of death.

Isaac Walton, speaking of the death-bed of Dr. Donne, said : "He lay fifteen days earnestly expecting his hourly change, and in the last hour of his last day, as his body melted away, and vapoured into spirit, his soul having, I verily believe, some revelation of the beatific vision, he said, ' I were miserable if I might not die ' ; and after those words closed many periods of his faint breath by saying often, ' Thy kingdom come, thy will be done.' "

Saints' tears are better than sinners' triumphs.

Saints would rather have holiness without comfort than comfort without holiness.

Salvation comes by faith, not by feeling.

Salvation by feeling would be variable as the weather. Faith embraces Christ, and in him finds salvation.

Salvation is a helmet for the head, and armour for the heart.

"Let us ascertain whether we have this helmet of hope on our heads or not. As for such paltry ware as most are contented with, it deserves not the name of true hope, no more than a paper cap doth of a helmet. Oh! look to the metal and temper of your helmet in an especial manner; for at this most blows are made. He that seeks chiefly to defend his own head (the serpent, I mean) will aim most to wound yours."—*Gurnall.*

Salvation is all of grace, but destruction is all of sin.

Both these statements are true, though some represent them as opposed. Sovereign grace and human responsibility are both true.

Sanctification is the best decoration.

Watson says, "Sanctification is the spiritual enamel and embroidery of the soul; 'tis nothing else but God's putting upon us the jewels of holiness, the angels' glory; by it we are made as the king's daughter, *all glorious within.*—Ps. xlv. 13."

Sanctified afflictions are spiritual promotions.

A choice sentence, full of consolation to those who seek that every twig of the rod may be made a blessing to them.

Satan as a master is bad, his work worse, his wages worst of all.

This is the worst form of Down-Grade: everything runs down to the lowest deep. In a sermon by *Tauler,* who lived and preached in Strasbourg, in the fourteenth century, occurs the striking expression, 'The devil's martyrs'! Such are many sinners, suffering both here and hereafter in Satan's service.

Satan cannot constrain, if we do not consent.

He tempts with a crafty bait, but he cannot compel us to bite at it. The will of the weakest, if helped to resist by grace, can lock the devil out of the heart. *Brooks* says, "As Satan must have leave from God, so he must have leave of us. That is a remarkable passage in Acts v. 3: 'Why hath Satan filled thine heart to lie to the Holy Ghost?' Peter doth not discuss the matter with Satan; he doth not say, 'Satan, why hast thou filled Ananias's heart to make him lie to the Holy Ghost?' but he expostulates the case with Ananias. He said, 'Ananias, why hath Satan filled *thine* heart to lie to the Holy Ghost?' Why hast thou given him an advantage to fill thy heart with infidelity, hypocrisy, and obstinate audacity, to lie to the Holy Ghost? As if he had said, Satan could never have done this in thee, which will now for ever undo thee unless thou hadst, thyself, given him leave.''

Satan doth more hurt in a sheepskin than when he roars like a lion.

Subtlety is ascribed to the serpent in Genesis, and it is still the main strength of our arch-enemy. Better by far a roaring devil than a canting one: the first we overcome, the second comes over us.

Satan sometimes accuseth *us* to God, and sometimes accuseth *God* to us.

He would make us think hard things of divine providence, and wicked things about divine grace. Let us not believe his slanders of our heavenly Father, for our Father does not heed what he says against us.

Satan tempts in life, and taunts in death.

After recklessness comes remorse, and both are the creation of the same evil hand. He makes men live without fear, and die without hope. Let us flee from the seducer to the Saviour.

Scarlet sinners may become milk-white saints.

"Wash me, and I shall be whiter than snow."—Ps. li. 7.

Scripture silence speaks solemnly.

It becomes us to be silent where God speaks not. We must not venture to rush in where God hath hung a veil.

Secret meals make the soul fat.

Private communion with God, and secret study of Scripture, cause the soul to grow exceedingly, and become strong in the Lord.

See the face of God before you see the face of man.

First speak with God in prayer in the morning before you have a word to say to your fellow mortals.

Seek all in Christ, and Christ in all.

Seek the Lord on earth, and you shall see him in heaven.

Sermons are not made for critics to look at, but for Christians to live upon.

The critic stands outside the window and judges the meat, but the hungry man enters and enjoys the food. We don't keep shop for lookers-on, but for such as will "buy and eat."

Sermons should be weighty, but not heavy.

> We fear they are frequently heavy, but not weighty ; ponderous, but not persuasive.
> *Lady*—"Mr. —— is really a wretched preacher."
> *Husband*—"My dear! Mr. —— is one of the most sound, orthodox preachers I know."
> *Lady*—"He may be very orthodox, but he is very heavy."
> *Husband*—"Gold is heavy."
> *Lady*—"Yes, but gold is bright."

Signal piety shall be crowned with signal power.

> *George Whitefield's* prayer was, "O Lord, make me an extraordinary Christian." He sought extraordinary grace, and he was answered by extraordinary usefulness.

Simple faith in God is worth
More than all the gains of earth.

> Faith makes us possess the Most High God, who is the possessor of heaven and earth.

Sin always ruins where it reigns.

> Therefore it must be dethroned ; and none can do this but the strong Lord of love, who casts it down, and breaks its reigning power in the heart which he enters.

Sin and shame came into the world together, and they are fit companions.

Sin dies most when faith lives most.

Sin forgiven
Is dawn of heaven.

> The shadows flee away, and the eternal light breaks in upon the soul, when free grace blots out our sins.

Sin hath turned our houses into hospitals.

Sin is a sovereign, till sovereign grace dethrones it.

Sin is honey in the mouth, but gall in the belly.

> *Secker* wrote: "Though Satan's apples may have a fair skin, yet they certainly have a bitter core."

Sin is like a river, which begins in a quiet spring, but ends in a roaring sea.

Sin keeps no Sabbaths.

> It has no holidays, but works day and night.

Sin may sleep long, but it will wake at length.

> If it is only lulled asleep by reformation, it is still there.   It needs to be slain, and only the two-edged sword, which goeth out of Christ's mouth, will do it.

Sin puts hell into the soul, and the soul into hell.

Sin, the worst disease, needs the best physician.

> "Lord, I am all diseases : hospitals,
> And bills of mountebanks, have not so many,
> Nor half so bad.   Lord, hear, and help, and heal me.
> Although my guiltiness for vengeance calls,
> And colour of excuse I have not any,
> Yet thou hast goodness, Lord, that may avail me.
> Lord, I have poured out all my heart to thee :
> Vouchsafe one drop of mercy unto me."
>   *Christopher Harvey.*

Sin's misery, and God's mercy, are beyond measure.

> Thus the latter exactly meets the need of the former.   As *Bunyan* said: "It must be great mercy, or no mercy, for little mercy will never serve my turn."

Sin's service is slavery.

> "An exiled king had learned this truth; for James II., on his death-bed, thus addressed his son: 'There is no slavery like sin, and no liberty like God's service.'   Was not the dethroned monarch right?   What think you of the fetters of bad habits?   What think you of the chains of indulged lust?   The drunkard who cannot resist the craving for the wine, know you a more thorough captive?   The covetous man, who toils night and day for wealth, what is he but a slave?   The sensual man, the ambitious man, the worldly man—those who, in spite of the remonstrances of conscience, cannot break away from enthralment—what are they, if not the subjects of a tyranny than which there is none sterner, and none more degrading ?"—*Melville.*

Sincerity is the salt of the sacrifice.

> Without it the offering can never be acceptable to the Lord.

Single coals do not burn well.

> Holy company increases the warmth of piety.   Join a church, and speak often with holy men, that you may be helped to greater earnestness.

Sinners fare the better for saints.

Laban confessed that he had learned by experience that the Lord had blessed him for Jacob's sake. So we read "The Lord blessed the Egyptian's house for Joseph's sake." As *Bishop Hall* says, "His very presence procures a common blessing; a whole family shall fare the better for one Joseph."

Sinners, spider-like, suck poison out of the sweet flower of God's mercy.

Whether spiders do get poison out of flowers we know not, but assuredly he is a sinner indeed who perverts mercy into an argument for further sin.

"None shall in hell such bitter pangs endure
As those who mock at God's way of salvation.
Whom oil and balsams kill, what salve can cure?
They drink with greediness a full damnation."—*Herbert.*

Sleepy Christians never awaken dead souls.

God uses suitable instrumentality. He gives life by the living. We cannot snore men into the kingdom.

**So let me live, so let me die,
That I may live eternally.**

This answers to the precept. So live that thou mayst live for ever. Let your life be the life which is life indeed.

Some men speak two words for Christ, and ten for themselves.

Those fine passages and poetical perorations must be for their own glory among men, for they serve no other end. Truth, which glorifies the Lord Jesus, is often kept back.

Some preach the gospel as donkeys eat thistles—very cautiously.

Fearful lest the guilty should be too easily comforted, or wicked men should invent excuses for continuing in sin, they handle the word with trembling, rather than with boldness. Yet men always will pervert the gospel, and it is ours to preach it none the less freely because of this evil habit.

Some would wear Christ's jewels, but waive his cross.

This cannot be : the cross goes over with the crown.

Sorrow for sin as long as you have sin to sorrow for.

Do not part with that fair friend, repentance, till you reach the gate of paradise. *Rowland Hill* said: "If I may be permitted to shed one tear, as I enter the portals of the city of my God, it will be at taking an eternal leave of that beloved and profitable companion—Repentance."

Souls need care after they receive cure.

It is not enough to seek or even to find lost sheep, they must afterwards be tended, led, and fed.

Sport not with time, for there is no sporting in eternity.

Life should be cheerful, but at the same time earnest. Those who make life a comedy will land themselves in a tragedy.

Strength in prayer is better than length in prayer.

Long prayers may send people to sleep, but a strong prayer tends to arouse the listener. God does not measure our pleadings by the yard. Prayer must be estimated by weight, not by length.

Suffering is better than sinning.

"There is more evil in a drop of sin than in an ocean of affliction." Better burn for Christ, than turn from Christ.

Sunday is the spiritual market-day of the week.

Lay in store holy thoughts and feelings. Let the first day set the tune for the whole week.

Sunday is the summer of the week.

How are we when it comes round with its time of singing, flowering, and fruit bearing? Happy Sunday!

Suns have their spots,
And saints their blots.

"As if to stain the pride of man, the most eminent saints have, in some flagrant instance, failed in the very grace for which they were most renowned. In hours of darkness Abraham, the true, equivocates; Job, the patient, is insubmissive; Moses, the meek, strikes the rock in anger; Elijah, the fearless, hides in the desert from his foe; David, the seraphic, plunges into the sins of the senses; Simon, called Peter, 'a rock,' for his strong and stern decision, has to be reminded that he might rather be called Jonas, 'a dove,' for the weak, scared, fluttering spirit he displayed in the storm of temptation."—*Dr. Stanford.*

AKE a horse by his bridle, and a man by his word.

> If every man would follow his word as readily as a horse follows his bridle, it would be well; but if a man is not to be led by his word, it is hard to know how to hold him at all. Perhaps the other saying, "A man by his word and a cow by her horns," hints at a measure of difficulty. A word should be sufficient between man and man; but it is so frequently otherwise, that it is better to have an agreement in black and white.

Take a joke as a joke, and it will not provoke.

> "When the loud laugh prevails at your expense,
> All want of temper is but want of sense.
> Would you disarm the sneerer of his jest,
> Frown not, but laugh in concert with the rest."

Take a man's judgment for what it is worth.

> Give it due weight, but not more. All will depend upon who the man is, and what he knows about the matter under consideration.

Take a woman's first opinion, and not her second.

> She is very apt to come to a right conclusion by a leap of instinct; but when she corrects that instinctive judgment by reasoning, she may possibly be mistaken. This proverb does not always turn out to be correct: second thoughts of women and men are often their best thoughts; indeed, they should be.

Take away fuel, take away flame.

> If we say nothing upon which strife can feed, its evil fire must die down. In all disagreements, silence is the friend of peace.

Take care of coppers, and beware of pewters.

> Too often the pence are lost in the pewters. Cool pewters at night do not make cool coppers in the morning. Spend no pence to buy regrets.

Take care of the minutes; the hours will take care themselves.

> Economy of time on a large scale will grow out of the odd five minutes. Many valuable books have by their authors during intervals which others r
>
> > As the watch crieth tick
> > Each minute flieth qu

Take care of your lambs, or where will you get your sheep from?

If we do not win the hearts of the young, where shall we get another generation of Christians? Those who speak of them as "a parcel of boys and girls" are not wise. A Highland shepherd, when asked how it was that he took the prizes so frequently at the cattle-shows for the best flock, replied, "I look weel to the lambs."

Take care of your plough, and your plough will take care of you.

Thus you must share with your share. If you keep the plough going, it will keep you going. Those who would have cash must earn it.

Take very great care
Of your own grey mare.

Watch lovingly over your wife, who is to you as your own self.

Take heed of speedy friend and slow enemy.

The first is hasty, and may fail you; the other has weighed matters, and is not likely to alter, and, therefore, he is to be feared because of his determination. If your foe is deliberate, so much the worse for you; for he will persevere in his attack till he gets you in his power. Malice in cool blood is the bitterest form of it.

Take heed when thou seest no need of taking heed.

Moments of self-security are moments of great peril. A sleeping devil is dreaming of deadly mischief. Watch most when there seems least cause for it.

Take heed you find not what you do not seek.

Many by their unjust suspicions have made for themselves life-long sorrows. Why thrust in your hand among burning coals?

> While poking their noses
> Into other men's roses,
> Paul Prys have been pricked by the thorns:
> And no one supposes,
> That o'er the proboscis
> Of Pry any one of us mourns.

Take me upon your back, and you'll know what I weigh.

Carry my sorrows by actively sympathizing with me, and you will then have some idea of the burden of my life. If you wore my boots you would know where they pinch.

Take more time, and you'll be done the sooner.

No doubt a steady careful mode of working leads to a speedier end than a hurried superficial method, which does nothing thoroughly, but only seems to do it. *Punch* says, "What is the best thing to do in a hurry? Answer, Nothing." Go slowly to make haste.

Take no man's talk out of his mouth.

It is a shame to have to eat your own words, and it is not good to eat another man's words out of his mouth. It is as great a pleasure to another to speak as it is to you; let him have his turn, and do not forestall him.

Let every man say what he meant to have said,
Don't rob him of words any more than of bread.

Take no more on your back than you can carry.

Attempt as much as you can compass, but do not overtax yourself, lest all your work suffer. Undertake only what you can overtake. Be temperate in business as well as in drink.

Take not a musket to kill a butterfly.

The creature is too insignificant to be thus overwhelmingly assailed. Adapt the means to the end. Some theories do not deserve to be argued down, a jest may suffice to crush them.

Take not a wife from a wicked household.

Look to her parentage. You cannot expect to find grapes among thorns. If the well-head be foul, the stream will not be pure. Yet this is not always true; for the providence and grace of God have made some of the loveliest characters to grow up in the most degraded families, and it would be a shame to think ill of them because of a parent's sins.

Take not advice from a man who never takes advice.

If he is not wise enough to know his own need of counsel, he is not wise enough to counsel you. Who will not learn cannot teach.

Take not offence at the arrow, but look to the archer.

A dog bites the stick, and forgets that it could do nothing if it were not in a man's hand. Quarrel not with the second cause of your sorrow, but humbly cry to the Lord, "Show me wherefore thou contendest with me."

Take not the baggage for the sake of the bag.

Marry not a good-for-nothing woman to get her goods.
> If she be base, though she be rich,
> Keep thyself clear of such a witch.

Take pepper, but do not be peppery.

Very hot-tempered people are hard to live with. Some are as hot as the very strongest black pepper, with which they say hogs can be killed. Your eyes will ache if the smallest grain of them is in the air. Be not a Hotspur yourself.

Take the bit, and the buffet with it.

Accept a little buffeting for the sake of a livelihood. We must all put up with something. When a man intends real kindness, we must not notice the roughness of his manners.
> Though smitten sorely by thy God,
> Yet with the covenant take the rod.

Take the chestnuts out of the fire with a cat's paw.

We do not advise any such mean course of procedure ; but it is a very general practice. Monkeys generally imitate men, but in this thing man imitates the monkey, if the fable be fact.

Take the cotton from your ear
When the gospel cometh near.

We have read that when Queen Elizabeth compelled all her subjects to attend the Parish Church, the Romanists put wool in their ears that they might not hear. It is to be feared that Satan does this for many nowadays ; but it is an unpardonable thing to go to the place of hearing determined not to hear.

Take the pledge, and leave off pledging.

The temperance pledge, and absence from the pledge-shop, usually go together. It is not the total abstainer that keeps the pawnshop going.

Take the tide, it will not bide.

The tide will not be tied. Take it at flood, or lie high and dry while it ebbs. One to-day is worth a hundred to-morrows.

Take the world as it is, and try to make it what it ought to be.

Use men and things as you find them. Do not despair because they are not so good as they might be and should be ; but set to work to improve rather than censure.

Take thou good heed,
And thou wilt speed.

> At least, it is one of the ways of doing so. Nobody fails through being too careful. Mind, or thou wilt be behind.

Take time by the forelock.

> He is said to be bald behind, so that when time is past we can no longer seize upon it, and turn it to account.

> > "Shun delays, they breed remorse ;
> > Take thy time while time is lent thee ;
> > Creeping snails have weakest force ;
> > Fly their fault lest thou repent thee ;
> > Good is best when soonest wrought,
> > Ling'ring labours come to nought."—*Southwell.*

Take time in turning a corner.

> Or you may run into something, or be run into by something. When making a change in the manner of your life, consider all the bearings of it, and be in no haste to wheel about and turn about.

> > When thou a dangerous way dost go,
> > Walk surely, though thy pace be slow.

Take time while time is, for time is flying.

> > "Complete what wisely you've begun,
> > Or you may live to rue it ;
> > When once you know what should be done,
> > Proceed at once to do it.
> > "Those who with time will sport and play,

to-day,

Take you

Taken to excess, even nectar is poison.

> In all human things you must draw a line, and say, "So far is good, and all beyond is evil." In meats, and drinks, and recreation, this is specially true.
>
> > Take not more than enough
> > Of the wholesomest stuff.

Talk and tattle
Make blows and battle.

Talk is talk; but it takes money to pay bills.

> Blandly, with a great show of politeness, the gentleman shows the best of reasons for not being able to settle the little account to-day. All very fine; but there stands the debt. A little of the precious metal would be better liked than a cart-load of this precious talk.

Talk like Robin Hood when you can shoot with his bow.

> But to use big words and swelling phrases, when you have nothing to show for your greatness, is absurd.
>
> > Frogs may not bellow like the ox,
> > Nor robins crow like farmyard cocks.

Talk much, sin much; pray much, have much.

Talk of what God does for you, not of what you do for God.

> For this last is too small a subject; and, indeed, if it were greater, it would all be wisely comprehended under the first head. God works in us what we work for him.

Talk, talk, talk, and it brings in nought;
Work, work, work, and the bread is bought.

> Thus *Thomas Spurgeon* describes that perpetual chatter which is so useless and wearisome:
>
> > " Bibble babble, gibble gabble, rattle, prattle, prate,
> > They jabber, chatter, cackle, clack, at ever such a rate.
> > Talk about the magpie, the parrot, and the jay,
> > I'm very sure these gossips talk ten times as much as they.
> > Talk about your talkabouts—the gift of g, a, b,
> > Loquacity, verbosity, and volubility;
> > The beasts, the birds, the fishes, if all of them could speak,
> > Would say no more in fifty years than these folk in a week."

Talking comes by nature, silence by wisdom.

Talking pays no toll.

If it did, the County Councils would need no help from the Van and Wheel Tax. If only a penny a line could be charged, the Panama Canal could be finished with the money which would have to be paid in less than a week.

Tall trees catch much wind.

Eminent persons are sure to be criticized, envied, and abused. Let no tree aspire to be a poplar, and no man aim to be popular.

Tarry, tarry, tarry, tarry,
Think again before you marry.

One might push this tarrying too far, but we seldom meet with such a case. They rush at matrimony like a dog at a piece of meat. A quaint writer says, "I have seen women so delicate that they were afraid to ride, for fear of the horse running away; afraid to sail, for fear the boat might be upset; afraid to walk, for fear they might fall; but I never saw one afraid to be married, which is far more riskful than all the others put together."

Taste and try before you buy.

This is the costermonger's invitation. As a piece of advice it applies to many more things than fruits.

Teach your boy a trade
And his fortune's made.

But a clerkship, or a roving commission, or the genius which can do everything, will leave him in risk of poverty. He that hath a trade hath a settled estate, which no man can take from him.

Teachers' sins are teachers of sins.

Children, and indeed all sorts of people, follow the examples of their teachers if there is anything wrong about them. Thus faults are reflected and repeated if seen in men of light and leading.

Teaching others teacheth yourself.

A young man at Cambridge spoke to a wise man about taking a tutor to coach him, but the other said, "Rather take a pupil." To learn, and then to teach, is to engrave one's learning on the heart and memory.

Tears are powerful orators.

This flowing eloquence melts the heart. horns, are nothing in power to women's tea

Tears are liquid eloquence.

"Tears have tongues"; and as these appeal to eyes rather than ears, they have greater power than words.

> Tears are the noble language of the eye;
> And when true love of words is destitute,
> The eyes by tears speak while the tongue is mute.

Tease a dog till he bite you, and then blame yourself.

Worry servants or children till they rebel in their anger, and with whom will the fault lie? The same Scripture which bids children obey their parents, also says, "Ye fathers, provoke not your children to anger, lest they be discouraged."—Col. iii. 21.

Tell-all is thought a fool,
And everybody's tool.

They pump him for information, serve their own purposes by his tattle, and then laugh at him. Note this, Mr. Blabs.

Tell me the moon is made of green cheese.

I shall believe that fable quite as much as the silly tale which you are trying to palm upon me.

Tell me with whom thou goest, and I will tell thee what thou art.

> When I see thy company
> I will tell thee what thou be.

Tell the truth, and shame the devil.

If, indeed, he can be shamed. Nothing is less to his taste than the undiluted truth. His kingdom rests on falsehood.

Tell your affairs in the market-place, and one will call them black, and another white.

Every one will have an opinion. You thought everybody would agree with you, and see your wisdom. Alas! none see with your eyes, and therefore they neither see *as* you see, nor *what* you see.

Temperance is the best medicine.

For it is a preventive and a preservative, as well as a cure. Some do not like it any better than physic.

Ten children have eleven dispositions.

> This is a Hindoo proverb, and sets forth the variety which can be found in a single household. Should not the training of each child be adapted to its special character?

Ten fingers ought to be able to feed one mouth.

> And as a rule they will. Able-bodied persons without families ought not to be dependent upon charity. He who will not work for himself will not work for anyone else.
>
> > " Far, far before the slave of pelf,
> > Give me the son of labour :
> > The man who rightly serves himself
> > Will rightly serve his neighbour."

Ten honest "noes" are better than one false "yes."

> Yet people will go on begging of us for a promise when we tell them that it is not in our power to do what they wish. We persist in our "no," though "yes" would, for the time, be far more pleasant. Why cannot people take our " No," and have done?

Ten measures of talk were sent down from Heaven, and woman took nine.

> Shameful statement! It was invented by some horrid man! Was it the same cynical wretch, who, being requested to propose the toast, " To the ladies," said, " They require no eulogy; they speak for themselves "?

Tenderness matches well with manliness.

> > " Use a woman tenderly, tenderly ;
> > From a crooked rib God made her slenderly.
> > Straight and strong he did not make her,
> > So if you try to bend you'll break her."

Test the truth, and then testify the truth.

> No testimony can equal that of a man who has by personal experience certified his own soul of the truth to which he bears witness. Experience is the best college tutor. It is the sinew of the arm of persuasion, and the marrow of the backbone of confidence

Thank God that hath so blest thee,
And sit down, Robin, and rest thee.

> Spend not all your life in getting, and none are so eager to get a living that they never live us sometimes to sit down and enjoy life, and

" Thank you, pretty pussy," was the death of my cat.

Compliments and flatteries do us more harm than good.

Thankfulness makes much of little.

> Be the meal of beans and peas,
> God be thanked for those and these.
> Have we bread or have we fish,
> All are fragments from his dish.

Thanksgiving is a good thing, thanks-living is a better.

The one may die in words ; the other lives in acts.

That cake came out of my oven.

It is amusing to see on another man's table some of your own cakes : and so it is to see in a person's book or sermon a dose of your own thoughts, coolly taken, and never acknowledged.

That cat won't jump.

You need not try on that trick with me ; for I am not to be taken in by it. You can't lodge here, Mr. Ferguson.

That cruse of oil will not be less
That helps a brother in distress.

The widow fed the prophet, and the prophet's Master fed her.

That fish will soon be caught which nibbles the bait.

> The fish that nibbles at the bait
> Is very soon upon the plate.

Toying with temptation is extremely dangerous work.

That head is very sound that has no soft place.

There is a boggy spot on all headlands, and it is well for each man to know where his marshy places lie.

That is a good war in which no blood is shed.

> That was of all the very best fight,
> When never a man was slain :
> They ate their meat, and drank their drink,
> And then went home again.

That is vain which vanisheth.

Therefore fix thy heart on nothing but that which is eternal.

That is well spoken that is well taken.

> Much depends upon the mind and spirit of the audience. That which was accepted as overwhelming eloquence when spoken, may be dull enough when read in cool moments at home. In private talk we give offence at one time by that which would have been right enough at another, because our friend is in a bad humour.

That lawyer is honest who has hair on his teeth.

> This was in the olden times said of millers who tolled the corn brought to them for grinding. We dare say it was quite as true of the gentlemen of the sack as of the gentlemen of the long robe ; or quite as false.

That man is lost indeed who is lost to shame.

> There is nothing left to work upon. The creature's hide is too thick for us to make him feel. We shall have to let him run away, for he has become too hard in the mouth for our bit.

That man is surely badly bred,
Who's strong in the arm, but weak in the head.

> Of this bad breed there are many. Giants in muscle, and dwarfs in mind. Men weak in the head are generally head-strong !

That man most justly fool I call,
Who takes to scribbling on a wall.

> Cutting initials on trees, and writing on public seats, and so forth, is a vulgar habit, against which all decent men should set their faces. Quote this rhyme till it becomes a common saying, and something will have been done to mitigate the nuisance.

That quite alters the case.

> When it is yourself or a relative that is concerned, you are apt to alter your opinion upon the business. *Morton*, in his "Bengali and Sanscrit Proverbs," gives the following :—
>
> > "Said a clown to a Brahmin, 'Sir, tell me. [1]
> > For crushing a spider, what fine must
> > 'Why, friend,' he replied, "tis a gri
> > And demands an atonement of seri
> > 'Indeed—then, alas ! with deep
> > Your son, sir, a poor little spi
> > 'Out, fool,' cries the Brahm
> > For killing a spider there's

That thou mayest injure no man, dove-like be;
And serpent-like, that none may injure thee.

"When the fellow will not mind your dove," says one, "set your serpent at him"; but that is hardly the correct thing. Keep your serpent, not for offence, but only for defence.

That tongue which every secret speaks
Is like a barrel full of leaks.

There cannot be much in it; but it makes a great mess, and causes great loss.
> The blab no secret can retain;
> But what he hears he tells again.

That which a man causes to be done he does himself.

Masters cannot innocently take the profit of that which is done by those they employ in an evil trade. How can you have your barmaids serving out liquors while you yourself are at church?

That which comes with sin goes with sorrow.

Or, if it stays, it brings a curse with it. That which is hatched under the wing of a raven will peck at its owner's eyes.

That which covers thee discovers thee.

A man is known by his clothes, and a woman still more.

That which humbles us is always for our good.

That which is born of a hen will take to scratching.

Everything is according to the birth. That which is born of the flesh is flesh, and nothing better in the best of cases.

That which is evil is soon learnt.

And when learned, it so suits the disposition of the learner that he never forgets it. All the scholars in the school of sin are quick in getting hold of their lessons.

That which is got over the devil's back is usually spent under the devil's belly.

It goes as badly as it came, and usually in some form of worship of the belly god. *Nathaniel Bailey's* explanation of this proverb is, that "it is used of such covetous persons, who have, by unjust, fraudulent, and oppressive methods, amassed to themselves worldly riches. It intimates that such ill-gotten wealth is commonly wasted by a profuse heir, in riot and luxury, and seldom descends to the third generation."

That which is learned early is remembered late.

In our last days our memory is stronger concerning the facts of childhood than in reference to the events of yesterday.

That which is sharp is generally short.

This is comfortable to remember when in pain, or under slander, or in a thunder-storm, or when buffeted by a passionate man.

That which looks like a mountain may melt like a mist.

Have courage, and press forward; for tremendous difficulties will vanish as you advance.

That which lowers itself is beginning to fall.

When a man inclines to low company and questionable ways, he is likely to go into gross faults. When a tradesman stoops to trickery, he is probably on the road to bankruptcy.

That which will not be butter must be made into cheese.

If a thing cannot be used in one way, we must use it in another, and suffer no waste. We must also make ourselves of use to the good cause by ingenuity of earnestness.

> In some way or other, help, if you please:
> If you can't be butter you must be cheese.

That you may be loved, be lovable.

Else you cannot expect people to love you, nor should you even desire them to act in so unreasonable a way as to love that which is not worthy of love. Love, and be loved: being loved, love.

That's my good which does me good.

That's not good language that all understand not.

The proverb refers to the language of preachers of the gospel; they must not speak in an unknown tongue, but use market language. *Old Cobbett* said, "I not only speak so that I can be understood, but so that I cannot be misunderstood."

Thaw reveals what has been hidden by snow.

So, changes in nations and families bring many things to light. Injured reputations are often thus restored. On the other hand, when a man's riches melt away, many dirty things are seen which his wealth concealed.

The accomplice is as bad as the thief.

Sometimes he is worse. Jonathan Wild was a worse black than Jack Shepherd and the rest of the gang whom he protected, fleeced, and betrayed.

The account is correct, but not a sixpence appears.

Accuracy of accounts is most commendable; but when there is no income, no correctness of accounts can fill up the vacuum. However good the account, the estate is of no account when there is nothing to be counted. However, even if the balance is on the wrong side, keep the books correct to a farthing.

The adviser is not the payer.

That is to say, he who gives advice, as a general rule, has nothing to lose in the matter. Be chary of the counsel of one who carefully keeps on shore, but exhorts you to go to sea.

The ale jug is a great waster.

Toby Fill-pot fills his own pot, but he often empties the tea from the teapot, and the flour from the kneading trough. A drunkard's purse is a bottle, and everything runs out of it.

The ancients have run away with all our new ideas.

> " I pine to be original,
>   But this I cannot be ;
> For ev'ry one's done ev'ry thing
>   In long advance of me.
> I've come into the world too late—
>   I fear it must be so :
> Oh, could I but be born afresh,
>   A thousand years ago !''

The anvil fears not the hammer.

> In patience it stands still and bears,
> Till all the hammers it outwears.

The arm is the stronger, but the tongue is the longer.

When the strong arm is weary, the nimble tongue still runs its race. The more's the pity.

The ass that brays most, eats least.

Moral :—

> If you would be largely fed,
> Keep a still tongue in your head.

The back door is the one that robs the house.

There is an unknown leakage going on out of sight. Little lots of goods go off to other houses. Back doors for going out, and back stairs for going up, are of little use to honest men.

The beadle of the parish is always of the vicar's opinion.

Of course. Would you have the good man quarrel with his beans and bacon? He is bound to order himself lowly and reverently to his spiritual pastor and master.

The bear is not so bearish as folks make him.

Often when we come to know a man who has a reputation for roughness, we find him quite amiable: he "roars like a sucking dove." If you are not a bear, why wear a bear's skin?

The beaten road is the safest.

Keep to it, and let foolish speculators go over hedge and ditch, and meet with tumbles, and thieves, if so it pleases them.

The beginning prophesies the end.

So Christiana sings of her setting out upon the spiritual life :—
" Our tears to joy, our fears to faith,
Are turnèd, as we see ;
Thus our beginning, as one saith,
Shews what our end will be."

The bell does not go to service, and yet it calls everyone to it.

This is very right in the bell, but it should not be told of a belle, or any other of man or woman kind. Where we bid others go, we should lead the way, lest the following rhyme be applicable to us:
The sign-post duly points the way,
Yet standeth still from day to day.

The best cause requires a good pleader.

Such a cause as that of the Saviour and his cross deserves our best efforts ; and so long as men are desperately set on mischief, we shall need to plead with them on truth's behalf, as for our lives.

The best colt needs breaking in.

Your own delightful son requires it as much as other people's much inferior offspring. Perhaps if you knew all you would attend a little more to this very needful business. He that cockers his child makes a rod for his own back.

The best dog leaps the stile first.

All the pack will follow, but one hound leads the way, and, of course, he is the strongest and most daring. Those who aspire to leadership should take the first place in danger and in self-sacrifice. The holiest man will be first in protesting against evil.

The best eyes look inwards and upwards.

The best fish swim near the bottom.

Go deep into truth. Be not content with the surface of it; for in the depths lie the most precious thoughts. In soul-winning deal with the very worst, and you may bring to light, in many an instance, originality, force, fervour, and intense gratitude.

The best go first, the bad remain to mend :
Let bad beware, for patience hath an end.

Spared by long-suffering, we must improve, or else the God who has taken his saints home will send us to our own place.

The best ground bears weeds as well as flowers.

The best families have their " aunt-eaters and uncle-suckers."

The best harvest is the longest in being reached.

Archbishop Whateley said : " The man who is in a hurry to see the full effects of his own tillage, must cultivate annuals, and not forest trees." Only children will be in such foolish haste.

The best is the cheapest.

Because it lasts out so many of the sweater's good-for-nothing goods. Cheap is dear, and dear is cheap. We ought not to beat down the prices of first-rate articles : it is grinding down the workman, and forcing down the quality of the goods.

The best knowledge is to know God.

The best merchants never best each other.

They do not take each other in, but they deal fairly. If a man cannot become eminent by fair dealing, he had better keep in the background. Only small and mean traders look out for opportunities of taking undue advantage ; and such people never prosper.

The best of all acids is assiduity.

Use this wonderful chemical. It will eat its way through every difficulty. A great reduction upon taking a quantity.

The best of cloth
May harbour moth.

> The moth is no respecter of qualities. Sin assails the purest of men, and will work them mischief if it can.

The best of days for mending your ways.

> This very day is the best. Every moment you remain in sin you sin again. Till your debt is paid, your debt increases.

The best laid schemes o' mice and men gang aft a-gley.

> Because neither mice nor men can foresee all contingencies, and something happens which puts them out in their calculations. We do not wonder that mice fail: are men at all surer of success?

The best of men are but men at the best.

> When trial comes it is seen to be so. What fault one man commits another may commit. Those are not the best of men who forget that they are only men.

The best physic is fresh air ;
The best pill is plain fare.

> It is well to remember this, for else we may fly continually to medicine, and end like the man who put on his tomb, " I was well, I wanted to be better, took physic, and died."

The best surgeon is he that has been well hacked about himself.

> He knows how to sympathize, for he has felt the smart. What a physician we have for our souls in the Man of Sorrows !

The best swimmer is often the first to drown.

> Because he is venturesome, while others avoid the water, since they know they cannot swim. Another proverb says, "The strongest swimmer was drowned at last." Nevertheless let us all learn to swim.

The best throw of the dice is to throw them away.

The better thou be, the more careful must thou be.

> The proverb books add, "quoth Hendyng." Whoever that worthy may have been, he spoke sound truth. It is hard to live up to a noble character : it is like keeping up a great house where the expenditure is large.

The Bible is the book which has no errata in it.

> Neither in matters historical nor scientific does it blunder, any more than in matters theological. The worst mistake is with the man who thinks the Holy Spirit can be mistaken.

The big fish eat the little ones.

> This is the mischief of it, for then one fish devours quite a number of small fry. Now, if the little fish ate the big fish, one of them might satisfy the hunger of hundreds. It is not an economical system, but so it is. Please, don't eat me up as yet.

The biggest horses are not the best travellers.

> In fact, the little ones have the reputation of keeping on long after the big horses are knocked up.
>
>> The biggest ox may do least work ;
>> Yet little ones know how to shirk.

The biggest pears are not the best.

> On the contrary, those fruits which exceed in size generally fail in flavour, and a big pear when eaten reminds one of a turnip.

The bird that can sing, and won't sing, must be made to sing.

The birds see the bait, but not the net.

> So men see the present pleasure of sin, but not its fatal result.

The black ox treads on all our toes,
And every man his burden knows.

> Care and trouble come to all. We should be glued to this world if this were not the case.

The blade oft used no rusting frets :
The running stream no filth begets.

> Activity is health to the mind as well as to the body. Neither for our holiness nor our happiness is idleness helpful.

The blind lead the blind, and both fall into the ditch.

> Our old-fashioned fathers were wont to sing :—
>> " The Pope, that pagan full of pride,
>>   He hath us blinded long ;
>> For where the blind the blind do guide,
>>   No wonder they go wrong."

The blind man sees his neighbour's faults.

The blood of the martyrs is the seed of the church.

> From the ashes of the martyrs springs a new race of confessors. The policy of cruelty has failed altogether.

> > The church of Christ is like a camomile bed :
> > The more it is trodden, the more it will spread.

The "Blue Boar" is a great devourer.

> Romeo would never have asked, "What's in a name?" if he had but lived to take a tour in England, and become acquainted with the nomenclature of some of our inns. To us there is hardly a sign in the kingdom which is not thoroughly significant; and any traveller, we should think, who has his mental eyes about him, may see at a glance outside the way in which he will be taken in. Who, for instance, would expect to enter the jaws or doors of a *Lion* without being bitten, or to get away from an *Eagle* without considerable bleeding? A little matured, the *Lamb* becomes decidedly indicative of fleecing; while every *Bear*, we know, is naturally prone to squeeze as many as he can lay his paws on. Roguery in the *Fox* is what everybody looks for, and plucking and roasting are, of course, inseparable from a *Goose and Gridiron*. Nor is the *Blue Boar* an exception to the rule, for it most aptly symbolizes your complexion when you leave it ; and no one, we should think, would enter a *Green Man*, when reminded on the threshold of his verdancy in doing so. Of all our signs, however, perhaps there is none more suggestive than the *Magpie and Stump*, which anyone may see is merely a contraction for the far more significant *Magpie and Stump Up.*—*Punch* (more than twenty-five years ago).

The board slays more than the sword.

The boaster counts his penny silver.

> As for himself, he is a wonder. If you would but believe it, he is the greatest man that ever honoured the race by being born into it.

> > Of all speculations the market holds forth,
> > The best that I know for a lover of pelf,
> > Were to buy up our John at the price he is worth,
> > And sell him—at that which he sets on himself.

The body has two eyes, the soul must have one only.

> A single eye to the glory of God is essential to a holy life.

The bone of contention is the jaw-bone.

The bottle and the glass make many cry "Alas!"

"The bottomless pit is in Chancery Lane";
So said a man; and he spake very plain.

> Law is not good news, its agents are not angels, and it does not lead to bliss. The place where the legalities abound is not likened to the highest heaven. It's an ill chance which leads to Chancery.

The boughs that bear bountifully bow low.

> "Trees are bowed down with weight of fruit,
>   Clouds big with rain hang low;
> So good men humbly bear success,
>   Nor overweening grow."

The bow must not be always bent.

> When life's all labour, and has no intermission, it becomes slavery. Work without rest is like an unstuffed saddle, and cuts the rider to the bone.

The brain is ever sowing corn or cockle.

> It cannot be still. If you want to keep out bad thoughts, fill up the mind with good considerations.

The brains don't lie in the beard.

> Age goes before honesty, but not always after wisdom.

The bread of idleness should never be eaten.

> *Judge Haliburton* says, "The bread of idleness in a general way is apt to be stale, and sometimes I conceit it is a little sour." None but the meanest of the mean will eat a crumb of it. It ferments within a man, and breeds vice, roguery, and lechery.

The butcher looked for his candle, and 'twas stuck in his hat.

> He could not have seen except by that candle's light; and by that light he looked for the light! So, many are carefully looking for the grace of God in their hearts, though they would never have a desire to possess it unless grace had wrought that desire.

The cask is sure to smell of the wine it has held.

> Habits leave their impress upon the mind, even after they are given up. You cannot pour sin into the soul and out again without a taste remaining. The ill savour abides, though the sin is forgiven.

"The cat did it"; but the puss had only two legs.

> Alluding to the general explanation of breakages. There is a cat in every catastrophe of a domestic kind.

The cat invites the mouse to a feast.

> So the strange woman solicits the unwary youth.
>
> "Will you walk into my parlour? said the spider to the fly,
> 'Tis the prettiest little parlour that ever you did spy."

The cat knows more than the kitten.

The cat settled the dispute between the birds.

> By eating them both up.
>
> Does this differ a straw
> From the action of law?
>
> It is thus described:—
>
> "Then take, says Justice, each of you a shell;
> We live at Westminster on folks like you.
> 'Twas a fat oyster. Live in peace. Adieu!"

The cat that killed the rat is the cat for me,
Whatever colour that cat may chance to be.

> Utility is in many matters the test of value. Whether a cat be white or cherry-coloured, that is to say, black, if she catches mice, she is worth her milk.

The cat thinks one thing, and the mouse another.

> The mouse plays, but the cat preys. The mouse seeks the corn, but the cat seeks the mouse. Hence:—
>
> The cat's advice
> Is bad for mice.

The cats that drive away the mice are as good as those that catch them.

> The one object is to save the corn, and the way in which this is done is not material. The policeman who keeps thieves away is quite as useful as another who arrests them.

The chamber of sickness should be the chapel of devotion.

> But devotion should not be confined thereto. It would be that a man should need to be sickly to be saintly, and that promoter of devotion should be disease.

The chapter of accidents is the Bible of the fool.

He directs his course by his circumstances, and estimates the pleasure or anger of God by the incidents of Providence: this is a grave error. He believes a statement because others profess to believe it, but the Word of the Lord has no weight with him.

The charitable give out at the back-door, and God puts in at the window.

They give in secret, but receive in public. The rich are trustees for the poor, and if they execute their trust faithfully, the Lord often sees fit to put more into their hands; or, on the other hand, when he judges that their trust is fully discharged, he may see it best to release them from further worry and responsibility by allowing them to retire contented with a little.

The chicken is fed in the country, but eaten in the city.

One man has the labour, and another the enjoyment: let us hope that both are satisfied. One feeds the bullock, and another feeds on the beef: let us hope that neither of them finds it tough work.

The child is sure to hate the man unwise,
Who gives him everything for which he cries.

He has spoiled the child, and in due time his child will spoil him.

The child of the rabbit soon learns to burrow.

In all cases the offspring takes after the parents. How can we greatly blame our children for being faulty like ourselves?

The child says what he heard his mother say.

Of course he speaks his mother tongue. Let his mother mind what she says, or her talk will be her bairn's bane. A gracious mother writes: "Something having annoyed me one day, I said impatiently, 'botheration,' when immediately I heard the child-voice repeat clearly, 'bo-ther-a-tion.' I was greatly shocked, so dreadful did it sound on his little lips, that I felt as though I had thus heedlessly dropped into *his* soul the possible seedling of future blasphemy." Oh that all mothers were thus conscientious!

The chimney catches fire from within.

It would be hard to set it alight from the outside; but when the soot has accumulated, it is apt to burn. So temptation from without would be a very small danger to us if it were not for the soot within. Our corruptions are a greater danger than our temptations. How wise to keep the chimney well swept!

The cleaner the linen, the plainer the spot.

Or, " The fairer the damask the worse the stain." The faults of very good men are more noticeable than those of persons of inferior morals.

Keep thy snow-white garments clean,
For stains on such are quickly seen.

The coaches won't run over him.

He has got into jail, and is quite beyond fear of the accidents of the road. He has more to do with the turnkey than the turnpike. The wheel will not go over him, for he is over the wheel.

The coalheaver is king in his own cot.

So he ought to be. Shall we call him Old King Coal? Take no liberties in his majesty's dominions, but treat him with due respect, lest the coalheaver heave you out of the house.

" In England every man's cottage is held to be his castle, which he is authorized to defend, even against the assaults of the king; but it may be doubted whether the same privilege extends to Ireland. 'My client,' said an Irish advocate, pleading before Lord Norbury, in an action of trespass, 'is a poor man; he lives in a hovel, and this miserable dwelling is in a forlorn and dilapidated state; but still, thank God! the labourer's cottage, however ruinous its plight, is his sanctuary and his castle. Yes, the winds may enter it, and the rains may enter it, but the king cannot enter it.' 'What! not the *reigning* king?' asked the joke-loving judge." — *The Tin Trumpet.*

The cobbler's wife is badly shod.

Usually those who sell an article are ill supplied themselves. They say the doctor's wife takes no physic. It is bad when ministers' families are the worst brought up in the parish; and when the teacher of other people's children spoils his own.

The cock doth crow to let us know,
If we be wise, 'tis time to rise.

If we went to bed earlier, and then rose at cock-crowing, we should enjoy the best part of the day, which now we never see.

The cock shuts his eyes when he crows, because he knows it by heart.

Many a preacher might do the same; but probably he does enough of eye-shutting upon other people.

The coddled child is the sickly child.

Mother is afraid the wind should blow on her darling, and so she keeps the fresh air away from him. Poor dear! "Do him up in lavender." Take care that you do not soon have to do him up in elm !

Who killed poor Sam ?
His *Ma* called him "lamb " ; and with treacle and jam,
She killed poor Sam.

The common people
Look at the steeple ;
But the joy of the place
Is the gospel of grace.

What is architecture compared with the glad tidings from heaven ? A fine church without the gospel is like a silver cover and no beef under it, or a golden pump without a drop of water.

The constant drop will wear the hardest stone.

Let it keep on long enough, and even the most despised of holy influences will tell upon the most stubborn mind.

The course of true love never did run smooth.

It is,

Like new-laid pavement, rather rough ;
Like trade, exposed to losses ;
Or like a Highland plaid, all stuff,
And very full of crosses.

The cow in the meadow would like to be on the common.
The cow on the common would like to be in the meadow.

We are never content with our position, whether we be cows or men. The ins would be out, and the outs would be in. Apprentices would be journeymen, and journeymen would be masters. The unmarried would like to be wedded, and some of the married wish they were single.

The cow little giveth that hard liveth.

We must feed her well if we expect much milk. Nothing comes out which is not first put in. Even Ayrshire cows can't live on air, and short-horns will not thrive on short commons.

The crop will show how the field was tilled.

The crow calls the rook black.

He looks at his friend's blackness, and quite forgets his own.

The cut that is worst
Of a leg is the first.

> This alludes to a leg of mutton, where the first cut is simply a great gaping gash. He who is content with the first cut of a shoulder of mutton has no appetite. In trade the first cut is nothing: most men lose at first. It must be all out-going at the beginning, and for some little while after; the next cut is better.

The darker the day, the more we must pray.

The darker the days, the more we should praise.

The daughter of a good mother will be the mother of a good daughter.

> If she meets with a good husband. There is a great deal more in the stock from which a child comes than some suppose. Marry a daughter of a good daughter, and hope to have a good daughter.

The day hath eyes, and the night hath ears.

> Thus we are always under observation, and must not dare to sin.

The day is short, and the work is long;
To waste a moment would be wrong.

The day may be foggy;
You need not be groggy.

The day you do not clean the house some special friend will call.

> Mind this, Mrs. McTorker. It is always so, that when things are awkward, folks most respected, but quite unexpected, drop in.

The dead all slumber in the same bed.

> "Cover his head with turf or stone,
> It is all one; it is all one."

The dead, and only they, should do nothing.

> While there's life in us let us live to purpose. He who has nothing to do may as well die.

The devil can cite Scripture to suit his purpose.

> But it is always with a twist of omission or addition. He cannot really support lies with truth; but the language of truth makes falsehood go down with the unwary.

14

The devil comes to us across the fields.

> Just when and where we think he cannot get at us, his temptations are sure to find us out.
>
>> The devil will be where we think he's not;
>> Security's vale is his favourite spot.

The devil does most when men are doing least.

> Idleness gives the evil one a great advantage : he gets into the train while it waits at a station. The Turks say, "A busy man is plagued with one devil, but an idle man with a thousand."

The devil entangles the youthful with beauty, the miser with gold, the ambitious with power, the learned with false doctrine.

> He has his peculiarly adapted temptations. How true it is that the learned are specially inclined to heresy! You cannot get up a false doctrine without a D.D. to doctor the gospel for you. This is the case when their knowledge puffeth up, and they have not the love which buildeth up.

The devil falls in when saints fall out.

> Times of contention are great opportunities for Satan. He is the spirit of hate, and feels much at home where ill-will is rampant. Yet when saints fall out with error and worldliness, the evil one has his nest disturbed, and he likes it not.

The devil first plays the fox, afterwards the lion.

> First deceives, and then destroys. Thus error first pleads for liberty, and then lords it over truth, and rages at those whom at first it flattered.

The devil in a sheep's-skin is a devil indeed.

> His deceitful nature thus finds a fit incarnation, and he riots among those whom he delights to worry, and desires to devour.
>
>> Oh, what may man within him hide,
>> Though angel on the outward side !

The devil is a bad master, and he has bad servants.

> Yet his bad servants are obedient to him, zealous in his cause, and obstinate in following his ways. This evil master and his servants grow more and more alike the longer they are together.

The devil is a busy bishop in his diocese.

Nobody can ever complain that he does not hold Visitations and Confirmations. He is all over his diocese, and puts forth all his energy. Hugh Latimer has a pithy piece upon this "most diligent bishop and prelate in all England."

The devil is neither dead nor lame.

Of *Mr. Haynes*, the coloured preacher, it is said that, some time after the publication of his sermon on the text, "Ye shall not surely die," two reckless young men, having agreed together to try his wit, one of them said, "Father Haynes, have you heard the good news?" "No," said Mr. Haynes, "what is it?" "It is great news indeed," said the other, "and if true, your business is done." "What is it?" again enquired Mr. Haynes. "Why," said the first, "the devil is dead." In a moment the old gentleman replied, lifting up his hands, and placing them on the heads of the young men, and in a tone of solemn concern, "O poor fatherless children! What will become of you?"

The devil is old, but not infirm.

On the contrary, his age has sharpened his cunning to an intense degree. Thousands of years he has been tempting men, and who can hope to be a match for him?

The devil leads him by the nose,
Who the dice so often throws.

Gambling is so silly a vice, that it is fair to say that its votary is led by the nose; and it is so ruinous, that surely Satan must have a special hand in it. The ancients say, "The devil goes shares in gaming"; and yet again, "Play hath the devil at the bottom of it." Yet the devil does not demean himself to play.

The devil likes to souse what is already wet.

Where evil is already abundant, he sees good soil for the growth of more. The worse a man is, the worse he may become; and therefore Satan attends carefully to his education in immorals. Evil is not evil enough for him; he would increase it without measure. Every sin is excess, but he would make it more excessive.

The devil takes ill-care of his own servants.

For a while he seems to reward them, but it is to mock them. What is called "the devil's luck" is only disguised ruin. Satan has no gratitude; but those who serve him best are the greatest sufferers in the long run.

The ... ... would be:
The ... ... was be.

Sett ... ... repentance, and dies as ...

... ... Lord.

... ... the way to drive evil ... ... Those who bear children un... ... have are devils in.

... ... When ... ... I ... think you ... ... I ... should suffer as the ...

... ... him.

... ... tumble down ...

... ... slightly in its ...

... ... law
... ... new.

... ... Surrey.
... ... will be
... ... is the
... ... get a
... ... in the

... ...
... ... have
... ... whim

... ...
... ... rush to
... ... seas
... ... that rush
... ... noise.

The dog that minds not your whistle is good for nothing.

Without obedience what is the value of the creature you keep? From the dog up to the servant and the child, the master has a right to expect attention all round.

The donkey's gallop is short.

Some say, "short and sweet." Many men are soon over with their little game. They take up work fast enough; but they drop it quite as fast. There is no depending on them for half-an-hour.

The double-shuffle is the devil's dance.

He practises, inspires, and admires the arts of deceit.

The dove hates the least feather of the hawk.

Every pure-minded man will hate even the appearance of evil.

The drunken man's joy is the sober man's sorrow.

He wastes the substance of the family, and degrades its name; and for this, father, brother, and specially wife, have grey hairs on heads which should not so soon be thus whitened.

The ducks fare well in the Thames.

Where there is plenty of room, and an ever-flowing stream. They are not alarmed by the fear of Cookham or Eton; but they disport themselves in the green and peaceful streams, and nobody hears of their being injured by the abundance of water. Where there is " enough and to spare " is the place for me also.

The Dutch have taken Holland.

Wonderful! And an ass has eaten thistles! A dog has gnawed a bone! A " modern thought " apostle has denied the gospel.

The ear tires sooner than the tongue.

Few are tired of talking, but very many are wearied with hearing. And well they may be when we think of what they have to hear. Many sermons exercise the patience of the saints.

The emperor rules the empire, but the empress rules the emperor.

Oftentimes some favourite son rules the empress, and then the land is unhappy, for it is really governed by a child. It is wonderful with how little wisdom kingdoms are governed.

The devil was sick—the devil a monk would be ;
The devil was well—the devil a monk was he.

> Sick-bed repentance is generally sickly repentance, and dies as
> the man recovers.

The devil will not drive out the devil.

> Else would his kingdom fall. Anger is not the way to drive evil
> out of your wife or your servant. Those who beat children un-
> mercifully may drive one devil out, but they drive ten devils in.

The devil's apple has a bitter core.

> Beware of his tempting fruit. When he says "*Ave*," think you
> hear wisdom saying "*Cave*." Every child of Eve should sicken at the
> sight of the serpent's apple.

The devil's journeymen never want work.

> He makes work for them, and makes them work for him.

The devil's meal is all bran.

> His gains and profits are not what they seem, but dwindle down
> to the small end of nothing.

The dew of the morning sparkles with health.

> Those who have it often on their brows speak highly in its
> favour.
>
> Wash thy face in morning dew ;
> Thou wilt thus thy health renew.

The difficult thing is to get your foot in the stirrup.

> To begin is the difficult matter. Once mounted, riding will be
> simple enough. To get some men really into the stirrups is the
> hard matter : they hesitate and remain undecided. To get a
> livelihood, it is a great thing for a young man to get his foot on the
> ladder, even if it be the lowest rung.

The dog does not get bread every time he wags his tail.

> He would be far too fat if he did. We must not expect to have
> all our wishes granted us. Children ought not to have every whim
> gratified, or they will be ruined.

The dog is a better friend to man, than man to the dog.

> It should never be so. He is a cruel cur indeed who is cruel to
> his dog. They say, "Love me, love my dog"; but in some cases
> the difficulty would not be to love the dog, but the brute that owns
> him. "Is thy servant a dog?" No, he is nothing half so noble.

The dog that minds not your whistle is good for nothing.

Without obedience what is the value of the creature you keep ? From the dog up to the servant and the child, the master has a right to expect attention all round.

The donkey's gallop is short.

Some say, "short and sweet." Many men are soon over with their little game. They take up work fast enough ; but they drop it quite as fast. There is no depending on them for half-an-hour.

The double-shuffle is the devil's dance.

He practises, inspires, and admires the arts of deceit.

The dove hates the least feather of the hawk.

Every pure-minded man will hate even the appearance of evil.

The drunken man's joy is the sober man's sorrow.

He wastes the substance of the family, and degrades its name ; and for this, father, brother, and specially wife, have grey hairs on heads which should not so soon be thus whitened.

The ducks fare well in the Thames.

Where there is plenty of room, and an ever-flowing stream. They are not alarmed by the fear of Cookham or Eton ; but they disport themselves in the green and peaceful streams, and nobody hears of their being injured by the abundance of water. Where there is "enough and to spare" is the place for me also.

The Dutch have taken Holland.

Wonderful! And an ass has eaten thistles ! A dog has gnawed a bone ! A "modern thought" apostle has denied the gospel.

The ear tires sooner than the tongue.

Few are tired of talking, but very many are wearied with hearing. And well they may be when we think of what they have to hear. Many sermons exercise the patience of the saints.

The emperor rules the empire, but the empress rules the emperor.

Oftentimes some favourite son rules the empress, and then the land is unhappy, for it is really governed by a child. It is wonderful with how little wisdom kingdoms are governed.

The empty cask sounds most.

It is a common remark that men talk most who think least. When knowledge comes, chatter stops, just as frogs cease their croaking when a light is brought to the water's side.

The envious die, but envy lives.

The eye of charity should be open, as well as its hand.

To give indiscriminately may be almost as mischievous as not to give at all. Charity must never be blind; but it may see too much, and therefore close its hand. Keep the middle way.

The eye of the master does more than both his hands.

He may do but little manual labour, but his oversight of the work gets it done in quicker and better style than if he were away. The more servants a man has, the more will he need to stay at home and look after them.

The farmer's care makes fields to bear,
Yet God, we know, makes harvests grow.

How the omnipotence of God works through the labour of man we know, for we see it before us every day. We work as if we did all; but we trust in God, knowing that all power belongs to him.

The farther from Rome, the nearer to God.

And it even seems as if there were less Popery in Rome than thousands of miles away from the Vatican. Even the imitation of religion does not flourish in that harlot city.

> They truly say the Pope of Rome
> Is little thought of nearest home.

The farther in, the deeper.

The more we press into the centre of true godliness, the deeper shall we find its mystery, its power, its joy. Those who are up to the ankles in the river of life should go further in till they reach "waters to swim in."

The feet are slow when the head wears snow.

Old age must be content to leave running to youth and middle age.

The fewer to stare, the better the fare.

It is, to some of us, impossible to eat at banquets. We feel like the wild-beasts, whose feeding is a thing for the public to stare at.

The finest diamond must be cut.

Because it is so precious it must undergo this ordeal. God tries the heart he values. The more dear we are to him, the more shall we be chastened. Pebbles lie undisturbed, but jewels do not.

The fire that burneth taketh the heat out of a burn.

It is so on homœopathic principles. That grace which burns us with conviction of sin taking the fire out of the burns of sin. We are judged in conscience that we may not be judged.

The first dish pleaseth all.

In the beginning, appetite is not satiated: everyone is prepared to start fair. The first speaker at a meeting is borne with because the people are not yet wearied.

The first hour of the market for me.

When I am fresh, and my customers have not yet spent all their money. When the goods are fresh and I can have the pick of them as a purchaser.

The first three men in the world were a gardener, a plough-man, and a grazier.

Honourable employments these! Let no man think little of the various forms of husbandry. They are the most healthful and enjoyable of callings. Being made of the earth, we are earthy, and thrive best in those employments which take us back to the ground whence we were taken.

The first to end a fray
Is the best man, I say.

He who is the least to blame is the first to desire reconciliation.

The first who speaks of a suit at law is not therefore in the right.

No, he is frequently a bully, who wants to frighten his opponent. "I'll bring an action" is his frequent threat. "I don't care a fraction" is the answer which usually silences him for the time.

The fish which we did not catch is a very large one.

That which gave us a nibble was immense! That which ran away with the hook was simply enormous! Thus do we make capital out of our failures. What might we not have done if—— !

The flawed pot lasts longest.

When things are a little cracked it is wonderful how long they last, and the like long continuance is proverbial in sickly people. And yet if ever a dish is broken it was cracked before ; and that wicked Mr. Nobody did it, or possibly the cat.

The flesh is master when the mind is idle.

An awful tyrant it is. O sleeping mind, wake up and claim thy proper sovereignty !

The fly that playeth with the candle singeth her wings.

How many do so until they perish ! We know many moths and flies in the shape of young men and women who are already feeling the flame. Fly away, poor creatures !

The fool is fond of writing his name where it should not be.

> When I see a person's name
> Scratched upon the glass,
> I know he owns a diamond,
> And his father owns an ass.

The fool saith, " Who would have thought it ? "

When the reply might be, " Who would *not* have thought it ? " When simple souls run into evil, *they* may be surprised at the consequence, but no one else is.

The foolish alchemist sought to make gold of iron, and made iron of gold.

So it is with those who deal with outside brokers, and go in for " cover, and options," and so forth. They were going to turn their little savings into a fortune, and instead thereof they turned them into smoke. Keep out of the stocks, or you will lose your stock.

The foolish and perverse
Fill the lawyer's purse.

> There be many people so given to strife,
> That they'll go to law for a twopenny knife.

The fools do more hurt in this world than the rascals.

So it would seem. Our own worries come not so much from the wicked as from the weak. A defence of you by a fool may do you more harm than a slander. Save us from a fool's enthusiasm !

The fowler catches old birds as well as young ones.

The fox barks not when he would steal the chickens.

> No, he is as cautious and silent as a modern theologian who is scheming to mislead an orthodox church.

The fox of Ballybotheram was caught at last.

> He worried both dogs and men, led them a fine dance, and got away every time : but the hounds devoured him at length.

The fox praiseth the cheese out of the crow's mouth.

> Let the crow suspect the praise, which is not given for her own sake, but for her cheese sake. You know the fable : it is the picture of that which happens every day.

The friend of the table
Is very variable.

> So say the French, and many English have proved it to be true. He is a wooden friend who owes his friendship to your mahogany.
>
> > The friend who serves for feasts and gain,
> > And follows but for form,
> > Will pack when it begins to rain,
> > And leave thee in the storm.

The full man does not believe in hunger.

The game is not worth the candle.

> The Hindoos speak of a leaf falling into a well, and seven men falling in while looking for it. It is a mad world, and exhibits many instances of hunting mud rabbits with golden hounds. For a homely instance, let us note that when a woman went out to work and earned a shilling, but left her children to do and suffer ten shillings' worth of damage, her game was not worth the candle.

The getting out of doors is the greatest part of the journey.

> With some it seems the hardest thing to start. Once off, they go well enough. It is a task indeed to get them into going order. Nothing will ever be attempted if all possible objections have first to be overcome; and with many timorous people this is very much the case. They will get on if they get off.

The girl with a settlement will soon be settled.

> > That opposite effects may flow
> > From the same cause, 'tis clear's no hum ;
> > For money makes the *mare* to *go*,
> > And also makes the *men* to *come*.

The girl with a sneer
Shall never be my dear.

> I should think not. What if she should sneer *at me* after I had courted her ? She might, but she shan't.

The glutton's temple is the kitchen, and his belly is his god.

> His sacrifice is his health. His reward is early death. Gluttony kills more than war. The epicure heaps suppers upon dinners, and breakfasts upon suppers, and lunches upon breakfasts, without intermission, till it costs him more to choke up his interior than it would to keep a dozen healthy men and women. The following lines were written by *Lord Francis Hervey* in a pastrycook's shop :
>
> > " Be sure that when you've had your fill,
> > You beat a swift retreat ;
> > For Satan finds some dainties still
> > For idle mouths to eat."

The good are better made by ill,
As odours crushed are sweeter still.

The good-man is the last who knows what's amiss at home.

> He must be a singularly absent-minded husband who would allow everybody else to see what he cannot see himself. No doubt it is sometimes so : the man is long-sighted outside in the world, but sees not that which is just under his nose.

The goodness of news half lies in the hearer's ear.

> When people are anxious, and longing for tidings, they think every word precious.

The grace of God is gear enough.

> He that hath grace shall have all other things added to him. "Man wants but little here below " ; grace will secure us that little, and much more. This is a good wish for a friend—
>
> > A little health, a little wealth,
> > A little house, and freedom ;
> > And in the end a little friend,
> > And little cause to need him.

The great ship has also great dangers.

The greatest art is to conceal art.

> It is well to do a thing so naturally that no one would dream that you had followed any rule, or had even taken thought.

The greatest learning is to be seen in the greatest plainness.

This is so with a preacher. If a man cannot make you understand what he is saying, he probably does not understand the matter himself. Ignorance conceals itself behind hard words: true learning expresses itself with careful clearness.

The greatest man must be put to bed with a shovel.

From the graves of the cemetery comes this voice:—

Princes, this clay must be your bed,
In spite of all your towers;
The tall, the wise, the reverend head
Must lie as low as ours.

The greatest of all faults is to be conscious of none.

For this will prevent all hope of mending by making a man think that he is perfect. That must be the greatest of faults which protects all the rest.

The greatest things are done by the help of small ones.

The hand that gives gathers.

May God make it so to every generous giver! Giving is sowing.

The hard man gives no more than he that hath nothing.

Miserly persons, if they have wealth, are more looked after than beggars; and yet they are not worth a penny more to anybody.

The hard-hearted man is the first to complain of unkindness.

He feels for himself because he feels for nobody else.

The hasty angler loses the fish.

He must have patience, and bide his time, and let his fish have a run, or else he will go home with a bare basket. Let him go, that he may not be gone. Let him pull out, that you may pull him in. Humour men and women in much the same way.

The head grey, and no brains yet!

This expression of wonder might apply to a very large number. Better not let them hear it, or a part of their head may grow red. *Dr. Chatfield* has the following:—"I wish to consult you upon a little project I have formed," said a noodle to his friend. "I have an idea in my head"—"Have you?" interposed the friend with a look of great surprise, "then you shall have my opinion—*keep it there!*—it may be some time before you get another"

The heart of a fool is in his mouth; but the mouth of a
wise man is in his heart.

> When the heart is in the mouth, too much comes up; but when the
> .heart controls the mouth, communications will be wise.

The heart that trusts for ever sings,
And feels as light as it had wings.

> That is to say, when the trust is rested upon God alone the rest
> which comes of it is true and gladsome.

The hen that laid the egg ought to hatch it.

> Those who commence a scheme should see to its development,
> and other people should defer to them, and give them the option of
> working out their own methods. The "ought" in this proverb
> may mean either duty or privilege, or both.

The herbs in our own garden will not do for medicine.

> No, we must fetch plants from India. Herbs are not prophets in
> their own country. Our own mineral springs are just as good as
> those in Germany, but no one drinks such common and vulgar
> waters!
>
> > To German *bads* our sick ones roam:
> > Our water's quite as bad at home.

The higher the fool, the greater the fall.

> Fall he will, sooner or later; and what a smash there will be!

The higher the head, the humbler the heart.

> It should be so; but very often the opposite is the case.

The highest branch is not the safest roost.

> > For there the bird is soonest seen,
> > And shot at by some sportsman keen.

The hog that is filthy tries to make others so.

> He hastens to rub against his fellows, and foul them with his own
> mud. Bad fellows cannot bear to see innocence. By example or
> by slander they will either make others wicked, or cause them to
> appear so. By all means keep clear of swinish men.

The home may soon be full of gear,
If you will learn to save the beer.

> The beer-money looks little enough as you drink it away; but
> when it is saved it is wonderful how rich you seem, and how much
> you can buy. Going without the beer makes all the difference.

The horseshoe that clatters is a nail short.

The clatter of the tongue in many a head indicates the same melancholy shortness with regard to the mind; only we generally say, "there's a button short," or "a slate loose." The worst of it is, that you cannot keep a cracked bell still.

The hour of idleness is the hour of temptation.

The house gives the wife a character.

According to its cleanliness and order she will be esteemed. An ill-kept house will damage her good name, and make the neighbours speak lightly of her.

The improvident fight against providence.

They may say what they please about their faith; but as a provident man is not pleased with improvident children, so our Father in heaven loves not prodigality. Those fly in the teeth of providence who squander the provisions of God's bounty.

The jawbone does the mischief.

Whether by too much talking or by too much eating. Much jaw much jeopardy, and much meat much malady.

The joking of wits, like the playing of puppies, often ends in snarling.

The King of Terrors is a terror to kings.

Hence Louis XIV. built his palace at Versailles, since he could not endure that of St. Germains, because from the terrace he could see the tower of the abbey of St. Denis, where the French kings are buried. Death is a dreadful leveller. What cares he for crowns?

The king may bestow offices, but cannot bestow wit to manage them.

To the misery of the parties concerned, this has been proved true in sadly many cases. Desire to be fit for a post before you desire the post itself. If you cannot ride, why seek a horse?

The king must wait while his pudding's boiling.

Or some say, "while his beer is drawing." Like other mortals, he must have patience, for he cannot eat pudding till it is cooked. The Queen herself cannot drink tea till the water is made hot. She who is waited on must wait. Should not we wait also?

The knot you knit
Think well on it.

>Before you make the thing binding, consider and reconsider.

The last drop makes the cup run over.

>Just as the last ounce breaks the camel's back, and the last cruel word breaks the heart. We receive many good things as a matter of course, though we ought not to do so; but some little extra blessing makes us pour out our hearts in gratitude.

The latest fashion is often the latest folly.

The law of love is better than the love of law.

The lawyer grows fat, but his client is lean.

>"A country carter, driving his team, upon a time, along the highway, the foremost horse, it seems, was in very good case, and the rest could hardly crawl after him without the crack of the whip. 'Why, how now, honest man,' cries a counsellor, 'how comes it that your first horse is so fat, and the others so lean?' 'Ho, sir,' says he smartly enough, 'the leader is a lawyer's horse, and those that follow him are but his clients.'"

The lazy begin to be busy when it's time to go to bed.

>Just when the season is over, he proposes to work; and just as he might prosper, he dies. Many a man has gone to the grave when he expected his great baking of bread to come out of the oven.

The lazy man is the beggar's brother.

>Even the beggar is by no means proud of him, but bids him go and sing for his supper, like the rest of the gang.

The lazy man's dessert—roast nothing and no turnips.

>Scant is the table of sloth, and scant it ought to be.

The leanest pig squeaks most.

>Generally. If there is one man worth less than another, he is the fellow to agitate for more wages, or shorter hours.

The least said the soonest mended.

>Every ill-word makes a breakage. If there has been no tittle-tattle, matters can soon be set right.

The less men think, the more they talk.

The less brain, the more jaw. It was said of one verbose preacher—
> "Ten thousand thousand are his words,
> But all his thoughts are one."

The less the fire, the greater the smoke.

Frequently it is so : a little smothered fire makes huge volumes of smoke, where a vehement flame scarcely makes a puff. The less grace the more boast. The less solidity the more pretence.

The less the temptation, the greater the sin.

For it is the more wanton, deliberate, and personal. If we run after sin, and are not drawn into it, we show great depravity of heart. Adam's offence had a great aggravation in it, since he did not sin by depravity, or habit, or example, or from poverty, or persuasion, or force of fashion.

The less wit a man has, the less he knows his want of it.

In fact, where there is very little wit, the man sets up for a sage, and out of his empty skull brings forth oracles of wisdom.

The less you have of goods, the more you need of God.

But it is equally true, "The more you have of goods, the more you need of God." Viewed from different points, positions of poverty or wealth are equally perilous, unless unusual grace be granted us. We may be poor and envious, or rich and proud From each of these may grace deliver us !

The life of love is better than the love of life

The love of life is natural, the life of heavenly love is supernatural, and is created in us by him whose name is Love

The longest life is a lingering death.

This is a pessimist's view of things. A man with a bad liver made this estimate : the worth of the life depends on the liver

The loosest spoke in the wheel rattles most.

Those who are quietly doing their duty make no fuss, but the blameworthy are always in evidence.

The loudest are not the wisest.

But, on the contrary, the louder the bray, the big

The loudest bummer's not the best bee.

> In fact, he is no true bee at all, but only a bumble-bee.

The loudest to threaten are the last to thrash.

The love of money is worse than the lack of money.

> One can go to heaven without gold in the purse, but one cannot get there at all with gold in the heart. Not money, but *the love of it*, is the root of all evil. *South* says, " Mammon has enriched his thousands, but damned his ten thousands."

The love of the wicked is more dangerous than their hatred.

> They can flatter to evil, where their frown would have no effect.

The lowliest Christian is the loveliest Christian.

> No virtue adds such grace to a fair character as humbleness of mind. The lily of the valley is a lovely flower.

The mad dog bites his master.

> He is often the very first person he flies at. When persons are out of their minds, they often hate those most whom once they loved best. It is a token of great folly and wickedness when a man turns round upon the person who was his benefactor and his leader.

The man is what his wife makes him.

> The man who weds a loving wife,
> Whate'er betideth him in life,
>   Shall bear up under all;
> But he that finds an evil mate,
> No good can come within his gate,
>   His cup is filled with gall.

The man of courage knows not when he is beaten.

> Like the English drummer-boy, he does not know how to beat a retreat. He may be crushed down, but never crushed out.
>
> The good man, like a bounding ball,
> Springs ever upward from his fall.

The man of loose life
Shan't have me for a wife.

> Sensible woman ! Mind you stick to that resolution. If you do not, you will have yourself to blame when misery comes upon you.

The man that once did sell the lion's skin
While the beast lived, was killed with hunting him.

> He made too sure of destroying the enemy, and so became himself the prey. Also: never sell what you have not got.

The man who does not trust his own judgment is a man of good judgment.

> No man but a fool is always right. A wise man knows this, and fearing that he may err he is willing to be advised. On the other hand, the first degree of folly is to think one's self wise, the next to tell others so, and the third to despise all counsel.

The man who is everything is nothing.

> He resembles the man whom *Dryden* describes as—
>
> > " Stiff in opinions, always in the wrong,
> > Was everything by starts, and nothing long ;
> > But in the course of one revolving moon,
> > Was chemist, fiddler, statesman, and buffoon."

The man who knows most, knows most his own ignorance.

> When one ventured a compliment to the great philosopher and naturalist, Louis Agassiz, upon the extent and variety of his investigations into the secrets of nature, the Professor's ready and modest reply was, " My dear sir, the longer I live, the more I find I know nothing."
>
> > All things I thought I knew ; but now confess
> > The more I know, I know I know the less.

The master's eye puts flesh on the horse's bones.

> " A fat man riding once along the road, upon a starved and bony jade, was asked, in a banter, why he himself was so jolly and good-like, and his pad so scragged and lean ? He replied very pat to the purpose, ' Why, I feed myself, you must know ; but my servant looks to my horse.' "

The master's presence is the field's profit.

> His foot fattens the soil. When things are well looked over they are not overlooked. Who lives in his business will live by his business.

The meanest reptiles crawl up the highest pillars.

> You cannot, therefore, judge of a man by his position in society.

The meekness of Moses is better than the strength of Samson.

Moses conquered himself, which Samson could not do.

The middle course is usually safest.

Not that which lies between truth and error, or right and wrong; but that which lies between violent extremes. Desire neither riches nor poverty; be neither sceptical nor credulous; spend neither with prodigality nor with meanness. Follow the golden mean.

The mill goes click, click; but where's the meal?

Plenty of resolving to do, and boasting of what is doing; but what really comes of it all?

The mill will never grind with the water that is past.

> " Listen to the water-mill
>   Through the livelong day.
> How the clicking of its wheel
>   Wears the weary hours away.
> And a proverb haunts my mind,
>   And as a spell is cast:
> ' The mill will never grind
>   With the water that is past.' "

The mistress's eye keeps kitchens clean.

Let her leave the maids to themselves, and she will soon see more dirt than there is dust in March, or rain in April.

The more a donkey grows, the more of a donkey he is.

Even growth in knowledge does not remove the folly of a fool. We have heard of a man who went to two colleges, but he was likened to a calf which sucked two cows, and the more it sucked, the bigger a calf it grew.

The more a fool has, the more a fool he is.

He has the more opportunity of developing and displaying his folly. He is able to spend money on his whims, and so he multiplies and magnifies them. Who does not remember a " Smith's Folly," or a " Robinson's Blunder " ?

The more coin, the more care.

Yet most men will run that risk; for they hold, on the other hand, that

> To have no coin,
> Is more annoying.

The more cooks, the worse custards.

Indeed, it is possible that you may get none at all. One would not be surprised to learn that one had left it to the other, and the other to a third, and so the custard was forgotten altogether, or that mustard was sent to table instead.

The more froth, the less beer.

Those who foam, and fume, and fuss, have so much the less of real worth in them.

The more haste, the worse speed.

Four things only are well done in haste : flying from the plague, escaping quarrels, catching fleas, and forsaking sin.

The more laws, the more offences.

This statement is true upon the face of it ; and it illustrates the Scriptural doctrine, that the commandment, however good, works sin in our corrupt nature, exciting desire by its prohibition.

The more noble, the more humble.

It is usually so. A proud man has nothing to be proud of ; with the lowly is wisdom, and wisdom makes a man noble.

The more one has, the more one wants.

Sad truth, that in many cases the wolfish hunger of covetousness increases with the quantity which it has devoured.

The more servants, the less service.

Rather a petulant declaration, like that other saying, " the more servants the more plagues." Yet was a man ever better served than when he had one " gyp " to do everything for him ?

The more the good tree grows, the more shade does it afford.

When a good man's estate increases, he diffuses the grateful shadow of comfort all around him.

The more the merrier, the fewer the better cheer.

This is at a feast. The generous like to see many guests ; but those who are hankering after a great feed for themselves, calculate that the fewer the eaters, the more will remain for each one.

The more thou doest, the more thou canst do.

And the more thou wilt have to do; for in this world willing workers are driven most mercilessly. If thou wilt thou shalt.

The more understanding, the fewer words.

When a man knows his subject well he is able to give a brief description of it. A great preacher desired more time in which to study his sermon, that he might make it shorter. A few drops of otto of rose are worth a ton of leaves.

The morning hour has golden minutes.

All the day is the richer for a man's beginning it in good time. Another proverb says: "The morning hour has gold in its mouth."

> Up at five all alive—
> That's the way to live and thrive.
> Up at nine, the day is gone,
> Will not do to think upon.

The most positive are often the most mistaken.

Cromwell, writing to the Presbyterian ministers of Scotland, once said, "I beseech you, dear brethren, think it possible that you may be wrong." But we are too wrong to think we are wrong.

The mouth is the door of mischief.

Both for entrance and exit. Mischief goes into the mouth in the form of strong drinks, and comes out in the shape of weak words. He was wise who prayed, "Set a watch, O Lord, before my mouth; keep the door of my lips."—Ps. cxli. 3.

The myrtle among brambles is still a myrtle.

Even as the lily among thorns is a lily still. Where there is the grace of God in the heart, the necessary associations of this evil world shall not destroy the beauty of the divine creation.

The nearer the church, the further from God.

It is sad when this is the case. It is worst of all when those who serve in the temple are themselves ungodly, and when ministers' children are children of the devil. Yet it is too often so, that those who are almost in the church are yet leagues away from it, and nobody thinks of looking after them.

> The cobbler's wife, and blacksmith's mare,
> Among the barest go most bare.

The new-made knights
Have great delights
To hear the people call them " Sirs,"
And mark the jingle of their spurs.

The novelty of their promotion pleases the little men, as new toys charm little children. The new-made D.D. grows so vain that some think him M.D., with an A. between.

The north wind finds out the cracks in the house.

Affliction tests our religion, and lets us see our failures of faith, patience, and temper. Blame not the wind, but the wall.

The old gospel is the only gospel.

As there is but one God, one Saviour, and one Spirit, so there is but one gospel.

The older the crabtree, the more crabs it bears.

Does it ? Well, we fear it is so with human crabtrees. Age does not temper some tempers.

The only way to have a friend is to be one yourself.

And this is the way to keep a friend when you have him. This reminds us of an old country health, which a farmer gave at the house of a neighbour who had helped him to get in his crops :—

Here's health to you and yours,
Likewise to us and ours ;
And if ever you and yours
Need help that's in our powers,
We'll do as much for you and yours,
As you have done for us and ours.

The other man is to blame.

He is in the country now, and not to be got at. Jack says "Harry did it" ; and Harry says "'Twas Jack."

The other side of the road always looks cleanest.

Who has not noticed this? So we think that others are free from trouble, when it is possible that they are even worse off than we are. "It is common," says *Tacitus,* "to esteem most what is most unknown."

The owl of ignorance lays the egg of pride.

A very fine egg, but of coarse flavour.

The owl thinks all her young ones beauties.

> And so don't we ! How often parents are the only admirers of their own offspring ! Happy partiality ! "A beetle is a beauty to its mother."
>
>> Where was ever seen the mother,
>> Would change her booby for another?

The ox ate the corn, and they beat the donkey for it.

> Certain persons seem ordained to be the scape-goats for others. One boy does the wrong, but sneaks out of it ; and another seems always to be caught in the act, and yet is innocent.

The ox ploughs the field, but the man eats the grain ;
One does the work, and another gets the gain.

> This comes from the Chinese, and shows that there is injustice everywhere ; and where there is none, there is still grumbling.

The paleness of the pilot is a sign of a storm.

The parings of a pippin are better than the whole of a crab.

> Yes, a few cheery words from a genial friend are far better than an hour's scolding from a churl.

The parson's pig is as hard to drive as mine.

> The lot of the very best is not free from crooks.

The penny in the purse is sometimes handier than the pound in the bank.

> For immediate purposes, a little ready knowledge may be more serviceable than a mass of learning which cannot be used.

The perverting of words is the subverting of peace.

> Because misunderstandings are thus created. The man whose words are twisted is aggrieved ; and so are those against whom those words are supposed to have been uttered.

The philosopher's stone is " Pay as you go."

> It does not turn all things into gold, but it is the best way of preserving what gold you have. Do as little as possible with borrowed money. Even in building a house remember the lines : —
>
>> The man who builds and wants wherewith to pay,
>> Provides a home from which to run away.

The pink of gentility is often the poppy of pride.

The place to spend a happy day—Home !

The pleasure of love is in loving.

> Not altogether : one is pleased to be loved in return.

The plough goes ill when one ox pulls one way, and the other another.

> When husband and wife are not of one mind, family arrangements are disarranged, and specially when there is a difference about religious matters. "Be ye not unequally yoked together with un- believers," is a wise precept, which should in no case be disregarded.

The poor man fasts because he has no meat,
The rich man fasts because he cannot eat.

The poor man no one kens ;
The rich have many friends.

The poor man's budget is full of schemes.

> His plans are wonderful, but they end in plans.

The poor man's hand is Christ's treasury.

> Fill it.

The poorest truth is better than the richest lie.

The pot boils best on its own hearth.

> The writer cannot study well except in his own den. Men are cleverest in their own sphere. Home has a developing power ; for when men are at their ease, they are able to bring forth things new and old. The proverb is a good reason for declining either to lend or borrow a pot, or kettle. Your own goods are best at home.

The price of mercy is to prize it.

The prodigal robs his heir, the miser robs himself.

> It would be hard to say which is the bigger fool of the two, but surely the second in order is not second in degree.

The proof of the pudding is not in chewing the bag.

> No : nor does the proof of soundness in the faith lie in using the phrases of orthodoxy, and harping on mere words.

The proud man has no God;
The envious man has no neighbour;
The angry man has not himself.

The proudest nettle grows on a midden.

> That which grows out of a dunghill is apt to smell of pride. The lower the extraction, the more offensive the exaltation. He who has gained his wealth by unsavoury means seems all the more conceited because of his money-bags.

The quarrels of professors are the reproach of their profession.

> Let us contend for nothing but the faith once for all delivered to the saints. All other contention should end at conversion.

The quart pot helpeth not.

> Yet it is a notion with many that they cannot work till they have seen the bottom of it.
>
> > The thatcher said unto his man,
> > "Let's raise this ladder, if we can."
> > "Nay," said the man, "but first let's drink,
> > And then mayhap we can, I think."

The receiver is as bad as the thiever.

> Often he is the cause of the theft; for few would steal if they had no "fence" to conceal the goods. Some men can be both thieves and receivers. We heard of one concerning whose honesty it was said, "It would not be safe to leave him in an empty house if there were any soot in the chimney." What can be blacker?

The reward of one duty is the power to do another.

> He that carries out one work well, shall be entrusted with another. Even heaven is after this order: "Thou hast been faithful over a few things, I will make thee ruler over many things."—Matt. xxv. 21. It is so in nations: the general who won in Asia shall fight in Africa.

The rich and ignorant are sheep with golden wool.

> But they are sheep and nothing more, however much their fleece may fetch. Yet a prize sheep attracts attention.

The right way leads to the right place.

> Wrong roads can never do this, however much they may appear *to do so.* Beware of the green lanes which lead to destruction.

The road to ruin is as smooth as a bowling-green.

> ·Hence the travelling along it is very rapid.   When ready-money horses the coach, the prodigal makes a very rapid journey ; and the old rhyme is scarcely an exaggeration :—

> Tom Goodfellow came to his fortune on Sunday,
> And *friends* came to see him in dozens on Monday !
> On Tuesday were with him to dinner and sup ;
> On Wednesday in honour of Tom kept it up !
> On Thursday his *friends* set the dice-box afloat !
> This game pretty soon strips a man to his coat.
> On Friday, by some means, Tom lost his last guinea,
> And Saturday—Saturday ended the ninny.

The rougher March the fairer May.

> Of this we are not sure as a matter of weather : but, as a rule, after a period of trial comes a season of repose.

The rule of the road is a paradox quite,
In riding or driving along ;
If you *go to the left* you are sure to be right ;
If you go to the right you are wrong.

But the rule of the footway is clear as the light,
And none can its reason withstand ;
On each side of the way you must *keep to the right*,
And leave those you meet the left hand.

Or—

But in walking the streets 'tis a different case,
To the right it is right you should bear ;
To the left should be left quite enough of free space
For the persons you chance to meet there.

The saddest dog sometimes wags his tail.

> Poor Tray ! We will not portray his grief, but let us be glad that even he has his day, and when that day comes he rejoices, or, at least, his tail does.   It is an exemplary trait in Tray's character that he freely gives you a wag of his tail.

The sea, great as it is, grows calm.

> So say the Italians. Why should not we little folk be at rest ? What good can come of our storms ?

The seeds of great things are often small.

The serpent's eye is an ornament when placed in the dove's head.

> The wisdom and sharp-sightedness of the serpent make a fine blend with the tenderness and modesty of the dove.

The sheep look not at the hedge, but at the turnips.

> Not the arrangement of the sermon, but the spiritual food in it is what hearers care about. "What is a hedge," said a rustic philosopher, "but that which joins one field to another?" Such are the divisions of a discourse.

The ship does not go without the boat.

> The great carry the small with them. The glorious Lord bears with him his poor people.

The shorter the tongue the sweeter the speech.

> Especially when the speaker is in a bad temper. So those have said who have been subjected to the wifely discipline of the curtain lecture. No doubt, many husbands deserve it, but none of them like it. One of them wrote:—

> > " That marriage is an enterprise,
> > Experience doth show;
> > But scolding is an exercise
> > That married men do know."

The shortest day is too long to waste.

The shovel makes game of the poker.

> But why? They stand in the same fender, work about the same fire, and are very nearly related. Why does one worker make game of another?

The silent cat catches the mouse.

> If she were always mewing, her little game would be up and away.

The silver arrow hits the white.

> It is too true that a tip is the tip-top way to succeed where even justice fails: hence one says—

> > Fight thou with shafts of silver and o'ercome,
> > When no force else can get the masterdom.

The slowest insects have most legs.

Those men often do the least who seem to have most abilities and opportunities. They are all leg, and have no heart.

The slut forgets to mend the slits.

Therefore they grow bigger, and her dress comes very soon into the rag-bag. It is slovenly to allow little faults to grow.

The smaller the house, the sooner cleaned.

The smallest boy often carries the biggest fiddle.

Little men aspire to big works; and they always try to carry the big fiddle, even if they cannot play it.

The smallest fishes bite the fastest.

Little minds take up with the last absurdity. Many are waiting to be taken in, and would be unhappy if some new nonsense were not dangled before them. This proves the littleness of their minds.

The smith and his penny are both black.

So are the sinner and his righteousness.

The smith's dog sleeps while the sparks are flying.

Use is second nature. Our hearers learn to sleep while the law is hammering and the sparks of wrath are flying in their faces.

The smoke of my own house is better than the fire of another's.

Not always true. Only a home-bird will say quite so much. And yet most assuredly I would sooner see my own chimney smoking than see another man's house on fire.

> My home with houseleek on the thatch,
> Against a palace I will match.

The son of an ass is sure to bray.

Should he not follow his father? Do some people wonder that their offspring talk foolishly? What other style of talk do they hear? Alas! certain sons of wise fathers exhibit a folly which is not hereditary. Rehoboam was the son of Solomon.

The sooner the better;
Delay is a fetter.

In all good things, promptitude is a valuable element. If hard to-day, a holy act will be harder to-morrow.

The soul lives where it loves.

> A religious man who does not love religion is irreligious.   Life is where the heart is; and when the heart is in heaven, our life is in heaven.   Life without love is day without the sun.

The sourer the gooseberries the more need of sugar.

> Bad tempered people must be treated with great kindness.   When you have a sharp thing to say, mix much love with it.

The south wind brings wet weather,
The north wet and cold together;
The west wind always brings us rain,
The east wind blows it back again.

> So that, according to this venerable saw, it must always be raining.   We think this saw is rusty through too much wet, and needs re-setting.   Yet some years it does seem as if the weather, like the Queen, was always reigning, or say, raining.   Still, we do have dry days even in England.

The spur won't hurt where the hide is thick.

> We know persons who have a thin skin, and we have pitied them; but, having lately come across persons with no sense of honour or shame, we have altered our mind.   Give us the grace to be sensitive rather than the coarse nature which feels nothing. They say, where there's sense there's feeling; and certainly men who have no feeling have seldom much sense.

The stone is hard, and the drop is small,
But a hole is made by the constant fall.

The stone that lieth not in your way need not offend you.

> Don't go out of your road to find something to stumble at. What is the good of looking out for a grievance?

The string slips where the knot's loose: tie tight.

The sun moves on, whoever hides its light.

> It were great folly should it stop.   What end would it serve? Its answer to dark bodies is to shine on them.   My son, imitate the sun.

The superfine gentleman is nobody's money.

> " The son of toil will gain the spoil,
>   While delicacy lingers :
> That man's unwise, whoe'er he is,
>   Who fears to soil his fingers."

The surety is sure to be sued.

"He that is surety for a stranger shall smart for it" (Prov. xi. 15). Mark this, and save yourself many a mark.

The sweet and the sour,
The nettle and flower,
The thorn and the rose,
Our life-time compose.

Like the year, life has its changeful seasons. It wears a Joseph's coat of many colours. He that knoweth it through age and experience, may say of it, "I will sing of mercy and judgment; unto thee, O Lord, will I sing."—Ps. ci. 1.

The tailor that makes not a knot loseth a stitch.

The time that we take to make our work sure and lasting is by no means lost: in fact, it is an economy of time to do things thoroughly well. Yet in these days, such is the evil force of competition for cheapness, that tailors would not only sew with a red-hot needle and a burnt thread if they could, but they would prefer to throw the pieces of cloth together, and let them hold on by their edges as best they could.

The tale-hearer is as bad as the tale-bearer.

A witty divine once said that the tale-bearer should be hung up by a nail through his tongue, and the tale-hearer by nails through his ears. So, too, those who tell you stories, will tell stories of you. The dog that fetches is of the same breed as the dog that carries: they are much of a muchness, and would both be the better for being muzzled.

The tallest trees
Feel most the breeze.

Don't grow up aloft, for there you feel the full force of the hurricane. Wisdom would suggest that we keep near the ground, and run to fruit rather than to wood.

The tankard robs more than the thief.

It steals a man's senses, character, and hopes: in fact, it steals the man himself, and robs him both of the happiness of this life, and the eternal felicities of the life to come.

All his life was cankered,
Since he ever hankered
For the flowing tankard.

The tears of the oppressed plead hard with God.

Those pence earned by ill-paid labour, with tears, and sweat, and life-blood, are memorials before the Lord which he will not forget: the sweater shall find another sort of sweat upon his brow when God deals with him.

The thief can steal in a moment, but the watchman must watch all night.

Temptation calls for constant watchfulness: sin may undo in an unguarded second the character which needed years to form.

The thief comes when the candles are out.

Darkness suits all ill designs. Ignorance is the worst of darkness, and spiritual ignorance the worst of ignorance. Let us light up many a candle in our own beloved land, and drive the thieves away. Does not the proverb remind you of certain altars with unlighted candles on them? It would be well to carry light there also, not to light the candles, but to enlighten the men.

The thin end of the wedge is to be feared.

The big end cannot do mischief till the thin end has made way for it. Avoid the beginnings of evil. Alas! the many take no heed to minor errors, and so invite the greater heresies.

The thorn serves well to guard the rose.
The thread breaks where it is thinnest.

We fail where we are weakest: but where are we not weak?

The times be good when men are good betimes.

To the like effect is the other sentence, "The times would mend if men would mend betimes." Some are always crying out for "the good old times"; but these are the "old times," for time was never older than now, and the times would be good enough if we were so. *Sydney Smith* used to say:

"The good of other times let others state:
I think it lucky I was born so late."

The tongue bites sharper than the teeth.

The tongue cuts where the teeth cannot bite. The teeth cannot get at the heart, but the tongue can. Moreover, the tongue bites miles away, and the teeth must be near. What awful wounds a cruel tongue can inflict! and yet who can protect himself from it?

The tongue does more mischief than all the other members.

For its range is wider, and its power is more penetrating than that of hand or foot. It is a world of evil when it is evil.

The tongue is in a wet place, and easily slips.

Slips of the tongue may be as harmful as slips of the foot: we must guard well the movements of that powerful little member.

The tongue is not steel, but it cuts.

And its worst wounds are not with its edge, but with its back.

The tongue of idle persons is never idle.

Yet is it always idle: idly making a noise, and doing damage. *Peraldus* reckons up four-and-twenty different sins of the tongue; one for every hour of day and night.

The tongue turns to an aching tooth.

Sympathy moves it. Thus should all Christians feel for each other, and instinctively render what relief they can to those who suffer; for we are members one of another. Yet, I pray thee, Mr. Talkative, turn not thy tongue to me, however much I ache.

The tongue which slanders is worse than the hand which strikes.

Knock me down if you will, but don't injure my character. I can rise after a blow, but who can restore a blighted name? "What shall be done unto thee, thou false tongue?"—Ps. cxx. 3.

The tools to him who can use them.

And if he cannot use them he ought not to take them to play with them and spoil them. Books, pulpits, seats in parliament, pens and ink, and so forth, should only be trusted to those who can use them to good purpose.

The tree is sure to be pruned before it reaches the skies.

No man will always rise. Something will occur to keep him within due limits. Envy will gnaw his root if nothing else happens.

The tree of knowledge has often flourished where the tree of life never grew.

One may have all knowledge, but without grace what a vain thing it is! Alas, if knowledge bring not good, how it works evil!

The truly great man would not trample on a worm, nor tremble before an Emperor.

> He is neither crouching nor crushing.

The very name "husband," what does it say?
Of wife and of household, the band and the stay.

The vicar of Bray will be vicar of Bray still.

> Amid the changes of religion in different reigns, from Popish to Protestant, and back again, this ecclesiastic still held his post; for his doctrine was expressed in the chorus of the old ballad:
>
> > And this is law, I will maintain,
> > Until my dying day, sir,
> > That whatsoever king may reign,
> > I'll be the vicar of Bray, sir.

The vulgar count not your hits, but your misses.

> This is only fair after all; for you yourself will record your hits, but not your misses, and thus a complete chronicle becomes possible.

The waggon must go whither the horses draw it.

> So will national affairs, parish matters, ecclesiastical policies, and domestic arrangements, go in the way in which the most energy is displayed. It is a sad pity when the horses are head-strong, and take to the wrong road.

The waster delayeth, and lets the debt lie;
The prudent man payeth, the cheaper to buy.

> Doubtless prompt payment gives a man great advantage in the market. The small tradesman cannot afford to be in debt.

The way to be safe is to take nothing for granted.

> See it right yourself, with your own eyes.

The Welshman keeps nothing till he has lost it.

> Surely this is Irish! We suppose the Welshman is impulsive and generous, and only learns economy when he perceives that he has given more than he could afford.

The whole truth is wholesome.

> But a part of the truth may mislead, and cause us to make as great errors as if we had believed a falsehood. Half the truth is a lie; or say, "a half-truth may be a falsehood." Therefore, let us endeavour to have a fair full-faced view of matters.

The wife can throw away more with a spoon than the husband can bring in with a shovel.

> Little wastes can prevent the accumulation of large earnings. Still, the greatest danger is not from the wife's spoon, but from the husband's cup.

The wife must prepare what the husband provides.

> " John's wife and John were *tête-à-tête*;
> She witty was, industrious he.
> Says John, ' I've earn'd the bread we've ate.'
> ' And I,' says she, ' have *urn'd* the tea.' "

The wife that loves the looking-glass hates the saucepan.

> Not always true; yet the fear is that the folly which shows itself in dress and self-admiration should lead to neglect of household duties. Blessed is the wife that can cook well, for she shall have her husband home to dinner. Well was she commended of whom it was said :
> " Tell me a thing she cannot dress :
> Soups, hashes, pickles, puddings, pies,
> Nought comes amiss, she is so wise."

The wind in one's face makes one wise.

> We wish it did. Still we know what the proverb means : it is by opposition and trial that we learn. There is an old saying that "The Tracys always have the wind in their faces" : we don't know the gentlemen, but we heartily rejoice with them, for nothing is more refreshing than a bracing breeze.

The window opened more and more
Would keep the doctor from the door.

> How long will it be before people will believe in fresh air ?

The wing with the liver
To him who's the giver.

> Let him have the best part of the fowl, since he placed it on our table. Let anyone who has fowls to give away try us, and see if we will not carve him the liver-wing.

The willow will buy a horse before the oak will pay for a saddle.

> Willow branches are quick in growth, and bring in more by far than the slow-growing oak. Men of small parts may do more by speed and perseverance than greater men who are slow.

The wise man gets learning from those who have none
themselves.

> Therein showing what a wise man he is. Wise men learn more
> from fools than fools learn from wise men.

The wise man keeps on good terms with his wife, his con-
science, and his stomach.

> Either of these three can make his life a misery to him, and
> therefore he would keep them all in good humour.

The wise man knows the fool, but the fool doth not know
the wise man.

> Yet he must be a very wise man who thoroughly knows a fool,
> for the ways of folly are inscrutable. The proverb is true in its
> own sense ; but, like others, it needs a pinch of salt.

The wise with a tick,
The fool with a kick.

> A wink is enough to make the sensible understand, but the
> stupid need more impressive instruction. So some think. We
> kick no one : it wears out our boots.

The wisest are not always wise.

The wisest man does not think himself so.

> A famous Eastern judge, on one occasion, after a very patient
> investigation of facts, declared that his knowledge was not com-
> petent to decide upon the case before him. "Pray, do you expect,"
> said a pert courtier, who heard his declaration, "that the Caliph is
> to pay your ignorance?" "I do not," was the mild reply ; "the
> Caliph pays me, and well, for what I do know. If he were to
> attempt to pay me for what I do not know, the treasures of his
> empire would not suffice."

The wisest mouse keeps farthest from the trap.

> The most prudent man is most careful to avoid temptation, and
> the sin which comes of it.

The wittiest man laughs least.

> Because he has a high standard of wit, and is not affected by
> much which pretends to be facetious. Wit is not always grinning.

The wolf does not weep over the death of the dog.

> No, for he has now more liberty to prey on the sheep. A faithful
> minister's death is joy to the heretic, and his leader, the devil.

The wolf loses his teeth, but not his inclinations.

Old age leaves him still a wolf. He retains his taste for mutton, though he cannot now leap into the fold to help himself thereto. Apply the proverb to wicked old men.

The wolf offered to watch the flock for nothing.

But he meant to pay himself in mutton. Always suspect that those who offer to do work for nothing intend to do it for something. Errorists are seemingly generous till their ends are served.

The workman makes the work, but the work also makes the workman.

This reminds us of William of Wyckham's inscription upon a building erected for the king. THIS WORK MADE WILLIAM DE WYCKHAM. When the royal owner objected to it, he explained it to mean, not that he made the work, but that the work made him. Both readings were true.

The world at its best is a handful of shadows.

No, not even a handful; it fills nothing : it is altogether emptiness. The world's ALL is nothing at all.

The world is governed with little brains.

History often forces this reflection from its readers. It would even seem as if madness had been more common in rulers than in the governed. Many a crown has no head beneath it.

The world is too narrow for two fools quarrelling.

If they could shove each other over the edge of the universe, society would not suffer much. For two such big men an extra world or two would be convenient, that they might swing their big swords, and fulfil their terrible threats without harm to others.

The world over, crows are black.

Meaning that men are sinful everywhere.

The world owes me a living, providing I earn it.

Those last words are a qualifying clause, which many forget. What right can we have to live on other people's earnings? Yet many fancy that all the world is in debt to a lazy fellow who puts nothing into the public purse.

The world was not made in a minute.

London was not built in a day : great things are not accomplished in a hurry. We must learn to labour and to wait.

The world would be better if you were.

> The world is as you take it ;
> It will be what you make it.

The worse the carpenter, the more the chips.

He who does his work well, makes little fuss about it ; but the incapable workman buries himself under the rubbish he creates.

The worse the passage, the more welcome the port.

"Then are they glad because they be quiet." What music is made when the ship is in the harbour, and the chain of the anchor runs out ! He that was most sick is the gladdest to land.

The worst argument is an ill-name.

Bishop Horne says, "It is too frequent a custom to give ill names to those who differ from us in opinion." *Dr. Hammond* mentions a humorous instance of it, that when a Dutchman's horse did not go as he would have him, he, in a great rage, called him an " Arminian."

The worst wheel rattles most.

Always. Those complain most against whom most complaints could be laid.

Their fears are most who know not what they fear.

Belshazzar saw only a hand writing on the wall, and this mystery appalled him. The unknown is the terrible. Ungodly men flee when no man pursueth, for at bottom they are superstitious.

> The wicked walk in fear of bush and brake,
> Yea, oftentimes their shadow makes them quake.

Then's then, but now's now.

Then let your now be now. What you resolve to do one day do this day. To-day is *the* day.

There are calumnies against which even innocence loses courage.

Slanders may be too foul to be met except with tears ; or, they may be told with such an appearance of truth that they gain instant belief. When a man is so stunned by a wicked charge that he cannot contain himself, or make a reply, it is an argument for his innocence. The Lord save us from the arrow which flieth by day!

There are forty men of wit to one of sense.

> Without sense men can talk nonsense. Smart witty people are far more common than thoroughly sensible persons.

There are good dogs of all sizes.

> Condemn not this dog for being too large, nor that for being too small. If you know where to look for them, you may find good little men, and even good great men.

There are many things much in use, which are not of much use.

> Such as the excrescences of fashion in dress, and so forth.

There are more ways of killing a dog than hanging him.

> If a fellow cannot be overcome in one way, he may be ruined in another. Let the poor dog look out and sharpen his teeth, or his enemy will compass his death one way or another.

There are no fans in hell.

> So say the Arabs. It is a terrible proverb; but how true! Misery without mitigation is of the essence of future punishment.

There are other thieves besides those who are locked up.

> A worthy divine was robbed of his portmanteau in which were a number of his discourses. Some one wrote for him as follows :—
>
> > "The thief who stole my sermons,
> > On which I set such store,
> > May safely bring them back again ;
> > They were stolen long before."
>
> Another version of this story is more circumstantial, and savours more of slang. The Rector of Kingston-by-Sea, on his parsonage being entered and robbed, is credited with the following :
>
> > "They came and prigg'd my stockings, and my linen, and my store ;
> > But they could not prig my sermons, for they were prigg'd before."

There are toys for all ages,
For fools and for sages.

> The man's toys are the most expensive, and the sage's are the most mischievous. There are the Evolution humming-top, and the New Theology penny whistle, and a number of other childish things.

There are wedges for all woods.

If we will use our wits, we can conquer all difficulties, even as all logs can be split if we get the right beetle and wedge.

No man may grow carnally secure; for God knows how to bring him down. Who can stand before his wrath? The proverb may also mean that there are temptations for all men, and if they do not yield to one they may to another.

There is a devil in every berry of the grape.

So says the Koran. It is a striking way of setting forth the evils of intoxicating drink. It will not frighten English wine-bibbers, for their stuff does not flow from grapes.

There is a religious way to perdition.

And it is none the less sure because smoothly rolled with cere-monies and professions.

There is a remedy for all evils but death.

I have known two persons who boasted that they would never die; but I hope they are dead, for I am sure they are buried.

There is a salve for every sore.

> The thing's to find the ointment out, ·
> And that you should be quick about.

There is a snake in the grass.

Where? Well, just where you do not think there is one. Who is he? Well, he is one whom you could not suspect; therefore don't suspect anybody. The " he " may be a " she."

There is a special providence in the fall of a sparrow.

The same law governs the small as well as the great. This is noticeable in all the laws by which the Lord governs nature and providence; they affect the minute as well as the magnificent.

> The very law which moulds a tear,
> And bids it trickle from its source,
> That law preserves the earth a sphere,
> And guides the planets in their course.

There is a time to fish, and a time to dry nets.

Happy is he who knows when his hour is come, and does the work appropriate for that hour. To rest when rest is due is as wise as to labour when the hour arrives.

There is a time to wink as well as to see.

> Some things are best unseen, especially personal slights.

There is a world of meaning in a little text.

> One who tried to expound a passage said : "There's a wonderful deal in it, my friends, if I could only get it out."

There is more bitterness in beer than comes from the hop.

> Don't try it to see. Ask the publican ; or, better still, see some of his work taken home, or carefully laid by in the police cell.

There is more disputing about the shell than the kernel.

> Controversy often concerns minor points ; it seldom touches vital matters ; but when it does, it is serious work.

There is no banquet, but some dislike something in it.

> For it is said, "There is no feast without a fool at it." It is said that one, at least, goes away unfed from every feast. The only exception is the Lord's festival of grace.

There is no benefit in a gift that sticks to the fingers.

> If you give grudgingly, or taunt a man with it afterwards, the grace of the gift has gone like smoke.
>
> > He gives as if his blood he shed ;
> > Indeed, he would be sooner bled.

There is no better patch than one off the same cloth.

> The deceased wife's sister will often supply the place of the deceased wife better than anyone else, *unless she is a cross patch*. It is a pity that bishops have no deceased wives' sisters. They would then see beyond their sees, and read Leviticus with clearer eyes.

There is no corn without some chaff.

> Nothing is absolutely free from imperfection. Wisdom is mixed with folly, truth with error, holiness with imperfection.

There is no going from Delilah's lap to Abraham's bosom.

> Shorn looks, blinded eyes, imprisoned lives, and cruel shame from the lap of the strange woman. Even a Samson i- there. The young man must, above all things, keep of all wantonness if he would lead a happy life b-

There is no larder but may have its mice.

> However large or small, it needs watching; for where the cheese is, thither will the mice be gathered together.

There is no law but has a hole in it for those who can find it out.

> You can drive a coach and four through any Act of Parliament. A keen lawyer can find a way through every law but Mortmain.

There is no stripping a naked man.

> He that has nothing cannot be fined or robbed. But if he can't be stripped he can be whipped. He that cannot pay with his tin must pay with his skin.

There is no such flatterer as a man's self.

> How delicately he pleases his customer! He hates flattery; he is so humble! The dear old stupid, how he drinks it in, and leaves no heel-taps in the cup!

There is no use in blowing a fire that burns well.

> Exhorting those to liberality and industry who are already doing their best, is not the wisest way of using one's oratory.

There is no use in preaching to the hungry.

> Give them a dinner of at least one course, and then give them a discourse. Theology is cold stuff on an empty stomach. The belly hath no ears when it hungers.

There is nothing so like a good shilling as a bad one.

> Except it is another good shilling. Of course, hypocrites imitate true believers as far as they can, or they would get no gain by their hypocrisy. No wonder that we are deceived! Yet the existence of hypocrites does not prove the non-existence of true believers, any more than bad sovereigns prove that there are no good ones. The proof is all the other way.

There never was a five-pound note but there was a ten-pound road for it.

> One never has money without having ways of spending twice as much. It may not be so with millionaires, but so we find it.
>
> > How doth our little careful wife,
> > And children all alive,
> > Demand our money all through life,
> > And soon devour a five!

There never was a looking-glass that told a woman she was ugly.

It was never plain to a woman that she was plain. In fact, from some point of view, every woman has her beauties, and she has the art of seeing herself from that stand-point. Bless the dear mirrors of perfection; no wonder they admire themselves. It shows their good taste and ours also.

There will be no Mondays in heaven.

No weary Mondays for pastors; no wicked Mondays for drunkards; no worldly Mondays for the outwardly religious.

There would be fewer open mouths if there were fewer open ears.

Just so. If there were not a market for scandal, nobody would be a scandal-monger. Where there are heads on one side, there will be tails, or rather tales, on the other.

There's a way to heaven from the gates of hell.

The worst of sinners may be saved.

There's a way to hell from the gates of heaven.

The proudest professor may be lost.

There's always room at the top.

The best men are always wanted, and there's always a scarcity of them. One could find ten thousand middling workmen; but where shall we look for a first-class hand?

There's always water where a calf is drowned.

One would think so. If there is sufficient of anything to do mischief, there must be enough for a better purpose. The man who has wit enough to be a thief, might earn a good living.

There's crust and crumb in every loaf.

We must take them together. The rough and the smooth, the soft and the hard, make up life, and there's no use hoping to see it altered. The best bred are not all upper crust.

There's gold in quartz, I hear:
Mine's gone in quarts of beer.

This confession is seldom heard, but in many instances it is true as the Confession of Faith.

There's little roast
Where braggarts boast.

There's little tale-bearing on the right side.

> A good deed in common life gets no corner in the newspaper,
> and no gossip busies herself with informing her neighbours of it. Yet
> surely it should pay as well to hawk sweet fish as stinking ones.

There's mischief brewing when the wolf licks the lamb.

> Extraordinary displays of affection have their motive—a motive
> which means no good to the victim of their effusive love. Young
> women should note this proverb. Affectionate wolves are common.
>
>> Whose manner is so over-sweet,
>> Has cheated or intends to cheat.

There's more room without than within.

> A young preacher once told me that he had a great congregation,
> and, he added, "There were more people outside than in." I
> answered, that I fully believed it. He saw my drift. Old houses
> had the chimney built outside the house; was this because there is
> more room outside than inside? There is more liberty outside of
> some societies than you can expect within.

"There's ne'er a best among them," as the fellow said by
    the fox cubs.

> Among certain sets of men all are so bad that the question is,
> "Which is the worst?" and never, "Which is the best?"

There's never any cake
But there's some of like make.

> Nobody is so odd, or so bad, or so good, but what there are others
> to match, if you know where to look for them.

There's no evil, but it might be worse.

There's no flying without wings.

> Trading on credit, preaching without ability, and the like, are
> vain attempts. They all end in a downfall.

There's no garden without weeds.

> No character without faults; no church without false professors;
> no family without troubles. Weeds come without inviting.
>
>> In the garden much more grows,
>> Than the busiest gardener sows.

There's no getting oil out of a mill-stone.

> Nor wine out of a wall, nor money out of an outside broker. Extracting feeling from some men is quite as difficult as getting blood from a turnip. To get money out of misers is about as hard as getting butter out of a dog's mouth.

There's no happiness where there's no occupation.

> Want of something to do is downright misery. It is long since some of us could complain of that affliction.
>
> > The want of occupation is not rest,
> > A mind quite vacant is a mind distressed.

There's no making omelets without breaking eggs.

> We must go to some expense to effect our purpose.

There's no mother like my mother.

> No, not even the Prince of Wales's mother! "No, sir," said a child when he heard a visitor quote Pope's familiar line, "An honest man's the noblest work of God." "No, sir, my mother is the noblest work of God."

There's no need to fasten a bell to a fool; everybody will know where he is.

> If his tongue wags he will not need to be looked for.

There's no need to grease a fat sow.

> Yet many are eager to do it: everybody helps the man who does not need it. Somewhat bitterly one writes—
>
> > By all observers it is known,
> > And daily seen on every hand;
> > The prosperous in life alone
> > Have proffer'd service at command.

There's no place like home.

> It is a great pity when either husband or wife is forced to answer, "I'm glad there isn't."

There's no piety where there's no morality.

> He that has not the pence of morality cannot possess the pounds of godliness. Sir J. Lubbock says of the aborigines of Australia, "They do not believe in a supreme Deity, or in the immortality of the soul; nor is morality in any way connected with their religion." Alas, that this should be true of so many nearer home!

There's no profit in teaching a pig to play the flute.

> Even if the pupil could learn, others would do the business better.
> There are persons who have no capacity for learning a certain art,
> and teaching it to them would be lost labour.

There's no reaping where there's no sowing.

> Thou canst not gather what thou dost not sow :
> As thou dost plant the tree, so will it grow.

There's no remedy for consumption of the purse.

> Why not? Brace the economical system by pulling the strings
> tighter. Administer an elixir of extra earnings. Try thrift.

There's no riding to heaven on a feather bed.

There's no security where there's a Committee of Safety.

> Though in the multitude of councillors there is safety, it lies in
> the direction of their never doing too much—if they ever do any-
> thing. A committee is like armour, an excellent device to pre-
> serve a society from harm, and to prevent its doing much of
> either harm or good.

There's no taking snakes with sugar-tongs.

> Hitting them over the head is far more effectual. Had Luther
> handled error daintily, the Reformation would never have come
> off. Some bad things need vigour and rigour rather than dainti-
> ness. Luther threw an ink-bottle at the devil's head, whereas
> another preacher, when Satan tempted him to doubt, set a chair for
> him, and bade him sit down and have it out : a rash experiment.

There's nothing impossible to perseverance.

> We copy the following from *Aunt Rachel's Advice to her Niece:*—
> "Mr. Medhurst, who was formerly a missionary in China, gives in
> his book a curious story—which reads more like a fable than a fact
> —of a woman, whom he saw one day rubbing a small iron crow-
> bar on a stone, at which she had been engaged for a very long
> time. And when he asked what she was doing it for, he was
> informed that she wanted a needle, and not being able to meet with
> one, she was grinding the crowbar down to the proper size; a
> singular instance, *if true*, of energy and perseverance."

There's nothing like leather.

> Pardon me, good sir ; that beef-steak upon which I wearied my
> teeth the other day was extremely like it. Every man cries up his
> own wares, and hence the tanner cries "Nothing like leather."

There's poor profit in flaying flints.

> Don't attempt to get money from the very poor. Some people seem to live upon what they can extract from the dregs of poverty: it must be a wretched business. The miserly are, however, worse to deal with than the very poorest: they are flints of the hardest kind, and are neither to be flayed nor chipped.

There's time enough where there's will enough.

> At any rate, good sir, you have all the time there is ; and when you have made up your mind to use it, there will be more. " I have no time " should frequently be interpreted " I have no will."

There's too much weighing meat about it.

> Spoken of trades and transactions in which there are a great many things upon which a loss will be sustained. It comes from the former habit of butchers, when selling prime joints, to throw in a bit of an inferior part, or perhaps a bone, under the idea that nobody could expect to have all the best of the meat, and none of the rougher portions.

These evil days bring sorry jokes
To simple men like Johnny Nokes.

> " *John a Nokes* was driving his cart toward Croydon, and by the way fell asleep therein. Meantime, a fellow came by and stole away his two horses, and went fair away with them. In the end, John, awaking and missing them, said, 'Either I am *John a Nokes,* or I am not *John a Nokes.* If I am *John a Nokes,* then have I lost two horses ; and if I be not *John a Nokes,* then have I found a cart." Simple persons need a friend to look after them, or they will be sorely troubled.

They are like a ha'p'orth of soap in a wash-tub.

> Or like a chip in the porridge : of no great consequence : too little to be of use. Like the gospel in certain modern sermons.

They love but little who can tell how much they love.

> In no case can love be subjected to either the rod or the scale. It is too ethereal for inches and ounces. No real lover of the Lord can measure his love ; but he wishes it were far more.

They may point at a star, but they cannot pull it down.

> Evil persons may ridicule a truly good man, but they cannot pluck him from the position wherein providence has placed him.

They never wrought a good day's work who went grumbling about it.

No one can work well when his heart is not in his labour : he is sure to fail in quantity or in quality. Give me the man who works with a will, and is not always looking for six o'clock.

"They say so," is half a lie.

Because it may be that we lead people to think that it is the universal opinion, when, perhaps, "they" means only myself and another fool.

> If thou wouldst tidings understand,
> Take them not at second-hand.

They say there is a skeleton in every house.

I have added "they say" to this proverb, because otherwise it is far from true. There are Christian homes which have nothing to conceal, no shameful secret, no Blue-beard cupboard.

"They say, they say," and donkeys bray.

Common talk is really no more to be regarded than the braying of asses. The theoretical talk of infidel scientists may be put in the same category. Think of this as taught by science :—

> Man was an ape in the days that came early ;
> Centuries after his hair became curly :
> Centuries more gave a thumb to his wrist,
> Then he became man and a Positivist.

They should be more thankful that give an alms, than they that receive it.

Certainly they are the more favoured of the two, and most in-debted to the goodness of God. A worthy Quaker would hear nothing of thanks for money given by him to charitable objects. His reply to those who thanked him was : "Friend, I am much obliged to thee for thy trouble in applying this money to good use."

They that hide can find.

As a rule this is a truism. But he that hides his religion may one day find that he has none to hide.

They that walk much in the sun will be tanned at last.

Exposure to evil influences tells upon the character, and before long the result is visible in the conduct.

They that wash on Monday have all the week to dry ;
They that wash on Tuesday are not much awry ;
They that wash on Wednesday there's no need to blame ;
They that wash on Thursday wash for shame ;
They that wash on Friday wash for need ;
They that wash on Saturday—oh, they are sluts indeed !

> These rude lines are a warning against putting off things to the very last day. The habit of delay begins with some when children, and then they are assailed with—
> "Dilly, Dilly, dollar,
> Ten o'clock scholar."
> This continues through life, and leads to Saturday washing and general tardiness. If those who "first come are first served," dilatory persons are served right when never served at all.

They who cannot have what they like should learn to like what they have.

> A tough lesson, but well worth learning.

They who have money are troubled about it,
And they who have none are troubled without it.

> So that neither poverty nor riches will ensure perfect repose.

They who will not be counselled cannot be helped.

> Refusing to be guided, they must even "gang their ain gate." It is said, "If you have your own way you won't die in a pet"; but on the other hand, such are very likely to fall into the pit.

They wonder at the cedar when it is fallen.

> They had no idea that the man was so good and great until he was dead; and then they knew the miss of him, and regretted that they had allowed him to be among them, and to be so little esteemed.

They wrangle about an egg, and let the hens fly away.

> Too often in disputes between master and men, trade is ruined, and so the hen flies away. In controversies over trifles, the spirit of love is driven away from a church, and the main thing is thus lost.

They wrong themselves, that wrong others.

> At some time or other the evil done falls upon the doer of it. The ball thrown against the wall comes back into the sender's hand. He that watereth a path with vitriol to kill the grass, is pretty sure to burn his own boots.

Thick sown and thin come up.

In some places the gospel has been faithfully preached by many ministers, and yet few are converted. On some men much teaching has been expended, but they know nothing. Their fathers spent much money upon them at college, but they are forced to cry, " We put gold into the fire, and there came out this calf."

Things forbidden have a secret charm.

This is sadly true. " I had not known lust, except the law had said, Thou shalt not covet." Adam might not have cared for the fruit of that one tree had it not been forbidden. In a smaller way, this is the cause of smuggling, poaching, and many other offences.

·Think and thank.

There is only a letter of difference between the two words. Surely we should never do much thinking without rising to thanking.

Think kindly of the poor
When it's cold out of door.

But let your thoughts be practical. A hundred thoughts will not warm them half so much as half-a-hundred of coals.

Think not, the husband gained, that all is done—
The prize of happiness must still be won ;
And oft the careless find it to their cost,
The lover in the husband may be lost.

What a pity it is when people leave off their courting manners as soon as they are married ! Should they not take more pains to be agreeable when they see each other all day, than they did when they had only occasional meetings ?

Think of ease, but work on.

So long as there is any life in the old ox, let it keep to the plough. It is more easy to think of ease, than to make yourself easy with nothing to do. Work for amusement if not for emolument.

Think thrice before you marry once.

Let the thinking be on both sides. Then the verse we are about to quote may come true.

> Abel wants to marry Mabel ;
> Well, that's very wise of Abel.
> But Mabel won't at all have Abel ;
> Well, that's wiser still of Mabel.

Think twice before you speak once.

> Then you will speak twice as well, or possibly you will do better, and not speak at all.
>
>> Wise men reflect before they speak,
>> Fools speak, and then think after.
>> Wise men's words are full of light,
>> But fools' are full of laughter.

Think twice over a great bargain, and then leave it.

> For in what seems a great bargain the chances are that we are taken in, or else we are making a market out of some poor man's pressing necessities. Beware of painfully cheap purchases.

Think well before you tie what you cannot untie.

> Enter upon marriage with courage, but with caution. Yet no one would go so far as the old bachelor of Elizabeth's days, who said—
>
>> If that a bachelor thou be,
>> Thou wilt keep so if ruled by me,
>> Lest that repentance all too late,
>> Reward thee with a broken pate.

Think well of a man
As long as you can.

> Frequently the rule would seem to be—
>
>> Think ill of each man,
>> The first time you can.

Think well of men if you would mend them.

> Nobody will let you suggest an improvement in his conduct if you begin by abusing him, or if he can see that you despise him.

Think when you speak, but speak not all you think :
Drink when you thirst, but thirst not after drink.

> Some are troubled with a constant running at the mouth ; others with a constant drought in the same place. Of the latter, *Livingstone* wrote :—" The Ptolemaic map defines people according to their food—the Elephantophagi, the Struthiophagi, the Ichthyophagi, and the Anthropophagi. If we followed the same sort of classification, our definition would be by their drink, thus : the stout-guzzlers, the roaring potheen-fuddlers, the whisky-fishoid drinkers, the vin-ordinaire bibbers, the lager-beer swillers, and an outlying tribe of the brandy-cocktail persuasion."

Thirst grows by that it feeds on.

The more drink, the thirstier is the drinker. The mouth is never satisfied with liquids. One glass makes room for another. Some soak in beer, some swim in wine, some splash in spirits; and all of them are apt to complain of being very dry. Some men are mere funnels.

> According to this kind of taste
> Did he indulge his drouth;
> And being fond of port, he made
> A *port*-hole of his mouth.

Thirty days hath September,
April, June, and November,
February has twenty-eight alone;
All the rest have thirty-one,
Except in leap-year, then's the time,
February's days are twenty-nine.

By this rhyme John Ploughman has been able always to know the length of the month. He recommends it to Sam Straw, and Hob Carter, and other country gentlemen.

This gift is small, but love is all.

This line is a posy for a ring. Another is, "Love the giver"; and another, "Not the gift, but the giver."

Thistles and thorns prick sore,
But evil tongues prick more.

Many hearts have been pierced, and lives rendered wretched, by the cruel words of slanderers. He that will stab a man with his pen would stab him with his penknife, if he dared.

Thistles would never become roses, even should you plant them in Paradise.

Position will not change disposition. A thistle in a garden is only so much the bigger by the richness of the soil in which it is planted. Bad men in high places become all the worse.

Those are very poor whom nothing will satisfy.

For their poverty is in their soul rather than in their pocket, and there is no filling such a great gulf.

> When want is in ourselves begun,
> Then whither from it can we run?

Those beans won't boil in my pot.

So say the Telugus. They mean much the same as when we say, "That cock won't fight," or "That game won't pay," or "You can't come over me."

Those on whom you most rely,
Can do you greatest injury.

In this respect we need to be saved from our friends even more than from our enemies.

The man whom we fear and suspect for a cheat
Can hardly delude us with art and deceit ;
But he in whose faith we sincerely confide,
May come round with impunity on our blind side.

Those who are hot-headed should keep in the shade.

Yet they generally put themselves very forward, and threaten to set every business on a blaze with their heat.

Those who are in the same boat should row together.

If they don't, they will be likely to be upset, or the boat will turn round and round, and make no progress, People who do not row together are very apt to *row* together.

Those who are past caring are past curing.

Those who are soon hot are soon cold.

Those who are soon wound up soon run down.

Yet among speakers, those who prepare least usually keep on longest. In other matters, the man who would do everything on a sudden, has done his everything quite as suddenly.

Those who do ill, dread ill.

Very naturally they do so. Judging others by themselves, they expect to be lashed with their own whip. They expect that when their dogs come home they will eat their masters.

Those who do nothing will soon do worse.

The preparatory school for rascals is idleness ; and well they bring the youngsters on in that academy.

Those who do well themselves think well of others.

Familiarity with good work makes them expect to see it in other men's shops. They are so busy in keeping their own work up to the mark, that they have no time in which to pick holes in others, but take it for granted that others are doing their level best.

Those who eat most are not always the fattest.

So those who read most have not always the most knowledge; they may even overload their minds with ideas, as men may fill their stomachs too full of food; and this may lead to mental dulness, as, in the case of the body, it causes indigestion.

Those who expect what in reason they cannot expect, may expect.

They have liberty to range the world in their idle fancies, but their dreams will never be realized. This is a poor way of deceiving one's self.

Those who fry in words often freeze in deeds.

Those who itch to know will ache to tell.

Curiosity has talkativeness for its vis-à-vis.

Those who know nothing are generally very knowing people.

It is disagreeable to see the airs of superiority they give themselves. The blind man said, "Stand back: let me see!"

Those who learn much should teach much.

Else they will be mere hoarders of information, and before long their heaps of knowledge will ferment, and be good for nothing. So, too, we may say that those who teach much must learn much, or their teaching will soon be lean as a gridiron.

Those who love you for little may hate you for nothing.

We flatter ourselves by forgetting this evident fact, and hence we are surrounded by a set of flies whose affection for us is really *nil,* but their buzzing around us is incessant while the warm weather lasts. That love which blazes soon, like straw, is very apt to die out as the fire of straw does.

Those who love you for silver may leave you for gold.

When once the sordid motive enters in,
Such friendship is not worth a headless pin.

Those who paint you before will black you behind.

Those who flatter will slander.

Those who promise mountains perform molehills.

Those who shift often, will often be put to shifts.

> Changing so often they cannot get on. Moving costs them as much as their goods are worth. The time wasted in learning a little of a new trade would have made them perfect in their old business.

Those who take offence, usually make offence.

Those who talk always, think seldom.

Those who think to catch are often caught.

Those who thunder in preaching, should lighten in living.

> None of us must say, "Do as I say, but not as I do." The real force lies in the man's personal character; apart from this, his words are only words; and words are wind.

Those who will not hear reason have no reason.

Thou must get thee some pelf by fifty and three,
Or reckon thyself a drudge for to be.

> By fifty-three a man should have something, or he may conclude that he will finish his days in poverty.

Though a lie have seven-leagued boots, truth will over-
take it.

> Not always soon enough to undo all its mischief, but in time to expose it to the contempt of those whom it has duped.

Though an ass shakes his head, his ears don't come off.

> He does not lose his donkey characteristics by shaking his head after the manner of learned divines. "Ah!" said one, "how wisely he shakes his head!" "Yes," said another, "he may shake his head as long as he likes, but there's nothing in it."

Though I'm down in the dust,
Yet in God I will trust.

Though old and wise, yet still advise.

Though one grain fills not the sack, it helps.

Though the cat winks, she is not blind.

> We can see more than they think we see; and very impertinent mice should remember that even when the cat sleeps she has one eye open. Presume not upon the incapacity of your superiors.

Though the heavens be glorious, yet they are not all stars.

In the happiest life there are special days of bliss. Among the best of men some are peculiarly holy. Even in the Scriptures certain passages convey to us more gracious instructions than others.

Though the serpent has little eyes, he sees very well.

The small eyes of the envious are terribly piercing. Craft, also, is like a weasel for penetrating into secrets.

Though the speaker be a fool, let the listener be wise.

The rampant orator may say what he likes, but you must sift it, and be all the more judicious because of the wildness of his talk. Many open their mouths and shut their eyes, and swallow all that is put before them. No wonder their minds are poisoned.

Though the sun shines, don't give away your coat.

You will need it yet. Do not in a hurry part with your business, or other source of income, because you are very flush of cash.

Though thy hands be rough, let thy manners be gentle.

Courtesy will raise the poorest to the highest rank. The king returned the bow of the sweep, rightly observing, " Would you have a sweep more polite than a king? " " My boy," said a father to his son, " treat everybody with politeness, even those who are rude to you. For remember, that you show courtesy to others, not because they are gentlemen, but because you are one."

Though you dip in the sea, you take up only as much as your vessel will hold.

Great as the gospel is, we can but grasp a part of its fulness.

Though you've lost the ring, you have the finger.

The garnishing may be gone, but the essential member is left. We sorrow if we lose our estates, but this is little if our souls are saved. We add another consolation—

'Tis this—a line that does not need a verse;
Nought is so bad but that it might be worse.

Three helping each other are as good as six.

They double their results by division of labour and mutual support. Christian workers pulling together accomplish far more than if they were mere units.

Three removes are as bad as a fire.

> So much damage is done in the removal both to the business and the furniture. *Poor Richard* says :—
>
> > " I never saw an oft-removèd tree.
> > Nor yet an oft-removèd family,
> > That throve so well as those that settled be."

Through being too knowing the fox lost his tail.

Throw a stone into mud, and it will splash your face.

> Of course it will. Why not let the mud alone? If people must needs interfere they will get bespattered.

Throw no stones at thine own window.

Thy friend has a friend, and thy friend's friend has a friend: be quiet.

> Thy secret is safe with thyself, but not with thy friend and his friend, and his friend's friend's friend *ad infinitum*.

Thy hand is never the worse for doing thy own work.

> " In London no man thinks of blacking his own boots," said a haughty Briton once to the late Mr. Lincoln, whom he found polishing his calfskin gaiters. " Whose boots does he black?" quietly responded Uncle Abe.

Thyself accuse; thy friend excuse.

> A great preacher said, " Every excuse a man makes for himself is something taken from his manhood; and every excuse he makes for his fellow-men is something added to his manhood."

Thyself know, that thou mayest know others.

Time and patience turn mulberry leaves to satin.

> In time the mulberry leaf becomes a silk gown, and a silk gown becomes a lady.

Time and trouble try the truth.

> Whether a man is really good or not is discovered by his perseverance in a good way. It is easy to run well just for a spurt, but to keep up the pace for years is the difficulty.
>
> > Long journeys prove a horse's strength;
> > And life is tested by its length.

Time and words can never be recalled.

Therefore be careful of them. Be wise at once, and lose no time. Play not so late that thou hast to go to bed in the dark. Thou canst not recall a lost moment, much less a lost life. Time is but a part of eternity; live so in time as thou wilt wish to live in eternity. As to words, speak advisedly; for thou canst as soon call back a bullet which has been shot from a gun, as a word uttered from thy mouth.

Time covers and discovers everything.

We need not have everything decided in the next five minutes. If we can wait a little, the hidden truth will come to light.

Time enough is little enough.

He that lives longest has no time to spare. No one has more than the present hour.

> Time flieth away
> Without delay.

Time is a file which works without sound.

Shakespeare makes one say, "I wasted time, and now doth time waste me." It works away at our bones, and undermines our constitutions. The tell-tale of its doings is frequently seen upon the head. One facetiously said:

> "My hair and I are quits, d' ye see;
> I first cut it; it now cuts me."

Time is a ship that never anchors.

Time is long enough for him who has grace enough.

> Time is quite long enough, for all useful ends;
> He who labours for God, its limits extends.

Time is not tied to a post, like a horse to a manger.

Time is not wasted in sharpening the scythe.

Time moves slowly to him whose employment is to watch its flight.

Time is too long for the doing of nothing, and too short for the doing of something: but to sit and watch it dribble from an hour-glass is dreary work indeed. As good have no time as have nothing but time.

Time passes slowly when sorrow presses heavily.

> " How like the fleeting wind, away
> Whole years of joy depart !
> But, oh ! how slowly does the day
> Move to the mournful heart ! "

Time, tide, and train, for no man will remain.

> Pursue thy work without delay,
> For the short hours run fast away.

Time trieth truth, but truth outliveth time.

Time will bring the roses,
Though cold bites our noses.

> Have patience : the snows will soon be thawing, and the cuckoo
> will be back again. Sorrow endeth, joy cometh.

Tin plates don't mind dropping on the floor.

> A man prepared for rough usage puts up with a great many
> things which would break other people in pieces.

Tired men are quarrelsome.

> Tired men tread hard, and tried men feel hard.

'Tis a good fish if it were but caught.

> Many a scheme is first-class, but it is not practicable.

'Tis a good knife; it will cut butter when 'tis melted.

> What must a bad knife be ? Some people fix their standard of
> good knives and good men very low indeed.

'Tis a good penny that earns a groat.

'Tis a thriftless thing to be sad.

> Because it mends nothing, and does not bring in a penny piece.

'Tis a very good world to live in,
To spend, or to lend, or to give in ;
But to beg, or to borrow, or get back your own,
'Tis the very worst world that ever was known.

> This is the witness of many ; and we have heard it given with
> savage emphasis. It is a pity that it should be so sadly true.

'Tis better to buy love than law.

> But how is it to be done? Here, you sir, let me have the equivalent to this five-and-four-pence in downright love, and you may give the law to the dogs.

'Tis better to sit with a wise man in prison than with a fool in paradise.

'Tis education forms the youthful mind;
Just as the twig is bent, the tree's inclined.

> "Spare me a little longer," said the young vine to the gardener, as he laid hold of one of her tender branches, to guide it to the prop he had provided. "I'll grow any way you like next year, if you'll only let me have my own way now."
> But the gardener shook his head.
> "Why not?" murmured the vine; "it's hard I may not have my freedom a little longer; it will be time enough, when I am older, to be guided and trained." "Ah!" said the gardener. "that only shows how little you know about it. Each year your branches will grow harder and less flexible, and where one nail will hold you now, it would take a dozen in a twelvemonth's time."

'Tis good buying wit with another man's money.

> How is it good to be mean? Some learn nothing from anybody.

'Tis good to be merry and wise;
'Tis good to be honest and true;
'Tis good to be off with the old love
Before you be on with the new.

> None of our readers will, we hope, need this warning. Very, very awkward it is to hang one's hat on two pegs at once, or to have two bonnets on your peg. Breaches of promise are bad, but a pair of breeches of this sort will prove very ugly wear.

'Tis good going on foot when you lead a horse by its bridle.

> You don't mind walking when you know that you can ride when you like. We are willing to do without a luxury if we feel that we could have it if we very much wanted it.

'Tis grievous to be poor in purse,
But poor in love is greatly worse.

'Tis hard to sail over the sea in an egg-shell.

> To speculate without capital is very unwise. To attempt to reach heaven by our own works and unaided strength is a notable instance of full-blown folly.

'Tis harder to unlearn than to learn.

How difficult to forget evil! How well-nigh impossible to be rid of an ingrained habit! To pick up Parisian French is rendered hard by the French of the school of Stratford-at-Bow, which was drilled into us in youth. Better learn nothing than learn wrongly. Blank paper suits an author; but to write over old manuscript is very unpleasant and unsatisfactory.

'Tis merry in hall when beards wag all.

When they are all eating and drinking, and otherwise agitating the lower jaw, and so causing the beard to move, of course, the whole of the jesters are in a merry cue. It was not quite so merry
When black-jacks all drained,
Each other they brained.

'Tis not all saved that's put in the purse.

It may be the occasion of loss, especially to men in trade; for as the Chinese say, "If a little cash does not go out, much cash will not come in." I knew a farmer who did not cultivate his fields because he thus saved the wages. His farm soon saw him saved all further trouble in husbandry.

'Tis not every question that deserves an answer.

We heard one say to an inquisitive person, "I move the previous question." The interrogator said, "And what is that?" "Well," replied the other, "the previous question is, 'Ought you to ask such a question?'"

'Tis not the food, but the content,
That makes the table's merriment.

'Tis said, that from the twelfth of May
To twelfth of July all is day.

The light never quite ceases during that time.

'Tis skill, not strength, that governs the ship.

Rule skilfully rather than wilfully. Tact is master.

Tittle-tattle, give the goose more hay.

That is, say and do any silly thing, those of you who are given to frivolous talk. We do not endorse this sarcasm: still, one is provoked to make some such remark when small talk annoys.
Pretty little damsels, how they chat!
Chit-chat, tittle-tattle-tat:
All about their sweethearts, and all that,
And chit-chat, tittle-tattle-tat.

To Adam, Paradise was home; to us, home is Paradise.

And this, we boldly assert, is usually the case with Christian people, notwithstanding the trials of our lives, and the faults of our characters. We do not believe the old satire—

"Ah, madam! cease to be mistaken,
Few married fowl peck Dunmow Bacon!"

To advise a fool is to throw water on a goose.

Still we would say as much as this to him : You have no right to make a fool of yourself so long as you have a mother or a sister to be put to the blush about you.

To angle all day, and catch a gudgeon at night.

Some don't even catch that. This gives point to the definition of an angler—"a long pole, with a worm at one end and a fool at the other." Such a fool have I been, and would like to be again.

To all give ear, but do not all believe,
For some there be who would a saint deceive.

To all good wives we wish long lives.

At home each happy husband sings :

" God bless my gracious Queen,
Long live my noble Queen ! "

To and fro, come and go;
All our earthly life is so.

"Here we have no continuing city, but we seek one to come."— Heb. xiii. 14.

To be angry with an angry man makes two angry men.

To be good among the bad is commendable;
To be good among the good is pleasurable;
To be bad among the bad is horrible;
To be bad among the good is abominable.

Of course a man's character must be measured in connection with his difficulties or advantages. There is more virtue in some men's being a little good than in others being greatly so.

To be hale in October drink no October ale.

To be idle is to be evil: diligence nourishes delight.

To be proud of your learning is to show your ignorance.

To be secure never be security.

To be washed white and to be white-washed are very different things.

> One longs for the first, but loathes the second. When washed white, we are alive unto God; but the white-washed are sepulchres full of corruption.

To believe a business impossible, is the way to make it so.

> If a thing is right, the word "impossible" must not be in our dictionary. Believe that it can be done, and it will be done.

To boiling pot flies come not.

> When a man is busy and earnest, he takes no notice of trifles. This is much the same in meaning as "Running dogs feel no fleas."

To bowl down hill is easy.

> I heard of one who threw a stone half-a-mile, but the reason was that he stood on a hill where there was a continuous descent, and nothing to stop a falling object. One might easily throw a stone five miles if he cast it over a boat's side into the depths of the ocean.

To brew in a bottle, and bake in a bag.

> Very little brewers and bakers these! They are emblems of little minds, which do everything on the very smallest scale, and are quite content to have it so. One convert in a century delights them.

To build high, dig deep.

> Nothing is like a good foundation. In religion, deep repentances contribute largely to stability and elevation of character.

To catch a Tartar.

> This is a bad thing in matrimony. You look for a Celestial to make your tea, and find a Tartar to make you a pickle.
>
> > Better be a lonely martyr
> > Than be married to a Tartar.

To change and to mend are two different things.

> We read of King Saul, that he had "another heart"; but what he needed was a new one. Some men when converted are like fair weather, when it changes for the worse.

To come out of "the shires."

This is how eastern counties people commonly talk of those poor folk who come from other parts of the country. They emerge from those barbarous and uncivilized regions called "the shires." Essex, Suffolk, Kent, and so forth, are real counties, of considerable account; but East Anglia seems to think it sheer folly to expect much from those divisions of the country which are merely "shires."

To covet more,
Makes rich men poor.

It is easy to be really rich! Do you think me trifling with you? Be contented, and you have it.

To cry with one eye, and laugh with the other.

This is a queer condition; yet have we been in it. The comic side of the terrible, and the awful side of the mirthful, will sometimes turn up, and the mind cannot tell to which to yield.

To-day man lives in pleasure, wealth, and pride,
To-morrow poor—or life itself denied.
To-day married, to-morrow harried.

Of course you shall have trouble in the flesh. Does not Scripture say so? At the same time, one does not want trouble in a wife: no one wishes for nettles in his bed.

To *do* good, one must first *be* good.

"A corrupt tree cannot bring forth good fruit."—Matt. vii. 19.

To every bird its nest seems fair,
My home's a palace rich and rare.

To fall in love and to be wise are very different things.

An old writer, under the heading LOVER, says, "See lunatic. A lover is a man who in his anxiety to possess another, has lost possession of himself." This is rather too bad.

To follow crowds but death I deem:
The live fish swims against the stream.

Drifting with the multitude down the broad way is commonly chosen; but to go singly along the narrow road, and push aside all obstacles, is the gracious choice of the gracious man.

To fool the world tell the truth.

So accustomed are men to chicanery, that plain honesty appears to them to be the subtlest form of deceit. *Bismarck* has the credit of this proverb; and it shows his shrewdness.

To forget a wrong is the best revenge.

Lord, teach us to forgive : to learn of thee !
How very little to forgive have we !

To fry in his own grease.

By no means an elegant expression. Did not the Prussian speak of "Paris stewing in its own juice"? No bad man can have a worse doom than to be left altogether to himself.

To get by a thing, as Dickson did by his distress.

We must surely know this Dickson. He made quite a fortune out of the decease of a venerable horse. By petitions and begging letters, he gathered in enough to horse the Brighton coach. We must set the Charity Organization Society upon Dickson.

To give is honor,
To ask is dolor.

He who gives has abundantly more cause for gratitude than he who receives. He who refuses to give ought to come to begging.

To give one a mouthful of moonshine.

A very common thing. Attend a lecture upon a scientific fad, listen to a political schemer, or hear a "modern thought" divine, and you will have a clear idea of a mouthful of moonshine.

To give to the poor increases our store.

Others say, "To give to the poor will bless your store." Both proverbs have truth in them. None of us can afford to cease giving. The rich should give that they may remain rich, and the poor that they may not be poorer. Want of generosity is unthrifty.

To go rabbit hunting with a dead ferret.

Working with useless tools or lazy servants, is a dreadful business. To have a friend to help you who is quite useless, is like working with a broken arm. Better alone than with an inefficient partner.

To go to law is to go to sea.

When will you come to shore again? You will soon be sick of it. When you see the sharks around your estate, you will wish yourself on land again.

To grin like a Cheshire cat chewing gravel.

I have never seen the domestic pet in this condition. I know how one stone in my teeth serves me, and a cat chewing gravel may very well grin if her sensations are like mine.

To harbour enmities is to plant miseries.

This is from the Chinese. Put it in your tea, and drink it.

To have a wolf by the ears.

"When a man hath a doubtful business in hand, which it is equally hazardous to pursue or to give over, as it is to hold or let go a wolf which one hath by the ears."—*Ray.*

To have an M under your girdle.

To treat a person with proper respect, to call him *Master* so-and-so. People forget to do this. There is a Creole proverb, "Behind dog's back, it is 'Dog'; but before dog, it is 'Master dog.'"

To have slanders forgotten by others, forget them yourself.

If you remember them, and continue to advertise them by answering them, they will live for years. Let them die a natural death.

To hear as hogs do in harvest.

That is, not at all. They are in fine feeding order, and they do not wish to hear the orders to quit the field. They have on their harvest ears, and can hear nothing.

To keep the sea back with a pitchfork.

A very absurd enterprise: yet not more so than attempting to stop the will of the people by the use of force.

To kill little birds is to multiply caterpillars.

No doubt; and yet farmers, both here and in America, are of opinion that there may be too many sparrows. One would think that even these must be better than worms and grubs.

To kill two birds with one stone.

Occasionally a person is able to accomplish two objects by one act. One would rather like the proverb to run, "To feed two birds with one hand," or, "To move two stones in one barrow."

To know little is bad; not to wish to know more is worse.

> *Bishop Ames* was once presiding over a certain conference in the West, when a member began a tirade against universities, education, &c., and thanked God that he had never been corrupted by contact with a college. After proceeding thus for a few minutes, the Bishop interrupted him with the question, "Do I understand that the brother thanks God for his ignorance?" "Well, yes," was the answer, "you can put it that way if you want to." "Well, all I have to say," said the bishop, in his sweet musical tones, " is, that the brother has a great deal to thank God for."

To know right, and to do right, are different things.

> As different as a *menu* and a dinner.

To live in peace, hear, see, and·say nothing.

> Another form of it is: "To live in peace, we had need be blind, and deaf, and dumb." We do not go all this length; but, certainly, one can be too quick of observation, and fall into bickerings thereby. To prevent shying, wear blinkers.

To look for a needle in a bottle of hay.

> Rather hopeless work. "Bottle" is the old word for bundle. A needle in a haystack would be hard to find.

To mad words turn a deaf ear.

To marry a woman for her looks, is like eating a bird for its song.

> Since you do not marry her to look at, but, to have as a companion and help-meet, observe the formation of her mind as well as the features of her face.

"To-morrow"—the day on which idle men work.

> But it never comes. The work they are going to do is wonderful. These gentlemen take three weeks' holiday every fortnight, and work hard in the time which remains.

To nought it goes that comes from nought.

> "*Sir James Macintosh* had no fewer than sixteen proofs of one of his works before he would allow it to go to press. The biographer of John Foster shows us through what agonies the perfection of style in his essays was attained. They say that Tennyson has spent days in the composition of a single line of poetry. A great musician was asked why he insisted on devoting so much time to the preparation of an apparently simple piece. He replied that, *without such care, nothing whatever could be expected to live.*"

18

To publish another's obligations, is to discharge him from them.

This is not the rule with good and grateful men; but it is the rule of the world, and there is a rough justice in it. When a man twits me with what he has done for me, he withdraws his claim upon my gratitude.

> To John I owed great obligation :
> But John unhappily thought fit
> To publish it to all the nation :
> Sure, John and I are more than quit.

To read without reflecting, is to eat without digesting.

It is one good point in *this* book that it would be hard to read page after page of it mechanically. But, perhaps, someone has already done so, as another read the Dictionary, and observed that it was a very nice book, but he could not quite see the connection.

To revenge a wrong, is to do a wrong.

> How hardly man the lesson learns,
> To smile, and bless the hand that spurns :
> To see the blow, to feel the pain,
> And render only love again !

To rob Saint Peter to pay Saint Paul
  Is shameful work for man to do ;
But surely it is worst of all
  To rob both Paul and Peter too.

Yet we know fellows who neither pay Peter nor Paul nor anybody else, but rob all saints and all sinners alike. As they have opportunity, they do harm unto all men.

To scare a bird is not the way to catch it.

Fierce, threatening preaching will not win men for Jesus.

To search for truth is commendable, but to enjoy truth is more comfortable.

One said that he loved the search for truth better than the finding of it : there is no accounting for tastes. We suspect that he was not over-fond of truth, but loved it best at a distance.

To see the sun rise is good for the eyes.

It is to be feared that many Londoners have never tried this golden ointment. Even lie-a-beds commend early rising.

To set up shop on Goodwin Sands.

> Does it mean that the shop-keeper is to win good as the sands of time run out? Or, does it mean that a certain person has so little capital that he builds his trade on the sand, and will be shipwrecked by being shop-wrecked?

To speak to purpose, one must speak with a purpose.

> To spin a yarn to fill up space is wretched work. He that speaks against time will find time speaking against him.

To spend and spend
Brings cash to end.

> Stop spending, then, if your purse is getting low. But what is the use of money if it is not spent? It is the circulating medium, and was meant to flow out as well as in.

To stop the tongue of slander, stop your own.

> We greatly question whether slander will ever cease till the last gossip is in her grave, or say, in *his* grave; but if anything will quiet it, it will be the silence of the person assailed.
>
> > If on the spark you do not blow,
> > Out, of itself, it soon will go.

To stroke with one hand, and stab with the other.

> Often done by cruel dissemblers. They praise the gospel and undermine it. They call you "fine gentleman," and cut your throat. This is what is done by strong drink; in fact, some drinkers, when they have wished the bottle passed, have cried, "Stab yourself, and pass the dagger!" Significant, is it not?

To subdue the passions is hard: to satisfy them impossible.

To swallow an ox, and be choked with the tail.

> This is done when men commit a great crime, and stickle over details; or when they embrace a huge error and boggle at a word.

To sweeten your morsel, share it.

> Selfishness turns sugar into sickly lusciousness; but generosi'y changes the quartern of bread into a sugar-loaf.

To take the wrong sow by the ear.

> Don't do that: better let the right sow escape you. Charges must be accurately laid, or not at all.

To talk without thinking, is to shoot without aiming.

To the wasp say, " Neither your sting nor your honey."

> Half measures will not answer with malicious minds.

To think is well, but to know is better.

To wash an ass's head is waste of soap.

> And it wins a chance of feeling the ass's heels.   To correct some men is labour in vain, for it only provokes them.

To win a cat you lose a cow:
It may be wise ; I see not how.

> To risk a great deal to gain little is the height of folly.

Tom Timid was drowned in a teacup.

> He went in as a spoon, made a little stir, and was never heard of more : he is generally supposed to have sunk in matrimony.

Tongue breaketh bone,
And herself hath none,
   Quoth Hendyng.

> Some make no bones about telling lies: in many cases there is nothing solid about what is said, but all is oily, slippery, worthless. I have heard that a well-dressed tongue needs five hours' boiling: I would like to see what half-an-hour would do with some tongues I wot of.   They make my blood boil often.

Tongues are the best and worst meat in the world.

> So *Æsop* taught.   We add a selection of proverbs referring to the tongue.
>
>> " The boneless tongue, so small and weak,
>> Can crush and kill," declared the Greek.
>> " The tongue destroys a greater horde,"
>> The Turk asserts, " than does the swoid."
>> The Persian proverb wisely saith,
>> " A lengthy tongue—an early death " ;
>> Or sometimes takes this form instead,
>> " Don't let your tongue cut off your head."
>> " The tongue can speak a word whose speed,"
>> Say the Chinese, " outstrips the steed."
>> While Arab sages this impart,
>> " The tongue's great storehouse is the heart."
>> From Hebrew wit the maxim sprung,
>> " Though feet should slip, ne'er let the tongue."
>> The sacred writer crowns the whole ·
>> " Who keeps the tongue doth keep his soul."

Tongues run all the faster when they carry little.

Like every other machine, what the tongue gains in speed it loses in power. Great talkers not only *do* the least, but they even *say* the least, if their words are weighed instead of being counted. Talkative tongues are like the plague of frogs in Egypt: those creatures did not bite, but they wearied by their endless croaking.

Tongues seldom ache through lying still.

Paul Chatfield tells us of a chatterbox who said, "I talk a good deal, but then I talk well." "Half of that is true," said one who knew him. When a man has learned to keep silence he loves it.

Too far East is West.

Your nice man is nasty, your severely righteous man is unfair, your ultra-democrat is a tyrant, and your liberal thinker is a bigot.

Too late to spare when all is spent.

Too little for one, may be too much for another.

Too many cooks spoil the broth.

Or *spill* the broth; or forget to make any.

Too many "night-caps" make a man's head ache.

The night-caps we refer to are of a spirituous kind.

Too much breaks the bag.

Too much courtesy, too much craft.

Too much may be said on the best of subjects.

Let "Finally" stand within measurable distance.

Too much of a good thing is not a good thing.

Too much of one thing, too little of another.

Sam Slick wisely said: "Them that have more than their share of one thing, commonly have less of another. Where there is great strength, there ain't apt to be much gumption. A handsome man, in a general way, ain't much of a man. A beautiful bird seldom sings. Them that has genius have no common-sense."

Too much oil puts out the lamp; too much wood puts out the fire.

Too much book-learning puts out the man himself. He has no room for his mind to turn in, for he has blocked up the space with books. Too much fluency may be the death of eloquence.

Too much palaver, too little honesty.

> You know the gentleman—all smiles and blarney: and as a dentist extracts your teeth under gas, so has he extracted your sovereigns by his empty pufferies.

Too much pudding will choke a dog.

> So, one may be lectured till he cannot endure it. Is it not so, Mr. Caudle? And one may be dunned with the same subject till you wish yourself deaf. The proverb is rather a currish one, and may have been started by some young dog who had been over-done with stick-jaw pudding at Dotheboys Hall.

Too much sail suits not a small boat.

Too much sugar may spoil the pie.

> A man who is all molasses, and "dearie, dearie," is a little too too, and we get sick of him.

Too much taking counsel ends in doing nothing.

> The Committee sat, and sat, and sat, till every sensible plan was crushed as flat as a pancake.

Too soon is easy mended;
Too late can't be defended.

> If a person gets to an appointment before his time, a little waiting puts him right; but if he comes after the hour, he is unjust to the person whom he promised to meet.

Too too will in two.

> Don't test the fabric with too hard a pull, and don't select too tender a material. Don't test friendship too severely, or it may fail. Don't try temper too often, or it may give way.

Touch a galled horse and he'll kick.

> See how certain people lash out when you touch on a point about which their conscience is tender. Touch me not on my sore heel. Do not remind me of an unpleasant fact.

Touchwood! Touchwood! Mind the fire.

> Touchwood soon takes fire. Where there is peculiar susceptibility to a sin, there should be a careful avoidance of all that leads to it. Don't put your cat in the pigeon-house, nor your dog among young rabbits; and don't put yourself into the kind of company which has aforetime led you astray.

Tough meat needs a sharp knife.

When fellows will not attend, sharp words become needful.

Towers are measured by their shadows, and great men by those that are envious of them.

Tradesmen may be like bad eggs, which look very well till they break.

But when the breaking comes, the tradesman is not in good odour, and his composition is not much admired.

Train up a child in the way you should have gone yourself.

Tread on the ball, live to spend all ;
Tread on the heel, spend a great deal ;
Tread where you may, money won't stay.

The wearing out of shoes by wearing them most in this place or in that, causes a portion of those expenses by which we are kept up, and our savings are kept down. In olden times men changed their shoes from day to day from foot to foot, to secure an equal wearing of them in every part. An old gentleman of our acquaintance, having a gouty foot, was ordered by his doctor to cut the shoe, and he did so. The next morning he was found with the uncut shoe on the sore foot, and nothing could induce him to forego the long habit of changing the shoes. So both had to be cut. Dear old Tory !

Trials are the ballast of life.

The burdened vessel may sail slowly, but she sails safely. Without the ballast of trial men are apt to blow over. Ballast yourself with sympathy, if you have no trials of your own.

Trickery is a dog which comes back to its master.

Dishonesty comes home to men. The knave outwits himself before long, and gets tarred with his own brush.

Trifles are only trifles to triflers.

Think nought a trifle, though it small appears ;
Sands make the mountains ; moments make the years
And trifles, life. Your care to trifles give,
Else you may die ere you have learned to live.

Trifling with truth is like fooling with fire.

No one can guess what mischief may come of it.

Trinkets and trash run away with the cash.

Boys and girls had better leave flash jewellery to fops and flirts.

Trouble is soon enough when it comes.

Do not go forth to meet it by timorous apprehensions of its coming. Believe that with the trial sufficient grace will come.

Trouble often shows the man.

> Until the steel the flint shall smite,
> It will afford nor heat nor light.

True blue will keep its hue.

True blue will never stain.

The colours of pretence soon fade in shower and sun, but faithful honesty defies all circumstances and oppositions.

> What is dyed in the grain
> Will not run in the rain.

True fame is neither sold nor bought;
She sometimes follows where she is not sought.

A man's reputation is like his shadow: if it follows him, he will never leave it behind him; if it goes before him, he will never go beyond it. It is best to take no note of it, but to be what you would be thought to be.

True friendship's laws are in this line expressed,—
Welcome the coming, speed the parting guest.

True *hospitality* is meant. Be as particular to see your guest off in good time, as you were to receive him; and do not importune him to stay when he has once said that he must needs go.

True love never grows old.

Trust in God, and keep your powder dry.

This Cromwellian sentence has grand common-sense in it.

Trust is dead: bad pay killed him.

This is a sentence which I have seen written up in shops where the poor are wont to deal. *Willis*, in his "Current Notes," says that he saw in a public house, at Chichester, the following verse:—

> "Since man to man is so unjust,
> No man can tell what man to trust.
> I've trusted many to my sorrow:
> Pay to-day, take trust to-morrow."

Trust no fox with the care of your young ducks.

Send not your boys to a school taught by Father Roman, nor your girls to a parson who has a confessional. Trust not your young lambs to the care of the wolf, unless you really want them destroyed. Leave no gambler to play with your boys.

Trust not a boy with a sword.

Sooner or later he will hurt himself, or somebody else. High offices and mysterious discussions are dangerous in the hands of inexperience and incompetence.

Trust not a horse's heel, a dog's tooth, or a gossip's tongue.

Trust the last least. Mad dogs and kicking horses are better than slanderous tongues.

Trust not a smooth sea, nor a smiling world.

Few men in the world can be relied upon. "Put not your trust in princes." The sea has its sharks, but the land has its deceivers.

To safe-guard man from wrongs, there nothing must
Be truer to him than a wise *distrust;*
And to thyself be best this sentence known,
Hear all men speak, but credit few or none.

Yet, at the same time, suspicion is but a cowardly virtue.

Trust not the man who promises with an oath.

He swears too glibly for his oath to be worth anything.

Trust not the ship to one rope.

Divide the risk, and have more than one earthly confidence.
Good riding at two anchors men have told;
For if one break, the other still may hold.

Trust self, and lose all; trust God, and win all.

Man who on himself
Dareth to rely,
Is like a frail reed
When the wind passes by.

Trust to Providence, but lock the stable door.

This reminds us of Mahomet's observation, when one of his followers said that he would turn his camel loose, and trust it to Providence. "Nay," said Mahomet, "tie it up as best you can, and then trust it to Providence."

Trust when you can; but know your man.

Men nowadays want a deal of knowing: when you think you are at the bottom of them, a trap-door opens.

> When man is practised in disguise,
> He cheats the most discerning eyes.

Trust your eyes rather than your ears.

See for yourself: your ears have to trust to other men's eyes, and tongues also: you will do well to put your own optics to work.

Truth always comes by the lame messenger.

After liars have told their tale, in comes honest truth to their confusion. Yet truth's messenger in another sense is by no means lame. His feet are beautiful upon the mountains.

Truth and time against the world.

Philip of Spain used to say, "I and time against any two." The man who defends God's truth can afford to wait; for both time and eternity are on his side. God and his truth have great leisure.

Truth cannot be bound nor drowned.

> Truth may go down
> But will not drown.
> This challenge, then, be boldly hurled,
> "The truth alone against the world."

Truth finds few that love her *gratis*.

People will look about and calculate the consequences. Faithful men not only seek no gain by truth, but are willing to lose all for her sake. Yet are these the greatest gainers.

Truth gives a short answer; lies go round about.

Truth needs not many words, but a false tale needs a large preamble. Some in their roundaboutness make us feel that there is some bamboozlement intended. Yet to certain minds the curvilinear mode appears to be as natural as the straight line is to others. There is a tale in Kashmir about a man who was once asked where his nose was. He did not reply by at once putting his finger on that organ, and saying, "Here it is"; but he pulled up the right sleeve of his long cloak, and passing his right hand around his head, eventually and with great difficulty, touched his nose with it. We know more than one friend who must have been a pupil of this Kashmiri gentleman.

Truth never grows old.

> In the sense of decaying, or being out of date.

Truth in faith works holiness in life.

> Errors in the life breed errors in the brain,
> And these, reciprocally, those again.

Truth is beautiful, but men scratch her face.

> Truth seldom goes without a scratched face, for men love her not.

Truth is the best buckler.

> Carry it with you, on you, within you.

Truth is truth till time shall end.

Truth lies at the bottom of a well.

> *Douglas Jerrold* said, "I've heard people say, 'truth lives in a well,'; if so, I'd advise you to take an early dip in the bucket." A very good verse has been written on this saying of the Latins.
>
> > "Truth's in a well!" To get it out
> > You'll find there's this impediment,
> > That if you, blundering, probe about,
> > You'll stir up *doubt*—the sediment.

Truth, like oil, comes to the surface.

Truth may be blamed, but can never be shamed.

> Yet some would blame it because it blames them. They are like the lady in the American story. Eli Perkins tells of an old maid with her face covered with wrinkles, turning from the mirror, saying, "Mirrors nowadays are very faulty. They don't make such mirrors as they used to when I was young."

Truth may come out of the devil's mouth.

> And then it is truth still; but he puts it in such a fashion that he means it to support a lie, or look like a lie.

Truth needs nothing to help it out.

Truth oft oppressèd we may see ;
But quite suppress'd it cannot be.

> A modern form of putting the same cheering sent in *W. C. Bryant's* verse :
>
> > "Truth, crushed to earth, shall rise
> > The eternal years of God are her
> > But error, wounded, writhes with ,
> > And dies among his worshippers.

Truth seeks no corners, and fears no scorners.

Truth should not swim in the brain, but sink into the heart.

Truth will in the end prevail,
Though it creepeth like a snail.

> Its slow progress in a false world is not wonderful; but God is with it, and its victory is sure. It is not a snail, but a mighty angel of God. *Magna est veritas, et prævalebit.*

Truth will sometimes break out in unlooked-for places.

> As it did in the monastery with Luther.

Truths, like roses, have thorns about them.

> Hence one says, "Follow not truth too near at the heels, lest it dash out your teeth"; but this is evil advice. When the thorns of truth prick a man, they act as salutary lancets, and he may be thankful for the wholesome pain they bring.

Try and *Trust* will move mountains.

> Say rather—God will move the mountains if we truly trust him.

Try before you trust.

> "Take no man to your heart at sight,
>   But prove his friendship strong;
> The man who often says you're right,
>   May oftenest think you wrong."

Try to suffer with such patience, that those around you do not suffer.

> As they will certainly do if you grow peevish and exacting. This precept is not so easy as it looks. It is well to be ill well.

Turn away from sin before sin turns you away from God.

> Say to its pleasure, "Gentle Eve, I will have none of your apple." To hesitate is to yield; to yield is to go into bondage.

Turn over your store, and give to the poor.

Turn stumbling-blocks into stepping-stones.

Turn the cake in the pan.

> Cook one side as well as the other. Attend to the whole of your business. Change the topic of conversation. Don't keep always in one strain. As for yourself, be not as Ephraim, whom the prophet calls "a cake not turned." Be gracious in all ways.

Turn your tongue seven times before speaking.

Two blacks don't make a white.

> If the other party is wrong it will not make your wrong right. Mind this, and don't defend yourself by defaming others.

Two cannot quarrel if one won't.

> A coloured man related to a friend his plan for avoiding family jars in the following words: "I telled Betty, when we was wed, dat, if she saw me getting angry like, she must go to the bucket, and fill her mouth wid water; and if I saw her getting out of herself, I'd go to the bucket, and fill my mouth wid water. So we never had any quarrels, for one can't quarrel alone, and anoder can't quarrel wid you when his mouth's full of water."

Two cats and one mouse,
Two women in one house,
Two dogs to one bone:
These I let alone.

> We don't believe in this old saw, except in a special sense: and in that sense no good man would wish to have two women in one house. "No man can serve two masters."

Two cocks on one dunghill will not long agree.

> So that males as well as females fall out. Two big crowing men are best apart, for they are sure to fight. It would be well if they ceased from being so high and mighty, and then they might agree.

Two eyes are not sufficient to choose a wife by.

> Not even if the ears and heart co-operate. We have need to consult the sacred oracle, and use our coolest judgment.

Two eyes, two ears, only one mouth.

> See and hear twice, and speak but once.

Two fools in one family are two too many.

Two glasses of grog are two too many.

> If you can stand them, you can stand better without them.

Two halves do not always make one.

> A half and a better half ought to make one, but they do not. The fight is at times which one it shall be, and then things go to pieces.

Two heads are better than one, even if they are only sheep's heads.

Two feeble minds may keep right by mutual advice where one strong-minded person hurries into folly. Speaking of sheep's head reminds us of Douglas Jerrold. At a supper of sheep's heads an enthusiast cried out, "Sheep's heads for ever," and the wag replied, "What egotism!"

Two of a trade seldom agree.

Competition is too apt to breed contention; but it must not be so among Christians. Paul dwelt with brethren of his trade, "for they were tent-makers."

Two strings to your bow, and you'll miss the target.

Have two strings to your belle, or two belles to your string, and you will not very readily get so far as the ring; though you are far more likely to get wrung by some indignant father or brother.

Two to one in all things against an angry man.

We do not insert this as a bet, but as a fact. He is too hot to be of cool judgment: his temper will lose him friends.

Sayings of a more Spiritual Sort.

Tears of repentance are good for the eyes.

But more certainly good for the heart.
> The tears of saints more sweet by far
> Than all the songs of sinners are.

**Tell thy God thy wish and care :
Turn thy sorrow into prayer.**

So shall every want and wish become a way of approach to God, or at least a motive for communing with him. The supply of those wants will also be a way in which thy Lord will come to thee.

Temptations, like foul weather, come before we send for them.

Therefore, we should pray, "Lead us not into temptation"; and as that petition will not be universally and absolutely answered, we must add, "But deliver us from evil."

That garment which was worn to shreds on Adam's back will never make a complete covering for mine.

Human righteousness soon dropped to shreds on the back of one whose nature was unfallen; therefore it will never suit us who are already sinful, and dwell in a sinful world.

That is best for us which is best for our souls.

For our souls are the best part of us.

The ark of God always pays for its entertainment, wheresoever it dwells.

Every Obed-edom will bear witness to this. Lot let angels in, and the angels led him out.

The armour-bearer of sin is self-confidence.

The best way to live in the world is to live

Old Romish pictures represent saints in prayer as lifted up from the earth. This is true spiritually. Prayer and fasting produce an elevated condition of heart; and if this can be maintained, we escape the injurious tendency of our surroundings, and in a measure this corruptible puts on incorruption.

The cross of Christ is the key of Paradise.

The curse of the serpent rests on the seed of the serpent.

> *Leighton* writes : "Earthly men are daily partakers of the serpent's curse ; they go on their belly, and eat the dust."

The death of carnal hope is the beginning of spiritual life.

The death of Jesus is the ground of the believer's life.

> Let him stand upon it, and upon it only.   If he shifts his ground, and relies upon his own experience, it goes ill with him.

The dew falls in due season.

> Let us pray the Lord to send it on all holy ministries.
>
> > " If not full showers of rain, yet, Lord,
> > A little pearly dew afford ;
> > A little, if it come from thee,
> > Will be of great avail to me."—*Christopher Harvey.*

The earth will hide
Bright eyes and pride.

The excellent of the earth can see no excellence in the earth.

> " My soul, what's lighter than a feather ? Wind.
> Than wind ? The fire. And what, than fire ? The mind.
> What's lighter than the mind ? A thought. Than thought ?
> This bubble world. What, than this bubble ? Nought."
> > *Quarles.*

The fear of man weakens ; the fear of God strengthens.

The gem cannot be polished without friction, nor man perfected without trial.

The gospel breaks hard hearts and heals broken hearts.

The gospel is sweet music in a sinner's ears.

> Well it may be, for it brings life for death, pardon for guilt, peace for terror, and heaven instead of hell.

The great God sees even a little good.

> His mercy makes him interpret hopefully every sign of grace. He spies out the first spark of desire, and fans it.   If there be only a sigh of sorrow for sin it will be heard in heaven.

The heart must be broken *for* sin and *from* sin.

> There is a beautiful Persian aphorism to this effect : " Nothing that is broken bears any value, except the heart, which becomes more valuable the more it is broken."

The hope of the hopeless is Jesus our hope.

> Blessed be his name! We do well to put into his mouth those words :—
>
> " The foolish, the feeble, the weak, are my care ;
> The hopeless, the helpless, I hear their sad prayer."

The key of prayer can open any lock, and deliver any Peter from prison.

> Four fours of soldiers cannot keep the man whom God sets free in answer to prayer; nor could four armies succeed any better. The iron gate opens of its own accord when prayer opens the hand of God. It is harder for us to pray than for God to answer.

The least sin should make us humble, but the greatest sin should not make us despair.

The less of man, the more of God.

> " None of self " is sweetly joined with " all of thee." God uses weak instruments, that we may the better see his power.

The life of sin is the death of the sinner.

> " In South America there is a creeper which climbs, and enfolds, and hangs in pendant festoons about certain trees, poisoning as it goes ; it drinks the sap, sheds its destructive seeds, and multiplies its power of injury and death. It is called ' The Murderer,' for its well-known and fatal qualities. We cannot fail to think of the destroying power of sinful habits, how they commence in little things, yet creep and grow, spreading and hanging about character and life, drinking the strength, and poisoning vital energies."
> *M'Michael.*

The Lord will never help us to catch fish with dirty nets.

> He will have his work done in a cleanly style. " Be ye clean, that bear the vessels of the Lord."—Isa. lii. 11.

The Lord's-day is the lord of days.

> Regard it as a right royal day. The head of seven is crowned from heaven. The day of the Lord is the lord of days.

19

The loss of gold is great, the loss of health is more;
But the loss of Christ is such a loss as no man can restore.

A good verse to be printed on a card, and put into the hand of the careless.

The minister's life is the life of his ministry.

People will not mind his words unless there is a holy life at the back of them. We must burn in our acts, and shine in our sermons.

The ministry is the best calling, but the worst trade.

To preach for a living is wretched hypocrisy; to preach for the living God is noble service. A prostituted pulpit is an awful sight.

The more you draw from God's Word, the more you will find in it.

"I see the oil of thy word will never leave increasing whilst any bring an empty barrel. The Old Testament will still be a New Testament to him who comes with a fresh desire of information."
T. Fuller.

The only way to keep our crowns is to cast them down at Christ's feet.

The prayer of the heart is the heart of the prayer.

The language of the heart cannot be imitated. Talma, the famous actor, hearing of the death of his father, uttered a loud cry of distress. Soon after he murmured, "Oh, that I could cry like that on the stage!" Too many prayers are but stage performances; the voice of the heart is not heard in them.

The promises, like a well-drawn picture, look on all that look on them with an eye of faith.

The reading of the Scriptures is the terror of devils.

"It is written" is a weapon which the prince of devils dreads; but a man cannot readily quote or use what he never reads. "What's wrang wi' ye noo? I thocht ye were a' richt," said a ragged boy, himself rejoicing in the Saviour, to another, who a few nights before professed to be able to trust Jesus, but who had again begun to doubt. "What's wrang wi' ye noo?" "Man, I'm no richt yet," replied the other, "for Satan's aye tempting me." "And what dae ye then?" asked his friend. "I try," said he, "to sing a hymn." "And does that no' send him away?" "No; I am as bad as ever." "Weel," said the other, "when he tempts ye again, try him wi' a text; he canna staun that."

The same sun that melts wax, hardens clay.

The holy influences which accompany the gospel produce in some greater hardness of heart. As the man is, such is the influence of preaching upon him, till the Spirit comes with power.

The sermon is not done till the hearer does it.

Coming home from the kirk a little sooner than usual, the good wife was asked by her husband, " What ! is the sermon all done ? " She wisely answered, " No, Donald, it is all *said*, but it has not begun to be *done* yet." Many sermons are done with, but not done.

The Son of God makes us sons of God.

This is the true sonship. That universal fatherhood which is so much cried up gives the lie to the great doctrines of adoption and regeneration, and it is itself a lie of the first magnitude.

The soul is the life of the body.
Faith is the life of the soul.
Christ is the life of faith.

The strongest objection to the Bible is a bad life.

The tear of repentance beautifies the eye of faith.

The tears of the congregation are the hope of the minister.

But they are disappointing. Men weep at the theatre at the sight of a tragedy, or at a funeral in the presence of death, but they wipe their eyes and forget all. It is much the same under sermons. Broken hearts are better than flowing eyes.

The thorough Christian is the true Christian.

A man who was in the habit of saying that although he was not what he should be, still, upon the whole, he was a good average kind of Christian, had given orders to a Christian man to construct a fence around his property. Meeting this man some days afterwards, he asked him if he had made a good fence. "Well," was the reply " the fence is not as it should be—it is not very strong in certain parts, and there are gaps here and there ; but it is a good average kind of fence." The man at once, with great indignation, said, " What do you mean ? Why, a fence of that kind is useless !." " Quite true," was the answer, " and the man who is only a good average kind of Christian is not very much use either."

The true Sabbath is to rest in Christ.

His is that finished work which brings us endless rest. In Him we ease from our own works as God did from his.

The water without the ship may toss it; but it is the water within the ship which sinks it.

> Therefore, let not care leak into your soul. "Let not your heart be troubled," even though your house may be.

The way to Canaan is through the wilderness.

> Where there is no way God leads his people by a right way.

The way to heaven is by Weeping-Cross.

> Repentance, with her clear wet eyes,
> Leads her children to the skies.

The will is no more free than it is made free by grace.

> The free-will of a man who is under sin is sheer slavery; he that doth the will of God from the heart is free indeed.

The worst want is want of faith.

> Faith will supply every other want, but what shall we do should faith cease to draw from God All-sufficient?

There is an infidel in every man's bosom

> An *honest* doubter is rare enough; but we are all born doubters of God, and of that holy truth which troubles us in our sins.

There is no reason for grace but grace.

> God's motive for mercy lies within himself. He loved his people because he would love them.

There is no water till God strikes the rock.

> Often all is dry as the desert till the Lord interposes in his providence, and then he turns the thirsty land into a pool. So, too, there are no streams of repentance till the touch of grace creates a fountain in the heart of stone.

There's a mountain of matter in every line of Scripture.

> The moderns will not believe it; but the spiritual know that it is so. One of the fathers rightly said, "I adore the infinity of Holy Scripture." There is little fear nowadays that men will make too much of the Bible: the most of them make too little of it.

They are well kept whom God keeps.

They that feel themselves lost are soon found.

> This is one of the earliest signs of a work of grace in the soul. Nothing can be truly found which was not first lost. Christ himself does not go after those sheep which have never gone astray.

They who sin the sin must bear the shame.

They who trust Christ's death must copy his life.

> We may not divide Christ. "Not a bone of him shall be broken." He must be our Exemplar, or he will not be our Saviour.

Those who are alive to God's glory are dead to vainglory.

> Thus to seek earnestly the glory of God is the best preservative against pride and self-seeking.

Those who believe are those who receive.

Those who deal with God must deal upon trust.

Those who have heaven in their hopes should have heaven in their lives.

Those who love God love God's Word.

Those who seek God, find him; and those who find him, seek him.

Those who think much of themselves, think little of Christ.

Those who welcome Christ may welcome death.

Those who wish to cross the seas
Must not lose the favouring breeze.

> Those who would enter heaven must use the blessed influences of the Holy Spirit. He bloweth when and where he pleases, and we must not neglect a single favourable opportunity.

Those who would get to heaven must get to Christ.

Though God may frown in the providence, he always smiles in the promise.

Though love will perfect fear remove,
Yet most I fear when most I love.

> This is not that slavish fear which has torment which grows out of love, and is no enemy to joy.

To ask amiss is to ask and miss.

To be much like Christ, be much with Christ.

A painter in Rome was forbidden to copy a famous picture. Determined not to be balked, he sat down in front of the painting and looked closely and steadfastly at it for half an hour every morning. He then hurried home and transferred one line or feature to his canvas. So he attained his object. If we would spend but half an hour each day in contemplating the grace and beauty of our Divine Redeemer, by a spiritual process there would be a transference of those lines of grace and beauty into our characters.

To broken hearts Christ brings unbroken peace.

To die *in* the Lord, we must live *to* the Lord.

To God keep near throughout the year.

To have a portion in this world is mercy; but to have the world for our portion is misery.

To look upon a promise without a precept is the high road to *presumption;* to look upon a precept without a promise is the high road to *desperation.*

To see the King is better than to see a thousand of his servants.

Make it your desire, in going to the house of God, that you may behold the beauty of the Lord while you enquire in his temple.

To win Christ is the greatest gain.

TOO LATE is written on the gates of hell.

Trifling with sin is no trifling sin.

Trust not in the ordinances of God, but in the God of ordinances.

Trust God where you cannot trace him.

Especially leave the unknown future in his hands. What is the use of fretting beforehand?

> If evils come not, then our fears are vain,
> And if they come, our fears augment the pain.

GLY women, finely dressed, are the uglier for it.

Are there any ugly women? We cannot say; but some evidently think themselves so, for they put on showy apparel to hide their plainness. Their gaudy trappings advertise their want of comeliness. The plainer the dress, the more conspicuous the beauty of the wearer.

Unborn pups are doubtful dogs.

To the same effect is the other proverb: "Unlaid eggs are doubtful chicks." It is idle to reckon upon the uncertain future.

Uncle pays for all.

In America it is Uncle Sam, and here it is Uncle John Bull, so far as the nation is concerned. "Never mind the expense, Uncle Bull will clear the bill." The Italians say that public money is like holy water, everybody helps himself to it. In families, also, the principle comes into action, and economy ceases when a rich friend "stands Sam." A bachelor uncle is almost as good as a maiden aunt; and in some respects better. It must be nice to be uncle when all the youngsters reckon on your paying for all they choose to buy.

Under a cloak the devil is two devils.

He is able to do double mischief when disguised.

Under golden sheath leaden sword.

Too often true; great show and poor substance. "Under silk hat a soft head," and "under a coronet no head at all." These may both be true; and yet all are not wide awake who wear wide-awakes.

" Under the rose."

That is, secretly. Let us do nothing which requires to be hidden. "*Sub rosâ*" is a state of things which makes honest men afraid.

Under white ashes lie glowing embers.

Men may seem very gentle, and yet be indulging the fiercest passions. Courtesy may conceal furious malice.

Underhanded dealing
Stirs up angry feeling.

Do everything above board; for no man likes to feel that he has been taken in and done for.

Unfit to die, unfit to live.

That which is necessary as a preparation for the next world is equally needful for this present life. If we live as we should, we shall die as we would.

Unfortunate and imprudent are often two words for the same thing.

When a man is incorrigibly stupid, he lays his failure upon his bad luck. Providence may arrange matters mysteriously at times; but, as a rule, when men cannot succeed, there is a reason for it. Those who are long out of work are generally out *with* work.

Unkind words fall easily from the tongue, but a coach and six horses cannot bring them back.

Unlooked-for often comes.

It is the unexpected that happens.

Unready and Unsteady are two Ne'er-do-wells.

Unsaid may be said, but said cannot be unsaid.

Therefore, prefer to err by silence rather than to sin by speech.

Unthankful men are unnatural men.

The unthankful and the evil are leashed together in Scripture, like a couple of hounds of the worst breed. No Billingsgate woman could give a man a worse word than to call him ungrateful. Nature is grateful: all the rivers run into the sea, and the clouds repay the earth for its mists by heavy rains. The flocks and the herds repay their keeper; and he is worse than a brute who hath no gratitude.

Until the physician has killed one or two, he is not a physician.

So say the Kashmiris; but those poor, ignorant people, have no acquaintance with our allopathic practitioners, and intend no allusion to those worthy gentlemen.

Unused advantages are no advantage.

He that hath fields he doth not weed,
He that hath books he doth not read,
He that hath ears but doth not heed,
Of common-sense hath grievous need.

Unwilling service earns no thanks.

Unwise people learn nothing from the wise.

As the Burmese say, "A fool is like a wooden spoon, which does not perceive the flavour of the curry-gravy in which it is placed." Solomon says, "Ye fools, when will ye be wise?"

Up in the morning early,
And leave off being surly.

Beds make beggars. Lazy lovers of sleep find all things going wrong, and they are on the grumble all the day. Getting up late, they get out on the wrong side of the bed, and are all day as surly as bears with sore heads.

Up like a rocket, and down like its stick.

A gradual rise is likely to prove a permanent one; but a sudden rise is often temporary. This proverb has been applied by ill-will to many who have not yet dropped like a stick.

Up hill spare me, down hill forbear me.

This is a part of the good advice which the horse is supposed to give to his driver.

Upon an egg the hen lays an egg.

To him that hath shall be given. Get a nest-egg and more will come. The difficulty of saving lies in the first ten pounds.

Use as little vinegar as possible in talking of others.
Use friends as you would have them use you.

Expect no more from them than they might reasonably expect from you. Many people have no thought except for themselves.

Use is second nature.

It is said that a man might live up to his neck in a horse-pond if he once grew used to it. But there is a limit to the influence of habit; for when the miser was getting his horse to be used to live on a straw a day it died.

Use is the best estimate of value.

That learning and talent which cannot be put to any service is not much esteemed.

A candle that affords no light,
What profits it by day or night?

Use legs, and have legs.

Those who walk can walk. It is the same with other things: the exercise of a faculty or ability is the making of it. Many a man has capacities which he has not discovered, because they have not been called into exercise.

Use more wit, and less sweat.

Many things which cannot be wrought by violent exertion are easily brought about by using a little common-sense. In public speaking let no man mistake perspiration for inspiration.

Use neither too much bridle, nor too much spur.

Good counsel as to horses, and equally wise as to young people under training. Neither curb too much, nor demand too great exertion of the mental powers.

Use pastime so as to save time.

Amusement is useful when it causes the mind to be rested, so that it is able to do all the more when you return to work.

Use soft words, but hard arguments.

Suaviter in modo: fortiter in re. The suaviter and the fortiter should be mixed in equal proportions. Be gentle. The sea is held in check, not by a wall of granite but by a beach of sand. Many think strong language strengthens a weak argument; but it does not. A bully is by no means a conclusive reasoner.

Use sugar more than vinegar.

Be good-tempered. Be placid, and not acid. Don't show a litigious spirit. There is no surer way of setting everybody against yourself than that of setting yourself against everybody.

Use words with care, or ill you'll fare.

If one had arranged to dine at the "Green Man, Dulwich," and told the coachman to drive to the "Dull Man, Greenwich," he would miss his dinner. One may lose the habit of truth, and even of reasonableness, by being careless in the use of language.

Use your eyes if you would be wise.

Use your shoulders as well as your knees.

Work as well as pray.

Sayings of a more Spiritual Sort.

Unbelief is giving God the lie.

> That's the plain English of it. If a man has "honest" doubt, he will at least grant that God is honest too.

Undone duty will undo our souls.

> "Unprofitable servants" when we have done all; what are we when we have left all undone?

Uneven conduct makes uneasy conscience.

"Upward and heavenward" be always your motto.

Use not your Best Friend worst.

> Nay, use him better than your best has yet reached.
>
> > The glory of my glory still shall be,
> > To give all glory and myself to thee.

Use temporal things, but prize eternal things.

Use the world by making it thy servant; abuse it not by making it thy master.

Use what you have, that you may have more to use.

Utter to your utmost unutterable love.

AIN thoughts are vagrants, and must not be lodged.

"How long shall thy vain thoughts lodge within thee?"—Jer. iv. 14.

Vainglory blooms abundantly, but fruits sparingly.

Vanity has no greater foe than vanity.

In this case dog eats dog : one proud person hates another.

Vanity is a blue-bottle, which buzzes in the window of the wise.

Aristotle once said to a conceited fellow, "Young man, I wish I were what you think yourself to be, and my enemies what you really are." Even so great a sage was annoyed by a fool.

Velvet paws hide sharp claws.

Very soft and pretty speeches are often intended to cover hard and cruel meanings.

Venture a sprat to catch a herring.

Venture not on one night's ice.

It will rarely be strong enough to bear you. New schemes and methods should not be trusted hastily. See whether they are safe.

Very cheap is mostly very dear.

Very few herrings are caught on Newmarket Heath.

We must look for things in their proper places. We shall never find true pleasure in sin, nor rest in self, nor gain in gambling.

Very hard times in the wood when the wolves eat each other.

When men who live upon the public take to devouring each other, things are probably going very badly with them.

Very like a whale in a butter-boat.

Something very wonderful ; too much cried up to be true.

When any tell a mighty tale,
I answer, "*Very like a whale.*"

Vexation treads on the heels of vanity.

Vice is learned without a schoolmaster.

> Yes, and all the more surely without schooling.

"Virtue in the middle," said the devil, when seated be-
tween two lawyers.

> A very old proverb, referring to lawyers centuries ago (?).

Virtue is a jewel of great price.

> No doubt. But how do the poor come by it ? It is neither to be
> bought nor sold : but it is the work of God.

Virtue is the reward of virtue.

> By doing well we learn to do still better. Virtue ranks above
> rank.
>> Virtue will homage gain in humble shed ;
>> While vice enthroned becomes a nation's dread.

Virtue soiled is virtue spoiled.

Vows made in storms are forgotten in calms.

Vox Populi, vox Dei.

> The voice of the people is the voice of God. By no means certain,
> for the people cried, "Crucify him." Yet that which is generally
> desired by the people is pretty sure to come to pass sooner or later.

Sayings of a more Spiritual Sort.

Vainglory easily creeps in even at the door of mercy.

> "One says, such a nobleman drank to me, shook me by the
> hand, discoursed with me ; and hereby he insinuates to the hearers
> some worthiness in himself, for which he was so graced. So some,
> in declaring God's works and favours to them, have a conceit of
> merit in themselves, deserving such respect."—*Thomas Adams.*

Verity is of God, and vanity is of man.

AGERS are the last arguments of fools.

> Yet how common it is to hear a man clench an assertion with, "I'll bet you ten to one on it!"

> Men, till losing makes them sager,
> Back their judgments with a wager.

Yet there is no argument whatever in this swagger. Men bet because they have no better proof of what they say.

"Wait and see," as the blind man said.

> An answer to one who wants to wait and see, when the case is obvious and urgent. His plea for delay is absurd.

"Wait" is a hard word to the hungry.

Wake not a sleeping tiger.

> By no means. When a passionate man is quiet, pray let him be. Don't start a discussion with a contentious individual.

Wandering lights deceive.

> He who is not fixed in his teaching cannot be true in it; for truth never alters. Wreckers' lights shift: lighthouses are stable.

Want is no friend to wit.

> It drives some men out of their wits. It is hard to be witty when you are hungry. Even when the poor man is really witty, few care to notice it; for truly does *Juvenal* say :—

> > Want is the scoff of every wealthy fool,
> > And wit in rags is met with ridicule.

Want makes strife
'Twixt man and wife.

> Too often when cruel need is in the house, love is soured into mutual disgust. Love lives on, but none can live on love.

Want of common-sense is a fatal want.

> Learning and grace may be had; but if a man has no common-sense, where will he find it? We mean

> > Good sense, which is the rarest gift of heaven,
> > And though no science, fairly worth the seven.

Want of money loses money.

Without capital the man has no chance of buying well. Without means he is hard pressed, and cannot avail himself of opportunities by which he might have profited if he had paid cash.

Want of punctuality is want of politeness.

And want of honesty. As to politeness: I ought not to insult any one by supposing that his time is worth nothing, and that he himself is a nobody, who may as well wait for me as not.

Wanton jests make fools laugh and wise men frown.

One should be very sorry if he finds himself overpowered by his sense of the ludicrous when the joke is not clean. Smut is not to be smiled at, but to be denounced in the plainest manner.

Wash a pig, scent a pig, still a pig's but a pig.

Wasps attack the ripest fruit.

Slander assails the sweetest characters; and frequently all the more so because of their excellence.

Waste not a second: time is short.

Even those who would detain the traveller at their tavern disclaim all intent of causing delay. Outside a country inn hangs the sign of a gate, with this inscription—

This gate hangs high, and hinders none :
Refresh and pay, and travel on.

We question the assertion that none have been hindered.

Watch little expenses, or they will eat you up.

Observe how articles are consumed in the house, or there will be much waste unaware to yourself.

Keep you your keys,
And be at ease.

Water is strong drink; Samson drank it.

It drives mills, floats navies, creates harvests. What is there which water cannot do? Water never floated a man into the lockup; but wine and beer have ruined thousands. It was said of one—

All his life was cankered,
Since he ever hankered
For the flowing tankard.

Water plants before they wither.

Look after those in whom there are the first signs of grace. A kind word may cause the weakly plants to flourish and bear fruit. Once let them wither, and watering may come too late.

Waters all run to the sea.

It seems as if wealth went to the wealthy. Using the saying in another way : All our love should flow to God, who is love ; and all our grace should bear us back to God, from whom it came.

We all row in the same boat.

Said by those who are agreed about a matter. It is a pity when the boat goes the wrong way, and all the crew agree therein.

We are bound to be honest, but not to be rich.

We are not infallible, not even the youngest of us.

A neat touch of sarcasm for the positive youth.

We buy the news to see that nothing is new.

We fall on the side we lean to.

No one does good by accident, because that is not the way nature inclines ; but if we fall, we fall into sin. Oh, for a new nature !

We know what we are, but we know not what we may be.

We may be happy yet. Another saying is, "We know what we have, but not what we may get." He who has the bag may get the sack. Let us live in hopes, if we die in a ditch.

We must all eat a peck of dirt before we die.

That may be ; but we would like to have it very little at a time, and as the negro said, "If I must eat dirt, let it be clean dirt." We must endure a good deal that we don't like ; but we will not bear sin and falsehood.

We must let you speak if you cannot hold your tongue.

Some cannot be kept quiet any more than a bag of fleas can be made good neighbours. To them we must say :
> You are not dumb-driven cattle :
> Still you must go rattle, rattle.

We must not lie down and cry, "God help us !"

No, no : God helps us to help ourselves. "Up, guards, and at 'em."

We never know the worth of water till the well is dry.

What a folly! Will men never value health, and opportunity, the gospel and grace, till they are lost beyond recall?

We ought to be doing, and to be doing what we ought.

We remember what we would forget, and forget what we would remember.

We should eat to live, not live to eat.

"For if we make the stomach a cemetery for food, the body will soon become the sepulchre of the soul. One-half of mankind pass their lives in thinking how they shall get a dinner, and the other in thinking what dinner they shall get; and the first are much less injured by occasional fasts, than are the latter by constant feasts."

We should play to live, not live to play.

When men make amusement their avocation, they are childish, if not worse. Play should help us to work; and if it does not, it is a wicked waste of time. Men should put away childish things.

We think our fathers fools, so wise we grow;
Our wiser sons, no doubt, will think us so.

Secretly, we fear that in this opinion they may be justified; but we have also a conviction that, in some things, they might be wiser if they would follow their fathers, and leave well alone.

"The silver heads of wisdom, lassie,
Are wearing fast away;
Will the green ones coming up, lassie,
Be wiser than the grey?"

"We two have much to think about," said the fly on the head of a philosopher.

"How well we played to-day!" said the blower to the organist. Yet all this is not so ridiculous as when we imagine that our thoughts are necessary to carry out the thoughts of God.

"We'll wait a bit and see," as the puppy said when he was a week old.

Wealth and worth are different things.

Yet most people think, that if a man is worth fifty thousand pounds, he must be a man of worth. He might have all that, and yet be worth less; or even worthless.

20

Wealth is timid.

As soon as a man has a five-pound note in the savings bank, he looks with apprehension upon all changes in politics. He who has nothing feels that a revolution could not make him poorer; and possibly he hopes that if there came a smash, he might pick up some of the pieces. Consols are very consolidating.

Wealth makes wit waver.

Pounds sober puns, and silence satire. Who dares poke fun at a man who could buy you up, and twenty like you? There have been sensible men who were not minded to worship the golden calf; but even these feel some awe in the presence of half a million.

Wealth of wit makes stint of words.

It is not easy to find words for deep thoughts, and so a wise man is often slow of speech. Moreover, a sensible man often says little because he knows his company deserves no more.

Wear like a horse-shoe, the longer the brighter.

Not like a shoddy suit. Of such wear beware.

Wear your greatcoat till May,
For fickle is the day.

Wedlock is a padlock.

A padlock is a very useful thing to preserve treasure; but a thing much disliked by the very rogues who most need locking up.

Wedlock is either kill or cure.

If a man is not made sober by marriage, what will become of him? But to give a man a wife as a medicine is scarcely the right thing. Oh, that in every case the old service of the Greek Church expressed a fact! The priest says, "The servant of God marries the handmaid of God."

Weed your own garden first.

And your neighbour's when he asks you, and pays you for it.

Weep more for the lives of the bad than for the deaths of the good.

Well begun is half-done.

So much depends upon the start. A bad beginning may involve double trouble before the end is reached.

Well-earned wealth may meet disaster;
Ill-got goods destroy their master.

Well-laid out, is well-laid up.

> When the right thing has been done with the money, no man is the poorer for what he has wisely expended.

Well may she smell, whose gown is burning.

> No wonder that persons are in ill odour whose lives are not right.

Well won should be well worn.

> Not proudly, nor wantonly, but with gratitude to God, and in obedience to his laws, should we enjoy the reward of our industry.

Were he to toss up a penny it would come down a pound.

> Some persons appear to be favoured by fortune; but the general explanation of good luck is hard work, common sense, and frugality.

Were it a wolf it would bite you.

> Said of a thing which is very near, and yet is not perceived.

What a day brings, a day may take away.

> If trouble comes on a sudden, it may go away as suddenly as it comes. Great comfort this!

" What a dust I raise! " quoth the fly on the coach.

> We know that fly: he buzzes in our parish.

What a man has done, a man can do.

> The speech of a man of pluck. "Can you read Greek?" said a lawyer to Hodge. "I don't know," said Hodge. "Why," said the legal gentleman, "you know you can't." But Hodge coolly answered, "I don't know; for I've never tried." We will believe we can till we have proved that we cannot.

What a pity it is marrying spoils courting!

> After-life ought to be a long sermon upon the text of the honeymoon, and those who discourse it should stick to their text.

What a weary traveller eats, tastes well.

> So say the Africans, and experience proves the truth of the observation. Even dry bread is fine when hunger is fierce.

What can you expect from a hog, but a grunt?

What can't be cured must be endured.

What children learn abroad they tell at home.

> Yes, and what they learn at home they tell abroad.

What comes by the devil will go back to him.

> Gained by dishonesty, it is often spent in debauchery.　The devil, like everybody else, takes his own when he finds it.

What comes from the heart goes to the heart.

> This is the secret of true eloquence.

What costs nothing is worth nothing.

> As a general rule, that which is not won by honest labour or fair purchase turns out to be a bag of moonshine.

What does the moon care if the dogs bark at her?

> Why should she care?　Why should *you* care if men slander *you?*

What God makes he never mars.

What good is it to an ass to be called a lion?

> It only makes him the more ridiculous.　Even in a lion's skin his ears and his voice betray him.　Though you dub him F.R.S., men do not revere him if they clearly see him to be an A.S.S.

What greater crime than wasting time!

> It is a sort of murder, for in killing time it destroys the stuff of which life is made.　Yet there are many who do so little, that if they were tied up in a sack and cast into the Atlantic, nobody would miss them.　Is not this crime enough?

What has not been may be.

> It has not had its turn yet, and therefore we may look for it in due time.　Gentle reader, you may yet be taken in.

What I *was* is passèd by,
What I *am* away doth fly,
What I *shall be* none do see,
Yet in that my beauties be.

> Here, then, is room for faith, that we may enjoy by anticipation the joys which are yet to be revealed.

What is bought is often cheaper than what is given.

Because a gift involves an obligation, and to discharge this, one may have to spend ten times the worth of the gift.

What is bred in the bone will come out in the flesh.

Nature, despite nurture, will show itself. The inner man is never quite concealed, even by the finest garments of propriety.

What is done can't be begun.

It might be greatly improved upon if we could begin again in better style; but it is too late now: we must do our best with it.

What is God's will, can ne'er be ill;
In darkest night, he makes it light;
For those who trust, help them he must.

These thoughts may render comfort to some poor soul by the cottage fireside. Learn them, and repeat them.

What is in another's pot,
This deponent knoweth not.

And does not want to know. Yet I wish every man had a chicken in the pot once a week, and a pudding at pudding time.

What is learned in the cradle, lasts till the grave.

The first impressions remain to the last, both in the memory and on the mind. Let every teacher of the very young ask for grace to be very wise.

What is not wisdom is danger.

Folly is foolhardy. Even after wise thought, danger may remain; but if a thing is imprudent, it is certainly unsafe.

What is rotten will rend.

When the time comes, every evil will come to its climax: the impecunious will be bankrupt, the untruthful will be called a liar, the hypocrite will be put to shame, and "modern thought" will develop into infidelity.

What is sport to the cat is death to the mouse.

Quoted when persons make mirth without respect to the feelings of the victim of the jest. It is like the saying of the frogs to the boys in Æsop: "What is sport to you, is death to us."

What is the use of running when we are not on the right road?

> The faster you go, the more astray you get.   Earnestness in a bad cause makes a man's action all the worse.

What is true is not always probable.

> Indeed, it is the improbable which occurs.   I read, the other day, a Hindoo legend, and not long after, I saw in the daily paper a statement of fact which was in all respects a parallel to it.   Those pictures which we think to be overdrawn are often truest to what the artist actually saw.

What is worth doing at all, is worth doing well.

> Do thoroughly what you set about :
> If you kill a pig, kill it out-and-out.

What is wrong to-day will not be right to-morrow.

> Moral principles are fixed, and so are doctrinal truths ; but this age loves perpetual change.   Men have windmills in their heads.

What lies nearest the heart is first in the mouth.

> That which is in the shop is seen in the window.   When a man loves onions, his breath smells of them.   "Out of the abundance of the heart the mouth speaketh."—Matt. xii. 34.

What matters it to a blind man that his father could see?

> Or to a fool that his father was wise?   Or to a scamp that his father was honourable?   Hence the inconsistency of making men hereditary legislators.   The tenth transmitter of a foolish face is not necessarily qualified to be a ruler over wise men.

What must be must ;
Man is but dust.

> Death is inevitable. Other decrees of God will also stand, whatever man in his puny wisdom may determine to the contrary.

What owl will not hunt mice?

> What man will be averse to getting money?

What should we do if we had nothing to do?

> We should feed the worms in the cemetery ; at least this would be better than to imitate the social man, who has nothing to do but to go about wasting the time of those who are busy.

What small potatoes we all are compared with what we
might be!

Or might have been. Yet we do not think small potatoes of
ourselves. Do we?

What soberness conceals, drunkenness reveals.

What decency would have kept from mortal ears, the madness of
drink blurts out. Hence alcohol is the picklock which opens drawers
which had better have been shut.

What the eye does not see, the heart does not rue.

It is a blessing that many things escape our knowledge, and so
do not vex us. It is a blessing not to see too much.

What the puppy learns the dog will do.

What thou givest forget; what thou receivest remember.

What tutor shall we find for a child of sixty years old?

He must be able to fetch him along quickly, for his pupil's time is
short. Will the old boy stick to his book? If not, who is to
appoint him impositions, or keep him in after school-hours?

What use is it to read the Vedas to a wild buffalo?

The best of books are lost on the profane: it is preaching to a
mad dog. Cast not your pearls before pigs

What was worth borrowing is worth returning.

Unless the fellow has kept it so long as to have worn it out.
Even if only an umbrella or a book, we are thieves if we keep it.
Alas! we find that whatever sort of accountants our friends may
be, they are very sure bookkeepers.

Not that imparted knowledge doth diminish learning's store;
But books, I find, when once they're lent, return to me no more.

What we are afraid to do before men, we should be afraid
to think before God.

What we dinna ken we shouldna speak.

What we doat on by day we dream of by night.

The lawyer dreams of law's delays, the policeman of the cook
and cold mutton, the student of his tutor (?), the British workman
of his conscientious toil.

When sportsmen in the night do fall asleep,
Their fancies in the woods still hunting keep.

What will not a pig eat, or a fool say?

What fools say should not much trouble wise men. What can it signify? Yet sensible people are often sensitive people, and are as much worried by idiotic remarks as fair ladies by a wasp.

"What will you stand?" I'll stand outside the public-house.

Stand your ground, and stand nothing else. Treat your friend, but not to a pot of cold poison.

What you don't want is dear at a farthing.

Even as a gift it will only be lumber, and cumber.

What you put in the dough you'll find in the cake.

Mistakes made in the conception and rough hewing of a design will appear further on in the business. Sins of youth crop up in old age. Bad example seen by the child comes out in the man.

Whatever a man delights in he will do best, and that he had best do.

Follow the bent of your genius. Let not the man who would have been at home with the tailor's goose make a goose of himself by setting up for an orator. Whether to mould a pill, or watch a mill, or melt a bar, or drive a car, be your chosen pursuit, keep to it till you are the best hand at it in all the country side.

Whatever sea-room a shrimp gets it will never be a whale.

Give a little man all the chance and the sphere which he can desire, and he will be none the greater. In fact, his shrimpship will seem all the smaller in so wide a space.

What's a table richly spread,
Without a woman at its head?

It lacks its chief ornament, its life, its light, its music, its queen.

What's everybody's business is nobody's business.

But when every one minds his own business, work is done.

What's not your own,
That let alone.

A world of mischief and misery would thus be prevented; but *fools* will be meddling, and knaves will be pilfering.

What's the use of doing what is already done?

Enough of necessary work comes in our way without attempting to do what is already accomplished by somebody else.

> Why fight your battles o'er again,
> And three times over slay the slain?

What's the use of jumping high, and coming down on the same place?

Tremendous efforts made, and no consequent rise, are by no means remunerative. Sit still, or move for the better.

" What's the way to Beggars' Bush?" Ask at the first Gin Palace.

And when you have your answer, go in the opposite direction, down Water Lane, and up the hill of Thrift.

When a beggar grows rich he is apt to grow proud.

Have we not seen it? We must all go on our knees to the Duke of Ditchwater; so his grace seems to think, but we think otherwise.

> " When beggars on their horses ride,
> Their saddle's always stuffed with pride."

When a cow dances she does it in style.

It is so out of her line, that if she does go in for it, she must needs go for it all fours. Men overdo what they are not fit to do.

When a good man thrives, all around him thrive.

He is liberal in his payments, and promotes merit; he is kind to the poor, and does not run down weaker tradesmen. As he rises, he raises others and crushes none.

When a goose is fat it is still a goose.

Riches do not turn a fool into a wise man.

When a goose is in fine feather it is still a goose.

Those who trust to their fine clothes are all the more foolish because of their finery.

> A dandy is a thing that would
> Be a young lady if it could;
> But as it can't, does all it can
> To show the world it's not a man.

When a man is a fool his wife will rule.
When a man is a fool his wife *should* rule.

> These two oracles balance each other. We know a lady who rules, and we know her husband who is ruled, and it is our opinion that the thing is arranged by Providence for *his* good, if not for hers. He who is second is best in the second place.

When a man is going down hill, somebody is sure to give him a push behind.

> This is of a piece with the usual cruelty of man to man. The poet says of them:
>
> " Those that are up themselves keep others low ;
> Those that are low themselves hold others hard,
> Nor suffer them to rise, or greater grow ;
> And every one doth strive his fellow down to throw."
> *Thomson.*

When a man is half a fool he is worse than a whole fool.

> Fools and sensible men are equally harmless: it is in the half fool and the half wise that danger lies.

When a man is in a ditch, his first work is to get out.

> He may put on his gloves and brush his hat afterwards. Till our souls are saved, salvation should be our sole concern.

When a man is in the mud, the more he flounders the more he fouls himself.

> If he has got into a scrape, he makes matters worse by his excuses of himself and accusations of others.

When a man is wrong, and won't admit it, he always gets angry.

> This is to turn the scent. It's the old story of "No case: abuse the plaintiff." Make a dust that others may not see your weak point. Get angry, for fear the injured should get angry first, and get the whip-hand of you. This seems to be the notion.

When a mouse is in the meal-sack he thinks himself the miller.

> Those who profit by the brains of others are apt to impute the wisdom to themselves. He who has bought the invention of a poor man for a mere song thinks himself by far the cleverer person.

When a promise is made, let it be paid.

When a rogue kisses you, count your teeth.

> For he may have stolen one of them. Another form of the proverb says that he counts your teeth. He is looking out for a chance of theft. You'll want all your eyes to match a rogue.

When a thing is plain, don't make a mystery of it.

> Some people like to have a truth confounded, rather than expounded. They look for bones in an egg, and when they have cherries, they swallow nothing but the stones.

When a will's to be read, the sick leave their bed.

> Of course they make an effort to assist in that important ceremonial. Out of pure esteem for the dear departed they wish to hear his very last wishes. Their interest is touching.

When all is right, a man will be
Himself his own best company.

> Make a generous, educated gentleman of yourself, since you are bound to spend a great deal of time in his company.

When an ignorant man knows himself to be ignorant, he is no longer ignorant.

When an old dog barks, a wise man harks.

> For there's something in it. Pups yelp for nothing; but the old dog sees a thief, or he would not make a noise.

When April blows his horn,
It is good for hay and corn.

> This is a saying of the ancients, but it must be taken with a considerable quantity of salt. As a general rule, seasonable weather must be the best weather for crops.

When cat and mouse agree it is bad for the larder.

> If policemen are in league with thieves we shall have a bad time. So in all similar cases the two parties are best apart.

When cats grow fat
They catch no rat.

> Some men, when they make a purse, are of no more use for =
> When parsons marry rich wives their throats are f
> affected, so that they quit the pulpit, or go to Jerusalem

When caught by a tempest, wherever it be,
If it thunders and lightens, beware of a tree.

> Better get wet through than run to objects which attract the lightning, as trees so often do. Better damp than danger.

When Christ blesses the bread, it grows in our hands.

> Where God doth bless, in time abundance springs,
> And heaps are made of many little things.

When couples fall out they had better fall in again.

> And the sooner the better. If we clear up as we go on, and leave no back reckonings, we may live together for a century with growing love.
> > The kindest and the happiest pair
> > Will find occasion to forbear;
> > And something every day they live
> > To pity, and perhaps forgive.

When cracked is the bell
It soundeth not well.

> Evil comes out in the communications of the evil man. What a nuisance is a bell which is cracked, and yet keeps for ever clacking! A cracked man is worse than a cracked bell.

When dry as a herring, of publics beware,
And never go home as cross as a bear.

> Two good counsels; worthy of wide acceptation. Drinking beer will not improve the temper, nor long quench the thirst.

When every one minds his own business the cows get fed.

> The necessary duties of life are forgotten when no one is appointed to see to them. Nothing is worse for a family than muddle; even the cows suffer when personal work is neglected.

When everybody talks, nobody hears.

When everyone treats him as a pig, he is apt to go into
the sty.

When fools go to market pedlars make money.

> Have your wits about you in transacting business, lest this proverb be remembered, and proved.

When fortune wraps thee warm,
Then friends around thee swarm.

> Who has not found it so? The sugar attracts the flies.

When foxes preach, geese should not be allowed out to late meetings.

> Indeed, our young people and our old people also are safest when they do not hear the teachers of false doctrine, such as the advocates of superstition on the one side and of scepticism on the other. These are both foxes.
>
>> There be many foxes that go on two legs,
>> And steal greater matters than cocks, hens, and eggs;
>> To catch many gulls in sheep's clothing they go;
>> They might be destroyed; but I know what I know.

When good cheer is lacking,
Friends will be packing.

When good men quarrel, the devil cries, "Bravo!"

When Greek meets Greek, then comes the tug of war.

> "You stout and I stout;" there will be a great struggle for the mastery. Neither will give way, and so they must fight like the two dogs, of whom nothing was left but half a brass collar.

When heads are hot, brains bubble.

> And many things boil over which scald the hearers, or envelop them in steamy clouds. Keep your head cool.

When hogs fly, drunkards will prosper.

> That is to say, when you can roast snow in a furnace, or fat pigs on pebbles, or teach a fish to dance a hornpipe.

When honest men fall out, rogues come by what is not their own.

> No doubt: even as, on the other hand, when rogues fall out, the honest have a better chance of getting their own.

When Honesty is married to Poverty, they take Self-Denial to be their housekeeper.

> Then love sweetens dry crusts, and puts a delicious flavour into a dinner of herbs. But this said self-denial is mainly practised by the wife, if ever practised at all; and yet those male wretches make it out that the women are expensive, and they call them "*dear* creatures." Here is a pretence at verse by one of these monsters.
>
>> " Heaven bless the wives, they fill our hives
>> With little bees and honey!
>> They soothe life's shocks, they mend our socks,
>> But—don't they spend the money!"

When I'm dead everybody's dead, and the pig too.

So far as this world is concerned. This is the reverse of Paddy's reason for insuring his life, because he would thus become a rich man as soon as he was dead.

When I'm rich, friends ask assistance ;
When I'm poor they keep their distance.

When Jack is in love, he is not a fair judge of Jill.

Wisdom and passion very seldom meet,
Hence lovers' bargains seldom are discreet.

When jokes give pain,
The wise abstain.

When joy abounds, grief is within hail.

Nothing on this earth can be the ground of settled confidence, for it is so uncertain. Like English weather, nothing lasts so as to be reckoned on an hour. Sorrow is the footman of mirth.

When joy is in the parlour, grief may be in the passage.

When man and wife fall out, none but a fool will interfere.

They would be pretty sure to unite their forces upon the intruder; hence the wisdom of the verse :—

" When man and wife at odds fall out,
Let syntax be your tutor,
'Twixt masculine and feminine,
What should one be but neuter ? "

When mirth comes in, beware of sin.

Sin is so apt to mingle with our merry-making, that we need be doubly watchful. The house of feasting attracts evil spirits.

When musing on companions gone,
We doubly feel ourselves alone.

When one goose drinks, all drink.

Very true, both in natural history, and in the history of naturals.

When one horse will not go, all the team are hindered.

A whole factory may be thrown out of order by one man. No fellow has a right to interfere with the rights of others by hindering them in their work. In a family one person may upset all.

When one man's beard is burning, another lights his pipe at the flame.

This is the Oriental method of describing the total absence of sympathy among men of the world. There is a measure of truth in this description. The Bengali has it, "While one man is being impaled, another counts the joints of the stake."

When our vices leave us, we flatter ourselves we leave them.

Even as the Turks have it, " 'It is fast-day to-day, and I must not eat,' says the cat when she cannot reach the liver." It is a poor virtue which we follow because we have lost the power to be vicious. Some stoop down because they cannot sit upright, and others keep their ground because their legs will not let them run.

When peace goes to pieces it is hard to piece it.

A thousand difficulties arise when trying to settle an old quarrel. Cement and rivets are hard to apply to broken friendships.

When prosperity smiles, beware of its guiles.

More men are bribed to hell than are frightened thither. The Sirens are more terrible wreckers than the Furies.

When Satan goes to church, he goes to prey.

And when he leads any there, it is that he may make them more surely his own. A gospel-hardened sinner makes a fine armour-bearer for the great enemy.

When Satan goes to prayer, mischief is in the air.

The old form of it is, "When the devil says his paternoster he means to cheat you." If he patronizes religion it is to betray it.

When Satan talks of peace, double bolt the door.

The worst of war is in his heart when honeyed words are on his lips. The vilest enemies of Christ are those who praise his ethics, and undermine his doctrines.

When sorrow is asleep, wake it not.

When suspicion enters the family, affection departs.

When table-talk is stable-talk, 'tis time to stalk away.

By being in low company you suffer moral defilement, and you appear to countenance impure language. Part and depart.

When the beam is low, stoop your head.

Or you may get a knock. Mark how the ducks never go through a barn-door without ducking their heads. There is not much need; but they do it in case there should be. Few are too humble.

When the cat joins the weasel, there's mischief a-brewing.

Some cruel motive has brought these rivals into conjunction. When Herod and Pilate are friends, Christ is crucified.

When the cat's away, the mice will play.

To this may be fitly joined, the other old saw,

> When the cat has gone to sleep,
> Out of holes the mice will peep.

When the cock crows, the fox knows.

He is on the watch for him and his hens, and observes all their movements : besides, he knows by the cock-crow that day is dawning, and that foxes will be safest at home in the daylight.

When the cow dies, we hear how much milk she gave.

"What a dear, good man he was!" Why was this never said while he yet lived? If a tithe of the love expressed when the man is dead had been shown to him in life, how happy it would have made him! Was it not his due?

When the curate clears the platter, there's not much left for the clerk.

If you take all or talk all, what is anybody else to do?

> For the clerk there's little fish
> When the parson clears the dish.

When the devil is landlord, be not his tenant.

Not even with the view of living cheaply, and doing good. Be not thou a lodger where thou canst not invite thy God to visit thee.

When the dinner's done, the spoon is forgotten.

When we have served a man's turn, he forgets us.

When the earth is driest, look you out for rain.

Another form of, "Man's extremity is God's opportunity."

When the fat is in the fire,
Keep thou clear, and come no nigher.

> Never go where mischief and discord are afoot. The best conduct in a quarrel is not equal to being altogether out of it.

When the fields yield not, the saints have not.

> This refers to matters years ago ; but now our saintly clergy must have their tithes whether the fields yield or not. When the farmer's profit is nothing, can the parson's fair tithe be much?

When the fool has made up his mind, the market is over.

> He is so slow in deciding, that his chance has made off and gone before his mind is made up. Even this may not involve so much loss as undue haste, but it effectually bars all hope of gain.

When the fountain is full it will overflow.

> That which is greatly in a man's heart will before long show itself in his talk and life. The affluent of thought should be fluent.

When the fox dies, the fowls never mourn.

> One would think not. The death of Bonner was the cause of joy to the good Protestants of his day ; for by his death they escaped death, and did not become Foxe's martyrs. When a deceitful system is abolished, honest men wear no hatbands. I know several things which will not cost me a tear when I see them no more.

When the glass rises expect bad weather.

> We expect good weather when the weather-glass rises, but the proverb refers to another glass, which we would see fall never to rise. After a glass or two some men are very stormy.

When the good wife is away, the keys are lost.

> Nothing is to be found when she is out. She keeps all in order ; and without her the little kingdom is in a state of anarchy.

When the harvest is ripe it will be reaped.

> > Corn fully ripe is reaped, and gathered in ;
> > So must we be when ripe in grace or sin.

When the helm is gone, the ship will soon be wrecked.

> He that is not guided by discretion, will make a failure of life.

When the hen crows, there's trouble in the yard.

> The general arrangements are out of gear: one member of the family is where another ought to be, and the result is not desirable. Then we remember the old verse :—
> "A jolly shoemaker,
>   John Hobbs, John Hobbs,
> He courted Jane Carter,
> No damsel looked smarter,
> But he caught a tartar,
>   John Hobbs! John Hobbs!"

When the house falls, the windows are broken.

> No doubt. When all goes, we may be sure that the weakest parts do not escape. Art, and science, and religion suffer in the ruin of a great commonwealth.

When the house is finished, the hearse stands at the door.

> How often true! Great expectations and ambitious projects are at last realized, and in the moment of gratification the man dies. I knew a good man who had for years longed for a certain honourable position: it came, and with it a stroke of paralysis which made it of little worth. How vain are all things beneath the moon!

When the joke is at its best,
Then's the time to let it rest.

When the man will lie, never rely on the man.

> One leak may sink a ship, and one lie may wreck a man's character for trustworthiness.

When the mistress sleeps, the servant creeps.

When the monkey reigns, dance before him.

> Bad counsel. This is the policy of mean selfishness. No doubt it is prudent to keep on good terms with the powers that be. But think of dancing before Chimpanzee the First!

When the morn comes, the meal will come with it.

> God gives the daily bread for which he bids us pray.

When the mouse laughs at the cat, there is a hole near.

> Or she would be moved by very different feelings. When some people are saucy to their employers, it is because another place is open to them.

When the oven is hot, put in your bread.

> Seize on favourable occasions: success comes that way. If you don't bake your pie when the oven is hot, when will you?
> The active man will catch the ball
> Before it cometh to a fall.

When the pear is ripe it falls.

> If we exercise patience we shall have the blessing when it is meet.

When the pig has a bellyful, he upsets the trough.

> Which is very malicious of him; but wonderfully like a pig. May not others feed also? What harm has the trough done? We know evil persons who spoil the trade by which they have lived, and thus knock down the ladder by which they rose.

When the prior plays cards, what will the monks do?

> They will take liberty to gamble in any way they like: the leader's example is always excuse enough for the underlings.

When the shepherd is a sheep,
All the flock will go to sleep.

> Lacking power to lead, because there is no leadership in him, the people will either quarrel with their feeble minister, or everything will drop into spiritual lifelessness. Oh, for men! Oh, for men of God! But these are almost as rare birds as white crows.

When the ship is sunk, everyone knows how she might have been saved.

When the ship went down, the story ended.

> The catastrophe did as the Frenchman said, "cut his little tale off short." It might apparently have gone on till now if the ship had not foundered. A great many other things come to an end when death cries "Finis."

When the shoulder of mutton is going, it is good to take a slice.

> Not if it does not belong to you. Under the impulse of such a knavish notion, many have helped themselves out of the general wreckage of a great estate, and have been guilty of utter villainy.

When the sky falls we shall catch larks.

> Numbers of little consequences come out of a great event. It is an ill wind which does not shake apples into somebody's lap.

When the spider's web is broken, he mends it again.

Well done, spider! Persevere, and you will yet catch the fly. The French say, "Bad luck will tire if you don't."

When the stars set, the sun will shine.

Lesser comforts may go, but our God will come nearer.

When the sun is shining all around, some notice nothing but the shadows.

When the sun shines, nobody minds him; but when he is eclipsed, all consider him.

A man may spend any number of years in holy living, and be unknown; but let him transgress once, and all will note it. Again, God may shine on us all the day, and we forget him; but if he withhold his light for a while, we cry out in anguish.

When the tale of bricks is doubled Moses appears.

So it is said, "When the night is darkest, the morning is nearest." When things are at the worst, they must mend.

When hope seems drooping to the tomb,
The withered branch shall freshly bloom.

When the thief cannot steal, he takes to honest ways.

Yes, and goes out lecturing upon the rights of property.

When the waggon is tilting, everybody gives it a shove.

Few will help you up, but a crowd will help you down.

When the weather is stormy, we must weather the storm.

When the wheat is ripe, the sparrows peck at it.

When the will is present, the legs are lively.

The Germans say, "Will is the soul of work."

When the wine is in, the wit is out.

The counsels that are given in wine
Will do no good to thee or thine.

The negroes say, "Liquor talks mighty loud when it gets out of the jug." By such talk folly gets wind. But there must have been very little wit in the man at first, or he would not have let the wine in. When wit is in, wine is kept out.

When there's no fire in the grate, there's no smoke in the chimney.

Without grace in the heart, there will be no sign of it in the life. On the other hand, when there's fire in the soul, there will be sparks in the speech.

When thy neighbour's house is on fire, it is time to look about thee.

It will come to thy house next. When thy neighbour dies, prepare thy grave. He yesterday; I to-day.

When thou hast done piping, they will cease dancing.

We must not conclude that all our converts will last: some of them are dependent upon our personal influence, and when we have done preaching they will have done professing.

When thou hearest, hear for thyself.

> My friend, be sure you wear the caps
> You try to fit on others;
> Take to yourself the preacher's raps,
> And no more blame your brothers.

When three know it, all know it.

Or very soon will. One man can hold his own tongue, but he cannot hold the tongues of the other two.

When tongues do clack, I turn my back.

Especially if I can't get a word in edge-ways myself.

When two quarrel, there's two in the wrong.

When war begins, hell opens its gates.

Another form of it is, "When war begins, death feasts, and hell holds carnival." What evil can be worse than even the best war? Is there any best about wholesale murder?

When waste is in front, want comes on behind.

When wife will gad,
Then home is sad.

She must keep within and look to her home carefully, or disorder will vex her husband, injure the children, and make the family miserable. Dear Mrs. Trotabout, stop at home for a change!

When wise men play the fool, they do it with a vengeance.

Solomon, who was the wisest of men, showed gigantic folly.

When with neighbours we deal,
Ourselves we reveal.

When women consume gin, gin soon consumes them.

When you can see no way to go, go no way.

When you don't know what to do, it is a clear indication that you are to do nothing. "Their strength is to sit still."—Isa. xxx. 7.

When you have a good name, keep it.

If you can do so ; not by truckling to others, but by walking in your integrity. Do not lose it by forming bad associations.
Avoid a villain as you would a brand ;
Which, if it burn you not, will smut your hand.

When you have nothing to say, say nothing.

But few observe this rule: they explain why they have nothing to say, and how glad they are that others are there who can speak so well, and all sorts of rubbish. They fancy that they hide the nakedness of the land, whereas they publish it abroad.

When you see a snake, never mind where he came from.

Kill him first, and then discover the origin of the evil.

When you take another man's hoe to work with, you must clean it, and put it back in its place.

This is sound African logic. Reasonable and fair is the dark man's demand. We press it upon white fellows, especially "the mean whites." Return a borrowed thing in good condition.

When you try to warm, mind you do not burn.

Observe a medium in all things. When you mean to arouse people to energy, don't drive them to fanaticism.

When you turn over in bed, turn out of bed.

So said the Duke of Wellington, a strong man who needed no indulgence. He may have been too hard. Do we not too often err in the other direction of sloth? A verse says :
Six hours of sleep the human frame requires ;
Hard students may to seven incline ;
To eight the man whom toil or trouble tires ;
But lazy folks will all have nine.

When your head is broken you'll run for a helmet.

> Put the helmet on at once, and go to Paul's armoury for it. See Ephesians vi. 17. Go no more out with head unguarded.

When you're paying through the nose,
Very fast the money goes.

> There's no stopping this sort of bleeding. No agreement being made, and everything left to others, no estimate of the expense can be even guessed at. A house built on such terms will become the tomb of a man's estate. Always know what you are spending.

When you've drunk swallows' milk, but not till then.
You may expect good deeds from wicked men.

Where a man never goes, he will never be robbed.

> Neither can he be injured by company he never enters.

Where all are poor, it don't take much to make a rich man.

> If you retire into a village, you are quite wealthy on an income which, in a large town, would be called a miserable pittance.

Where gold avails, argument fails.

> Appeal to the man's palm, and you will gain his hand.

Where hens do crow I would not go.

> For there there is not much peace. Our forefathers were more eloquent about usurping women than against tyrannical men. Here is an old distich :
> > Wife a mouse, quiet house.
> > Wife a cat, dreadful that.

Where ignorance is bliss, 'tis folly to be wise.

> "I was a happy man," said one who looked very ill, "until my last birthday, when my wife made me a present of a microscope. In an evil hour I took it, and began examining the articles of food we eat and drink. I have been living for a fortnight on distilled water, it is the only thing that is not full of nameless horrors."

Where love is, there the eye is.

> The beloved object draws the glance, and before long fixes the gaze. Mind the eye of your mind. If we loved our Lord more, we should be more eagerly looking for his glorious appearing

Where might is right, right is not upright.

Where rosemary flourishes, the lady rules.

> Seeing the rosemary growing luxuriantly in a certain garden, I
> somewhat accidentally quoted this old saying to mine host. He said
> nothing; but when I went into his garden a short time after, *the
> rosemary was dead.* Then I drew an inference. Ahem! Ahem!

Where sin dines, sorrow sups.

Where the bee sucks honey, the spider sucks poison.

> We do not know if this is good natural history, but it illustrates
> the undoubted fact that from precious truths some gather grace, and
> others wrest them to their own destruction.

Where the best wine grows, the worst is drunk.

> It may be so. Who can get good milk in a village? Who
> expects patience or charity from a Perfectionist? Who looks for
> extraordinary spiritual edification from a Doctor of Divinity?

Where the bird was hatched it haunts.

> We retain a love to old dwellings, and old habits. A man loves
> to worship where he was converted.

Where the cat caught a mouse she'll mouse again.

> They say that thieves love to go to the spot where they made a
> great haul. Where a man enjoyed an evil pleasure, the temptation
> is to make a frequent pilgrimage.

Where the devil cannot go himself he sends drink

> He could not send a more effective substitute. Ardent spirits do
> the work of the evil spirit in a terrible manner.

Where the heart is past hope, the face is past shame.

Where the wasp has pass'd,
The gnat sticketh fast.

> One may force his way by his weight and energy, where another
> is hindered by his own feebleness and want of character.

Where the wolf gets one lamb he looks for another.

> If one poor creature has fallen into sin, the great enemy will
> labour hard to get another of the same sort.

Where there are hooks, there may not be bacon.

Show may be without substance. A man may carry a horsewhip and never ride; he may cut a dash and have no dollars; he may be a deacon, or a minister, or a bishop, and have no grace.

Where there are geese, there are usually goslings.

Provide for them. Take earnest care of the young. Let no population be without its Sunday-school.

Where there are lambs, there will be bleating.

"The next sight that we get into the cares and troubles that married life is heir to, is through the remonstrance of a Hibernian paterfamilias, who declares to his wife that he really wishes that the children could be kept in the nursery while he is at home, 'although,' he considerately adds, '*I would not object to the noise if they would only keep quiet.*'"

Where there are rings on the water a stone has fallen.

These are the outward signs of an invisible presence. We see by the movements of the face what is felt in the heart.

Where there is loud cracking, there are few nuts.

And those are mostly rotten.

Where there's a mouse hole, there'll soon be a rat hole.

The tendency of things is to grow worse and worse. We may tolerate evil till it becomes intolerable.

Where there's a will there's a way.

Where there's drink there's danger.

Write it on the liquor store;
Write it on the prison door;
Write it on the gin-shop ﬁne.
Write, oh, write this ——   ine—
    Where there's dr   danger.

Where there's no sore, there   r.

There's no use in comfort   in bringing the
gospel to the self-rights

Where there's very n
Sense is sure to be s

Where there's whispering there's lying.

In general, that which is not meant to be heard is not fit to be heard; and what is not fit to be heard should never be spoken even in a whisper. Whisperers ought to be shut up in the Whispering Gallery.

Where they cannot climb over, they will creep under.

Anything to get along. Dogged perseverance finds a way, or makes one. Self-seekers are not particular about methods : they can cringe and crawl where no upright man could go.

Whether or no the weather'll be fine,
No living man can always divine.

Almanacks know nothing about it, and those who pretend to be weather-wise are generally otherwise. In one of the Percy Society's volumes there is a rhyme by one Duncomb, of Houghton Regis, which shows how little there is in the forecasts of rustics :—

" ' Well, Duncomb, how will be the weather ? '
' Sir, it looks cloudy altogether,
And coming 'cross our Houghton Green
I stopped and talked with old Frank Beane :
While we stood there, sir, old Jim Swain
Went by, and said he know'd 'twould rain.
The next that came was Master Hunt,
And he declared he knew it won't.
And then I met with Farmer Blow ;
He plainly told me he didn't know.
So, sir, when doctors disagree,
Who's to decide it, you or me ? ' "

Which is the high road to Needham ? Turn to the left, at the sign of the Quart Pot.

So also the way to heaven is plain—" First turn to the right, just by the cross, and keep straight on."

Which way the wind blows, the dust flies.

Persons of no character and mind go before the prevailing wind of opinion. But then they are but dust.

Whichever way the wind doth blow,
Some heart is glad to have it so :
Then blow it east or blow it west,
The wind that blows, that wind is best.

This is optimism; and a grand faith it is. For some one or other, that which is an ill wind for others blows good. God's winds are the best he thinks fit to send to such a world as this.

While debts I owe, I sink in woe.

Unless you have been long a debtor, and in that case you try to borrow of somebody else, and are as bold as brass when thus trying to steal from your best friend. Without debt, without care.

While foxes are so common, we must not be geese.

While still at sea we must keep watch.

For as long as life lasts danger will be around us; and even the wisest and most experienced must be on their guard. At the very entrance of the Fair Havens there are rocks.

The seaman's greatest peril's near the coast:
When we are nearest heaven the danger's most.

While the big girl was stooping, the little girl swept the rooms.

Spoken in praise of little people: but it is hardly fair thus to undervalue tall girls. At any rate, they are more likely to be able to whitewash the ceilings without having a scaffold put up. Of course tall people lie longest in bed, but little people are often the biggest when they are up—in their own opinion.

While the cat winks, the mouse is gone.

Much more is it true, that "while cats play, mice run away." We must be very wide awake to catch anything nowadays, unless it be a cold. While we think to catch we are caught.

While the dogs are fighting, the wolves are rending the sheep.

A good reason for hearty union among lovers of truth and grace.

While the grass grows, the steed starves.

While the great bells are ringing, no one hears the little ones.

Yet their music may be very sweet. Let the less man wait l time, and his voice may yet ring out o'er hill and dale.

While the medicine is coming the man dies.

While we live we hope, for while we hope

Whisky drinking is risky drinking.

This is too charitable to the evil spirit.

Whisky is very harmless—if you don't drink it.

We remember one who poured it into his boots; and though we thought him foolish, we were glad he did not pour it into his legs.

Whisky whisks many to the grave.

Dr. Guthrie said, "There is nothing in this world like whisky for preserving a man when he is dead; but it is one of the worst things in the world for preserving a man when he is living."

White flour comes not out of a coal-sack.

A man of evil life cannot yield holy influences.

White walls are fools' copy-books.

They need not sign their names, we know who they are.

Who begins amiss, ends amiss.   Mind this, miss!

Who borrows, sorrows; who lends, learns.

Who brews a quarrel may bruise his head.

Let quarrels be brewed in some other party's boiler, but not in your teapot.   Keep away from strife.

> Leave foes alone, and give thine heart
> To such as will like love impart.
> The silly goat, so I have heard,
> Once kissed the fire, and lost his beard.

Who builds too fast builds not to last.

We have been inclined to christen certain rows of houses by the name of *Jonah's Gourds;* they are up in a night, and look as if they would perish in a night.

Who dainties love shall beggars prove.

The kitchen is the burial-place of the epicure's health and fortune. Queen Elizabeth, after going over a handsome mansion, observed, with her usual delicacy, "What a small kitchen!"   The owner wisely replied, "It is by having so small a kitchen that I am enabled to keep so large a house, and entertain your majesty"

Who doth sing so merry a note
As Jack that cannot change a groat?

So it happens that many poor hearts are merry where the rich are burdened with care.

Who cannot sing may whistle.

He can, in some way or other, express his cheerfulness, and increase the general harmony. We remember a man who was asked to lead the congregation, but he answered, " I cannot *sing* a tune ; but, if you like, I will whistle the Old Hundredth." What more could an organ have done ?

Who comes seldom is welcome.

A warning against wearing out your welcome by making yourself too common. People value you the more for being scarce.

Who eats his fowl alone may saddle his horse alone.

We cannot expect people to rush forward to help us in our work if we never give them a share in our pleasures and luxuries.

Who eats till he is sick must fast till he is well.

Too many alternate between repletion and depletion. They are like the alderman of whom it was said, " His talent is in his jaws, and the more he grinds the more he gets. From the quantity he devours, it might be supposed that he had two stomachs, like a cow, were it not manifest that he is no ruminating animal."

Who falls to-day may rise to-morrow.

Waldemar, King of Denmark, when struggling for his country, was accustomed to say, "There is yet another day," meaning that he would try again, and yet hope to succeed.

Who fears makes cause for fear.

" Oh, Mr. Coachman," cried a timid traveller by the York Mail in the good old coaching days, " Is there any fear ? " Jehu answered, " Plenty of fear, Madam, but no danger." But if Jehu had been afraid, there would have been danger enough.

Who felleth oaks must give great strokes.

The labour must be proportioned to the design. You cannot cut down a forest with a pair of scissors.

Who frets much because he hath little, will cert less.

Even if his property remains, it will bring les brings any. Fretting scrapes all the meat fro

I would not fret, if I were you,
Till fretting brings you meat to

Who gives his estate before he is dead,
Takes off his clothes before going to bed.

> Very unwise was King Lear, who did this. Wear your clothes till bedtime. Give away all you can spare, but retain the control of your property in your own hands, as long as you have hands.

Who gives not thanks to men, gives not thanks to God.

> He who is not grateful to his brother, whom he hath seen, how is he grateful to God whom he hath not seen? The least return we can make to benefactors is to be thankful.

Who gladdens not is not glad.

> For joy is pre-eminently contagious; and selfishness is its deadly foe. He who would shut the sunshine in, inevitably shuts it out.

Who goes softly goes safely.

Who halveth honey with a bear
Is like to get the smallest share.

> So to speak, the bear is sure to take the lion's share. He will be generous as to leaving you the bees and their stings, but your share of the honey will naturally stick to his paws.

"Who has drunk will drink."
I fear the charge is true;
And this it is which makes me think
You'd better wear the blue.

Who has made no mistake has made nothing.

> So natural is it to our fallible minds to make mistakes which are almost unavoidable, that he who has never blundered must have never acted; which, truth to tell, is the greatest blunder of all.

Who has never done thinking, never begins doing.

Who has no foes, has earned no friends.

> Usually we shall find that we may gauge our friends by our enemies. He who has warm opponents has warm advocates, and *vice versâ*. The energy of the man's personality, or its weakness, will be seen in its effects on those with whom he lives.

Who hath money to throw away,
Let him leave workmen alone all day.

> Wretchedly true in many cases. No master, no work. Talk of striking: it is more than striking to see how the pace quickens when the master is near!

Who has tasted a sour apple will have the more relish for a sweet one.

No doubt poverty endured makes wealth the more delicious when it comes; and he that has been long ill doubly enjoys health.

Who hunts two hares at once, catches none.

Divided aims ensure double disappointment.

Who is ill to his own, is ill to himself.

Especially in the case of wife and children: if a man does not make them comfortable, they will be no comfort to him.

Who is so deaf and blind as he
Who will not either hear or see?

Who judges others, condemns himself.

Who know don't talk; who talk don't know.

Frequently the case; though the rule has many exceptions.

Who knows where Crooked Lane will end?

It is easy to begin a tortuous policy; but to what will it lead you? It is easy to tell one lie, but very hard to tell *only* one lie.

Who laughs at crooked men had need walk very straight.

He invites criticism, and he deserves that it should be unmerciful. He strikes others, and therefore he ought to have it straight from the shoulder. His own measure should be returned into his bosom; and it should be " pressed down and running over."

Who lives at peace with God, and friend, and foe,
Shall rest in sleep when others do not so.

Who lives with a praying man may learn to pray.

He will, if that praying man acts as he prays, but not else.

Who loses cannot afford to laugh.

Poor man! he laughs on the other side of his face.

Who loves his son will chasten him; who hates him will pamper him.

The Chinese say that love will give the cudgel, and hate will cram with dainties. Let over-fond parents take note of this. Our Father in heaven does not err in this direction.

Who loves his work and knows to spare,
May live and flourish anywhere.

Who makes black white, will make white black.

> He justifies your wrong-doing, and he will as readily defame your well-doing. The flatterer readily becomes a slanderer.

Who many do feed,
Save much they had need.

Who must needs follow fashion may one day go naked.

> Things are looking that way already with ladies of the first quality, and hence a wag has said of them :—

> > "When dressed for the evening, the girls nowadays
> > Scarce an atom of dress on them leave.
> > Don't blame them; for what is an *evening* dress
> > But a dress that is suited to *Eve?*"

Who never tries, wins not the prize.

Who never warms, never burns.

> Some cannot be excited, and therefore never rise to action. We know some awfully cool fellows who might act as refrigerators for a shipload of New Zealand mutton. They might sit in an oven for a month and never get melted.

Who nothing save, will nothing have.

Who reckons without his host must reckon again.

> The host is sure to put down something which the guest forgets: he is not likely to abide by the guest's sole reckoning, and so the matter must be gone over again. Many come to conclusions without remembering all the main circumstances.

Who ripens fast, will seldom last.

Who rises late, must trot all day, and hardly overtake his
      business by night.

> Most true. One has been made to feel it if the bed has held him too long in its embrace. Yet there are creatures who snore out verses like this :—

> > Up in the morning's not for me ;
> > In the morning I am surly :
> > No fate can worse in winter be,
> > Than to rise in the morning early.

Who sees a pin and lets it lie,
May live to want it by-and-by.

Who sows beans, will reap beans.

> And it is the same with wild oats, and thistles. Our conduct brings its own reward or punishment.

Who steals a penny will steal a pound.

> If he can. He soon educates himself out of the roguery of taking paltry amounts, into the respectability of failing for thousands.

Who steals an egg would steal an ox.

Who strikes at mud will smear himself.

> If you assail an evil, you had better expect to be bespattered and evil entreated. It is part of the bargain in the case of every reformer. Don't take up the business if you can help it.

Who tells your fortune tells you lies ;
Who tells your faults has truthful eyes.

Who thinks himself singularly wise is a singular fool.

> Little harm will come of being stupid until the fellow thinks himself clever. Pretended wisdom is the worst of stupidity.

Who trifles with a loving heart,
Whip him at the tail of cart.

> Several parties have we known to whom this would apply. Jilting a loving girl is a crime for which flogging is too lenient a punishment. In love let us have sincerity. Say,
>
> > My hand and heart in one agree ;
> > I give my very self to thee.

Who trusts the morrow earneth sorrow.

> To-morrow is the tense of fools as to action, and the dream of the rash as to expectation. To postpone duty is to commit sin, and to make escape from it more difficult.
>
> > Let no man think he can repent too soon :
> > I found it midnight, ere I thought it noon.

Who undertakes very much will overtake very little.

> > Fools only make attempts beyond their skill :
> > A wise man's power's the limit of his will.

Who ventures to lend,
Loses money and friend.

Who wastes his time throws life away.

> " He liveth long who liveth well ;
> All else is being flung away ;
> He liveth longest who can tell
> Of true things truly done each day."

Who watches not catches not.

Many a golden chance goes by him unobserved.

Who weds a sot to get his cot,
Will lose the cot and keep the sot.

Thousands of times the little property has soon gone in drink, and the poor woman has had a drunken husband to keep all her life.

Who weds for dower resigns his power.

He sells himself to his rich wife, and is like a bull led by a ring in his nose. If she keeps my house up, she is likely to keep me down. The woman who buys a husband wastes her money.

Who will go far must not go fast.

Who will not be counselled cannot be helped.

As he refuses the wisdom of others, he has to learn it for himself when trouble overtakes him. The engine-driver who takes no notice of signals goes in for a smash. Yet many are angry at advice.

Who will not better the evil is an abettor of the evil.

By refusing to help a reform, he bolsters up the old wrong, and thus becomes a partaker in the evil deeds of the past by approving them, and in all similar deeds in the future by permitting them. Those who are not against sin are with it.

Who will not lend may come to borrow.

And when he comes to borrow, it will be of no use to come to those whom he refused his help. Who give no loan may want alone.

Who wills to fight will find a weapon.

Who work not the mill have not the meal.

That is a just rule, but it is not always carried out. Be a promoter of a company, then you may get the meal, and leave the mill to the shareholders, who will find it turn to *nil.*

Who would be great must first be little.

Sometimes it is greater to be little than to be great.

Who would deceive the devil must rise betimes.

Who would eat a good dinner, let him eat a good breakfast.

He had better get his food when he can. Moreover, he gets himself into condition by his breakfast, and will feel strong when dinner comes. We suspect that this is a proverb by which men of large appetite urge on their fellows, and excuse their own voracity. The old proverb is, "No breakfast, no man"; and if no man, there can be no dinner. No dinner, no stomach for the fight.

Who would have honey must put up with bees.

And in getting money, it would seem that men often put up with far worse things than stings. Many swallow much dirt while scraping up yellow dust. Let us hope that the lines are not true in which it is said :

"He who'd sit upon the woolsack, must be ne'er with conscience . curst,
And for *wool* to fill the cushion, he must take to *fleecing* first."

But, certainly, in certain methods of amassing wealth, there is more to put up with than an honest man will endure.

Who would heal a wound must not handle it.

In settling quarrels say as little as possible. Don't go over the ground again and again. Enter not into particulars which are of an exasperating nature. As a rule leave the details alone.

Why dig up a mountain to catch a rat ?

Why destroy a grand institution to destroy some minor evil ?

Why go bare to deck an heir ?

He will not thank you for it ; and if he does, you will not be there to hear him. Use your money for yourself, and the poor. Let not your heir call you a fool for being so miserly.

Why live poor to die rich ?

What is the use of dying rich ? O~
a certain miser had left a million of ı
shall leave more than that behí
the whole world, and all that ı
having to leave more than you

Why saddle your horse, if you will not ride?

> Why get an estate, and never enjoy it? Why get an education, and then do nothing with your learning?

Wickedness is great when great men are wicked.

> The poorer sort imitate them, and take great license from the kind of respectability which greatness lends to vice. It is bad enough in a private person to be vicious; but it would be worse in a peer, or a minister of state, or a magistrate, and worst of all in the chief of all.

Wilful makes woful, and such woe is the worst of woe.

Wilful people must have their own way.

> And that way will lead them into a churchyard, or a jail, or a county-court, or a workhouse, or a lunatic asylum.

Wilful pigs go forward if you pull them back.

> The more you say they shall not, the more they will. Invite them, and they will not come; refuse them admittance, and a regiment of soldiers could not keep them out.

Wilful waste makes woful want.

Will a black dog become a holy cow by merely going to Benares?

> Thus is the uselessness of merely outward religion illustrated among the Hindoos.

Will the headache be cured by changing the pillow?

Will to work, and work with a will.

> For in these days, wealth comes not by chance; but, as a rule,
>
>   Good striving
>   Brings thriving.

Willows are weak, but they bind other wood.

> So, many a gentle, tender woman is the bond of the family, and all feel that she holds them in loving union.

Wilt thou my true friend be?
Then love not mine, but me.

> Cupboard love is not worth keeping even in a cupboard. He loves me not who loves me for what I have, and not for what I am.

Win gold and wear it, is the motto of the vain man.
Win gold and share it, of the generous man.
Win gold and spare it, of the miser.
Win gold and spend it, of the profligate.
Win gold and lend it, of the broker.
Win gold and lose it, of the gambler.
Win gold and use it, of the wise man.

> If you never win gold at all, you may be all the better man.
> Better be a man *of* mettle than a man *with* metal!

Wind and tide for no man bide.

Windfalls are generally rotten.

> Persons who are waiting for legacies, or unusual strokes of luck, are almost always deceived. Pick your fruit yourself, and don't wait in idleness for that which may never come.

Wine drowns more than the sea.

> Alas, what wrecks it has caused! Souls here are lost for ever.

Winking sets me thinking.

> This old proverb makes me feel somewhat ill at ease in the presence of persons who have a knowing wink.
>
> > He that winks with one eye, and sees with the other,
> > I would not trust him, though he were my brother.

Winter finds out what summer lays up.

> Then come forth the " poor frozen-out gardeners," or those who pretend to be such. They did not lay up a shilling in summer, and in winter they appeal to the pity of the provident.

Wisdom does not always speak Latin.

> Words hard to be understood are marks of pedantry, and not of understanding. Friendship loves plain speech.
>
> > Not quibbling quirks, but simple speech,
> > True friends should deal in, each with each.

Wisdom is a good bargain, cost what it may.

> Especially the heavenly wisdom which makes wise :

Wisdom is the wealth of the wise.

> Wisdom is better without an inheritance
> without wisdom.

Wisdom must be wooed ere it is won.

Wisdom never forces herself on men. If we use lock and bolt to keep her out, she will make no forcible entry. If an empty bottle is corked up, you may throw it into the sea, but it will not be filled thereby. Wisdom will only flow in where there is a clear entrance for it. Few men will ever be hanged for being too wise.

Wisdom spun too fine is folly.

Mere pedantry is not true learning, and prudishness is not prudence. A man may be so exactly right as to be practically wrong; so unspeakably wise as to be a marvellous fool.

Wise men change their minds; fools have none to change.

Wise men give good counsel, but wiser men take it.

It requires more true sense to be willing to be guided, than to act as a guide. Humility is a scarce grace, but it is the hall-mark of genuine wisdom. Take counsel, that thy counsel may be taken.

Wise men sue for offices, and blockheads get them.

So that the blockheads were 'cuter than the wise men. Is that so? Or is this the snarl of a disappointed candidate?

Wise mice keep away from the trap.

They do not go near it to investigate it, and see how far they can go into it without peril. Prudent men keep clear of the temptation, that it may not overcome them.

Wise words and lengthy seldom agree.

One has wittily and paradoxically said, "The smaller the calibre of the mind, the greater the *bore* of the perpetually open mouth." The wise man is like a dealer in diamonds—his goods go in small compass. Great thoughts seldom fill a great space.

Wish and wish; but who'll fill the dish?

The Chinese say, "Better go home, and make a net, than go down the river desiring to catch fishes." You cannot slake your thirst by wishing for lemonade; nor obtain salvation by wishing you had believed; nor grow in grace by wishing for edification.

Wish to be what you are, and you have what you wish.

Wishers and woulders are poor householders.

Wishes are very small fishes for our dishes, and might-have-beens are poor vegetables to eat with them.

Wit is folly unless a wise man hath the keeping of it.

It may be wit to enter a stable and steal a horse in fun, but it is wisdom to let it alone. Practical jokers are fools in bloom.

Wit must be bought if it cannot be taught.
Wit once bought is worth twice taught.

Because you have really learned it, and are never likely to forget it. No doubt the birch has been the tree of knowledge to many a boy, and trial has been the same to many a man.

Wit without wisdom is mustard without beef.

It is the flavouring with nothing to flavour. It is no joke to be always joking. When a jest cannot be digested it is sickening. Stale puns ought to be made punishable offences : he who deals in them is as bad as the seller of ancient mackerel.

With a staircase before you, you look for a rope to go down by.

Some persons never will follow the ordinary and easy plan of going to work, but must find out some out-of-the-way way. Why, even in going to heaven, the plain way of believing is often set aside that silly speculations may be tried.

With gold spectacles, men see strange things.

> What makes all kinds of reasoning clear ?
> About five hundred pounds a year !
> And all seem black was white before ?
> Why, something like five hundred more !

With great caution choose a wife :
Once you're wed, you're tied for life.

Happy will you be if you find a wife like the lady whose epitaph thus describes her :

> She was——, but words are wanted to say what.
> Think what a wife should be, and she was that.

With lands, houses, and gold,
Men are rarely too bold.

Capital is tender and conservative. He who he fears no risk ; but he who has much to guard h himself in peril. "Throw stones, boys : I have

With morning prayer the day begin;
With evening prayer the night shut in;
With grateful thanks sit down to eat:
Thus much from Christian man is meet.

With seven nurses a child will be without eyes.

> Some serious omission or commission will injure the unhappy babe who has so many to look after it, and no one to be wholly responsible for it. With eight nurses it will have no head.

With shoes one can walk upon thorns.

> Being duly protected we can trample upon trouble. See how Paul would have our feet shod. Ephesians vi. 15.

With sour and sweet
We eat life's meat.

> Days change the flavouring, and the change is for our profit.

With tooth and nail
'Gainst debt prevail.

With truth at your back,
Though helpers you lack,
Yet fear no attack.

> But some, nowadays, will do anything but suffer for the truth. They must think the martyrs great fools; for they don't think any doctrine is worth living for, much less dying for. We cannot call them all heterodox, and yet they are not orthodox: to us they are a paradox, and to many they are stumbling-blocks.

Without economy none can be rich; but with economy few need be poor.

> Economy in the beginning of life, before marriage, is the only way of rising in the world. Economy is the price of comfort.

Without going you can get nowhere.

> This is a Chinese saying. It is self-evident; and yet inactive and hesitating people may need to be reminded of it.

Without the doctor one dies a natural death.

Without the sun, what can be done!

> To ripen the fruits of the earth, or to give health to the sick, the sun's shining is of the first importance.

Wits are often unwittingly wise.

Such men fall upon good thoughts by accident, but they are not in the regular line of them. They flash now and then, but they do not burn with a steady light: they seem to be saving it up for special displays, as *Butler* says of one of his heroes :—

> " We grant, altho' he had much wit,
> He was very shy of using it,
> As being loth to wear it out,
> And, therefore, bore it not about,
> Unless on holidays or so,
> As men their best apparel do."

Woe to him who worries the weary.

Woe to the house where children are never chidden.

Woe will surely come. Unchecked, the youthful savages will tear their parents' hearts. Without rule, without peace.

**Woes have come to courts and kings
Through neglect of trifling things.**

Woman is the Sunday of man.

She helps his rest, his joy, his elevation, his sanctification. We do not quote this because the proverb is " Women must be praised "; but because by experience we have found it true.

Woman, with all thy faults, I love thee still.

"But when is she still?" cries the ungallant bachelor. The old rhyme is worth preserving :—

> " A woman once, as it is sung,
> Could speak so loud without a tongue,
> That they could hear her full a mile hence.
> A greater wonder I can tell :
> I knew a woman very well
> Who had a tongue, and yet kept silence."

I also know some of the quietest of mortals, and it Still, it is a rare thing for a lady to be at a loss for

Women, on a sudden, are wiser than men.

They leap by instinct where men climb by rea'

Women talk less in February than in a]

Because it is the shortest month. This is but the women are not so ungenerous as to

Woo to win, and win to wed.

No man who is worthy of the name will act otherwise. Yet some like to play at wooing, and after a while cast off a tender heart as if it were an old glove.

> He who courts and runs away,
> May live to court another day;
> But he who courts, and will not wed,
> May find himself in court instead.

Words are good when works follow.

Otherwise, "Words won't feed cats." Mere words become like the snow which fell last year, and has left no trace behind it.

Words are not work, as froth is not beer.
Words are very like the wind:
Faithful friend 'tis hard to find.
Words buy no wheat, but make much chaff.

Words are sometimes the signs of ideas, and sometimes of the want of them. When men talk for the sake of fine words, they are playing with the tools they ought to work with.

Words once spoken cannot be wiped out with a sponge.

Oh, that they could be! Alas, they are spoken in a moment, but they may live through centuries. Our words diminish or increase the sum of human happiness throughout our own generation, and all the generations that are to follow.

Work as if thou'dst live for aye;
Pray as if thou'dst die to-day.

Give both this world and the next its due. Work as if all depended on *you;* pray because all depends on God.

Work is a fine tonic.

It braces both soul and body, and helps us to cast off those nervous forebodings which haunt the inactive.

Work warms when coals are dear.

And the warmth is much healthier and cheaper, too, than that which comes through roasting yourself at a stove. Some people in waiting-rooms take up all the fire, and toast themselves so that you wish you could find a fork to take them off with.

Work when you work, and play when you play.

Do one thing or the other. It aggravates an employer to see a fellow fooling when he should be steadily toiling. He who gives in work a little more than his master can claim is seldom sent adrift. Employers know when a man is worth his money.

> He that to be obliging tries
> Is sure of work where'er he hies.

A mixture of work and play is poor stuff. It brings a workman into disrepute. You are not hired to be a merry-andrew.

Workmen are easier found than masters.

Hands you can get by the thousands, but heads are scarcer far. A man can always find a servant, but a servant cannot so soon find a master to employ him.

Worldly good is ebb and flood.

It is for ever changing, like the troubled sea, which cannot rest.

Worldly riches are like nuts.

Many clothes are torn in getting them, many a tooth is broken in cracking them, but never a belly filled with eating them. If you have wealth, use it as you would wish another to use it if you had none yourself. Call other folks in to have a crack with you when your basket is full of nuts.

Would you be thanked for feeding your own pigs?

We cannot expect gratitude for serving our own turn; yet some seem to look for it. Let them look. Who serves himself may pay himself. Let his own pigs grunt his lordship's praises.

Would you live an angel's days?
Be holy, wise, and kind always.

Wouldst live in peace?
From gossip cease.

But the regular gossip cannot cease. She is a fifth of November cracker, and, being once let off, she must fizz and crack till there's nothing left of her but a spent case. Poor dear!

Wouldst thou rule the world, first rule thyself.

This is true royalty. The ambition which makes us seek self-conquest is a virtue.

Wranglers are never in the wrong.

They will not hear reason. They are in too much heat of temper to consider that there are two sides to a question. Don't wrangle with them; there's no use in it: as well try to teach a pack of hounds to say the Shorter Catechism.

Wranglers never want words though they may want matter.

It is wonderful what a lot of grievances you can conjure up when you try, and what faults you can allege when you are in the humour. What is the use of it? It may be well to be Senior Wrangler at Cambridge, but I would neither wish to be senior nor junior in that line anywhere else, except it were at Oxford.

> Be not angry with each other;
> Man is made to love his brother.

Wrinkled purses make wrinkled faces.

> A lonely penny in the purse,
> And need increasing worse and worse,
> Will make a man's face very blue,
> I know it well, and so may you.

Sayings of a more Spiritual Sort.

Wait for God's grace, for he waiteth to be gracious.

Watch against weariness *in* prayer, or you may soon be weary *of* prayer.

We are never right till we are right with God.

We are not saved by feeling, nor without feeling.

> We are saved by faith, and not by feeling; but being made alive unto God, we necessarily feel both joys and sorrows of a spiritual kind. He that does not feel does not live.

We are not to make our experience the rule of Scripture, but Scripture the rule of our experience.

We are undeserving, ill-deserving, hell-deserving sinners.

> A confession often made in the prayers of good men a generation back, but seldom heard now. Why the omission? Is it because the men of the present day are so much better and worthier than those of the past? Is it not rather because they have a less vivid perception of the evil of sin and of their own guiltiness? Not long since, one said frankly that he did not think himself bad enough to go to hell; and there is no doubt that many are of the same opinion. They agree with the Duchess of Buckingham, who wrote to Lady Huntingdon that "it is monstrous to be told that you have a heart as sinful as the common wretches that crawl on the earth." But there is no hope of any being admitted to heaven who are not brought to acknowledge that they might justly be sent to hell.

We become happier than others, not by having more goods, but by doing more good.

We believe, but God gives us faith.

> It is important to remember that we must ourselves believe. The Holy Spirit does not believe for us.

We burn our Master's candles; let mind our Master's work.

We cannot trust God too much, nor ourselves too little

We fear men much, because we fear God little.

We fell by standing against God ; we shall stand by falling before him.

We know the true fold by the presence of the Great Shepherd.

> This is the test of a true Church. Where the Shepherd is, there is the chosen flock and the true fold. Whatever be the place of worship or the form of church government, if the Lord Jesus is there, no friend of his need be afraid to be with him.

We lie to God in prayer, if we do not rely on him after prayer.

> Prayer without faith is a kind of mockery.

We may pray to live, if we live to pray.

> For prayer is of the utmost value to the church and to the world, that we may desire to live to bless our age by its means.

We must be born twice, or we shall die twice.

We must be self-searchers, but not self-seekers.

We must believe to see, not see to believe.

> By faith realize the great goodness of the Lord, and do not wait to see what God will do before you believe his Word. Faith which depends upon sight is no faith at all.

We must not let crosses load us down, but we must lift them up and carry them.

We need to feel the storm that we may know the worth of the anchor.

> The storm-tossed Christian proves the staying power of faith. When the promise has been tried and proved, we value it.

We serve the devil if we serve not Christ.

> "The poet has put an awful truth into the lips of the father of lies, when he makes him say to Cain—
>
> 'He who does not bow to *him* has bow'd to me.'"

We work, not *for* life, but *from* life.

> I would not work my soul to save ;
> That work my Lord has done ;
> But I will work, like any slave,
> For love of God's dear Son.

Weak grace may *do* for God, but it must be *strong* grace to *die* for God.

"Have you grace enough to be burned at the stake?" was the question once put to Mr. Moody, who answered in the negative. "Do you not wish that you had?" "No, sir, for I do not need it. What I need just now is grace to live in Milwaukee three days and hold a convention."

Weave in faith, and God will find thread.

Weekly services neglected, make weakly Christians.

There is a proverb in Scotland, that "Mony ane will gang a mile tae hear a sang that winna gang a foot tae hear a sermon." A certain United Presbyterian Church in the North of England was the scene of two evening meetings in one week, viz., an evangelistic meeting and a concert, or service of song. A Scripture reader in connection with the congregation, while on her diurnal rounds, came in contact with a douce old Scotchman, a member of the church. "Now, David," queried the good woman, "are ye comin' up tae the meeting this week?" "Oh, ay," exclaimed the canny Scot, "I maun come tae the meeting: for I ken some o' the folk that's gaun to sing." "Tuts!" exclaimed his interrogator, "it's no the concert; it's the ither meeting I mean." "Oh!" sighed the devout Scot, "I dinna think that I can come; for you see I am sae tired at night that I can hardly stir aff my chair."

Well doth the good old proverb speak—
"As the Sunday, so the week."

What God's purpose plans, God's power performs.

What is anyone the better for ordinances, unless he be bettered by ordinances?

For in themselves, the outward forms are valueless: unless they are the channels of blessing, they are of no more use than old lead pipes when the water is cut off.

What the Papists cry up as the mother of devi
we cry down as the father of superstitio

Ignorance will smother true devotion. Kno
worship. God asks not a blind faith; for suc'
faith of blindness and darkness; and "God is

What we neither feel nor see,
We by faith believe to be.

"Faith is the substance of things ho]
things not seen."—Heb. xi. 1.

What we weave in time we must wear in eternity.

What we win with prayer we should wear with praise.

Whatsoever is not above the top of nature is below the bottom of grace.

The work of grace, at its lowest degree, is above the highest effort of nature at its very best.

Wheat and tares may grow together, but they shall not remain together.

The separation which cannot be wisely attempted by man will be perfectly accomplished by the Lord. What a mixture all our assemblies are! How true are *Herrick's* lines:—

"In holy meetings, there a man may be
One of the crowd, not of the company."

Wheat in a barn is better than chaff in a church.

Just so. A few poor saints in the meanest room excel all the unconverted nobility and gentry of the district when assembled in the most magnificent cathedral.

When a saint at God's bidding can stand still, 'tis an evidence that he will soon go forward.

Thus Israel, at the Red Sea, learned to stand still and see the salvation of God, and then came the word, "Go forward."

When Christians are rusty they're apt to turn crusty.

Doing nothing, they growl at those who are workers.

When Christians dispute, worldlings deride.

They cannot say, "See how these Christians love one another!"

When clouds are heavy, blessings are near.

When God makes us his children, he makes us brothers.

When God wills, our ills are wells.

He brings good out of evil; and makes the bitter sweet.

When God would work, his tools are ready.

In fact, he can use any tool: he can use *me*. The Lord's strength gets glory through our weakness.

When God's Word is opened, may our hearts be opened.

We read, "He opened to us the Scriptures"; and in the same chapter, "Then opened he their understanding."—Luke xxiv. 32, 45.

When mercy is rejected, judgment may be expected.

When once a man becomes a god to himself, he then becomes a devil to others.

He is so lifted up with pride that he plays the tyrant. Because Nebuchadnezzar was so proud, he threw those into a fiery furnace who would not obey his will. Good to yourself, evil to others.

When prayer leads the van, deliverance brings up the rear.

When the leaf falls,
To repentance it calls.

Or, "When leaves are falling, wisdom is calling."

When the sea is without waves, saints will be without trials.

This will come when they stand on the sea of glass, and not till then. Were we without trials, we might doubt our sonship; for "What son is there whom his father chasteneth not?"—Heb. xii. 7.

When the sun is set, we are all in the shade.

General calamity impoverishes all. When the Lord's Spirit leaves the church, we all suffer through his absence.

When the world is bitter, the Word is sweet.

When we are in Satan's hand, *he* is in God's hand.

God has a chain on the enemy, even when he gives him most latitude. He may rule as he wills, but the Lord overrules him.

When weeds are uprooted, good plants are in danger.

Hence the need of great care in discipline, lest in removing tares we destroy wheat. We need equal care in rebuking error, lest we destroy truth with falsehood.

When you rest, rest from sin.

It is the only true rest, for sin is a troubled sea. Those who allow themselves to enter sinful places, because they are taking a vacation, disgrace their vocation.

when you play,
ent-day.

Where can that soul stay, which stays not itself upon
God?

Where death finds you, eternity binds you.

> Despite all that is said to the contrary, this is the plain teaching
> of the Scriptures of truth.

Where death leaves us, judgment finds us.

> All that men have done or said
> Lives when they themselves are dead.
>
> And when they are called to judgment they will find the things
> done in the body there to confound and to condemn them.

Where God becomes a donor, man becomes a debtor.

> Every gift of grace involves a debt of gratitude.

Where the Scripture hath no tongue to speak, we should
have no ear to hear.

> If we are wise above what is written, we are presumptuously
> foolish. What the Lord does not reveal we should not wish to
> know. Beyond revelation all is speculation.

Where there's no repentance there's no religion.

While guile remains, guilt is not removed.

> With forgiveness of sin there comes honesty of mind. "Blessed
> is the man unto whom the Lord imputeth not iniquity, and in whose
> spirit there is no guile."—Ps. xxxii. 2.

While thou livest, pray; and as thou prayest, live.

Who has charge of souls cannot carry them in bundles.

> Each one will need a special treatment for its peculiar case.

Who has no thirst, has no business at the fountain.

> Hence our needs give us a right at the mercy-seat. "*No admis-
> sion except on business*" is true of communion with God. None do
> come to God, and none *can* come to him, except on an errand of
> necessity. Necessity is the mother of supplication.

Who prays in grief, secures relief.

> And then he must take care to give glory to God for the gracious
> answer to prayer which has been vouchsafed to him.
>
> > Prayers and praises go in pairs:
> > They have praises who have prayers.

Whom free grace chooses, free grace cleanses.

Whom God calls, he qualifies.

> Hence we may be sure that a man is not called to an office for which he is utterly unfit. A being meant to fly has wings given it. If a man is meant for preaching he will have brain and tongue bestowed upon him.

Whom God will make, the devil cannot mar.

Woe be to him whose advocate becomes his accuser.

> When the Saviour shall witness against us, and our own conscience shall condemn us, how shall we escape?

Women were last at the cross and first at the sepulchre.

> " Not she with trait'rous kiss her Saviour stung,
> Not she denied him with unholy tongue ;
> She, while apostles shrank, could danger brave,
> Last at his cross, and earliest at his grave."

Worldlings make gold their god; saints find God their gold.

Worldly delights are winged delights.

> Soon do they fly away : why trust in them ?

YEARS know more than books.

Yielding is sometimes the best way of succeeding.

We may stoop and pick up victory. To yield a part for the sake of the whole is good economy. To yield one's right is often better than the right. We may gain by kindly giving way.

You a lady and I a lady, who's to clean the saucepans?

If everybody must be great, how will the common duties of life be performed? This is not a fit world for finery; yet people talk of their gentility.

"Genteel it is to have soft hands,
But not genteel to work on lands;
Genteel it is to lie in bed,
But not genteel to earn your bread."

You are not everybody in the world, and the man in the moon too.

But many a man talks as if he were cock of the walk, and king of the castle. He and his friends are all the plums in the pudding: if they were gone, the rest would be the commonest duff.

In men this blunder still you find:
All think their little set mankind.

You are rich if you want no more.

You break my head, and then bring me a plaster.

All very fine; but it would have been better if the wound had never been made. At the same time, if we have injured another accidentally, he ought not to resent our kindly endeavours to make amends. All we can say is:—

"Take all in good part, whoever thou be,
And wish me no worse than I wish unto thee."

You can break an egg without a sledge hammer.

Why speak so fiercely when a gentle word will do?

You *can* catch some old birds with chaff.

Though a proverb declares that you cannot, it is very often done. The very knowing are often very silly.

You can promise more in a minute that you can perform in a month.

You cannot call back yesterday.

You cannot climb a ladder by pushing others down.

> Some seem to imagine that if they lower another in public estimation, they thereby rise themselves. They are much mistaken.

You cannot dig a well with a needle.

> Adapt your means to your end.

You cannot draw a straight line with a crooked square.

> False doctrine will not produce good living.

You cannot drink and whistle at the same time.

> The child said, "I want to go home to dinner, and I want to stop here and sail my boat." Then he began to cry, because he could not have both his ways at once. We must not be so childish, but must give up one thing for another. Let us forego earth for heaven, and the praise of men for the glory of God.

You cannot eat your cake and have it too.

> If the cake be eaten, it cannot be brought out to-morrow. If the food is saved, the children will not be fat and strong. We cannot have the thing in two forms. If you spend money discreetly, there is the pleasure; if you save it frugally, there is the interest.

You cannot fill a chest with grace, nor a heart with gold.

You cannot get more out of a bottle than you put in it.

> That is an error. Besides what you put in, you can get out of it an aching head, a sick stomach, a lost situation, and perhaps a fine of five shillings, or a few days in prison.

You cannot have a good pennyworth of bad ware.

> However many bad razors you buy, you can't shave. However many rotten apples you get for your money, you can't eat them. Yet cheapness is everything nowadays, and things are made to sell, for they say :—
>> What is the worth of anything
>> But how much money it will bring ?

You cannot have a sandwich all of meat, nor a life all holiday.

You cannot have foreknowledge, but you should have forethought.

You cannot have two mornings in the same day.

Nor can you expect to be youthful twice. Opportunities do not return. Use your morning lest you have cause for mourning.

You cannot know wine by the barrel.

If men were honest you would, if you wanted to.

You cannot make good broth without meat.

Solid matter is required for the making of a good sermon.

You cannot pull hard with a broken rope.

Nor do much with a gospel in which you do not believe.

You cannot push a man far up a tree.

He must exert himself and climb by his own efforts. We can do very little for one who does not help himself, and he deserves even less than we can do.

You cannot scold a man out of his sins.

Let us try the gentler way, and see what can be done by prayerful, loving persuasion.

> Let's find the sunny side of men,
>   Or be believers in it :
> Wrath shuts the heart against the truth,
>   But love will surely win it.

You cannot swallow dates whole.

The stone must be taken out, and the fruit masticated. So it is with what we hear : we must discern and divide.

You cannot work in iron with a wooden file.

To deal with the sin of man you must have the solid truth of revelation, and of God's law, or you will labour for nothing.

You can't be lost on a straight road.

I am not sure of this. Some seem to have the heavenly road right before their eyes, and they do not know it. Still the proverb is a good one, in one sense. Keep straight in the straight road.

You can't burn the faggot and have it.

To the same effect is the other proverb, "You can't keep a fire and keep the coal too."

You can't catch a cow in a cobweb.

Nor hold your heart to virtue by vows and promises made in your own strength. Nor alter facts by sophistical arguments.

You can't catch hares with unwilling hounds.

No hearts can be won by us unless we heartily desire it. Earnestness is in most things essential to success.

You can't draw a waggon with a hair.

Things must be proportionate and adequate.

You can't drive a nail into nothing.

Where there is no mind to retain your teaching, labour is lost.

You can't drown me in a spoonful of water.

I am able to bear what little you can inflict.

You can't earn your breakfast by lying in bed,
And if you won't work, you shall not be fed.

You can't expect pippins from a crabtree.

Nor figs from brambles : every man acts according to his nature.

You can't get good chickens from bad eggs.

When the design is bad, we may not hope for good results from it. Bad doctrine will not produce good lives.

You can't hang soft cheese on a hook, nor drive a nail of wax.

Some people are too limp for you to do anything with them.

You can't kick when your leg is off.

When you have lost your power it is idle to threaten.

You can't lay eggs, so don't cackle.

He that cannot help should not criticize.

You can't make a silk purse out of a sow's ear.

> Nor turn a boor into a gentleman.

You can't make pork pies out of pig iron.

You can't pass a rope through a needle's eye.

You can't shave a man's head in his absence.

You can't sing the savageness out of a bear.

You can't steer too far off danger.

You can't swim across the Thames by hanging on to a dog's tail.

> Nor can you attain great things by following mean means.

You can't tell a nut till you crack it.

> So the street-sellers say, "Try 'em before you buy 'em."
> "Prove all things; hold fast that which is good."—1 Thess. v. 21.

You can't turn charcoal into chalk by a thousand washings.

> A change of nature is needed both in men and charcoal; and only a miracle can change one or the other.

You carry fire in one hand, and water in the other.

> Blessing and cursing cannot both be kept;
> Fire in your right hand, water in your left.

You come a day after the fair.

You come of the McTakes, but not of the McGives.

> Always ready to absorb, but never willing to disperse. Who cares for you?

You drink out of the broad end of the funnel, and hold the little one to me.

You feed me with an empty spoon.

> You promise, and flatter, but you give me nothing.

You have debts, and make debts still;
If you've not lied, lie you will.

> Debtors make false promises, to put off pressure for payment. Debt is the death of truth; true men should hate it.

You have hit once, but don't always be shooting.

You spoke well once : don't be for ever speechifying. One venture has succeeded ; but do not become the slave of speculation.

You have kissed the Blarney Stone.

Though never in Ireland, some men have learned the art of gammoning, and laying on butter with a trowel.

You have less than you desire, but more than you deserve.

Therefore, find contentment in the consideration of free grace.

You have no more sense than a sucking turkey.

A cutting speech for a downright simpleton. Some have not the sense they were born with : you might pass them through a sieve, and never shake a dust of wit out of them.

You have run long on little ground.

How many talk without end, and all about nothing !

You may be right, but do not fight.

You may gape long before roast chicken will fly into your mouth.

Chance and expectation lead to nothing. Earn what you want.

You may grow good corn in a little field.

In a small sphere, with slender abilities, one may achieve very noble results.

You may hide the fire, but not the smoke.

Your action may not be seen, but the consequence will appear. You may be quiet yourself, but people will talk.

You may hold an eel so fast as to let it go.

You may judge a girl by her mother.

For the daughter is very apt to copy the mother, and she is very seldom an improvement upon her.

Now, young man, before you court her,
From the mother learn the daughter.

You may know a foolish woman by her finery.

The silly woman lives at the sign of " The Flowery Bonnet."

You *may* live, but you *must* die.

The proverb, "Young men may die, but old men must," has another shade of meaning. This applies to all alike: "It is appointed unto men once to die." Prepare for the necessity of death, and you will be prepared for the contingency of living. It would be a huge calamity if we were bound for ever to remain in this poor life.

> "I couldn't live for ever;
> I wouldn't if I could;
> But I needn't fret about it,
> For I couldn't if I would."

You may lose in an hour the work of a lifetime.

One false move throws away the game. A whole life-story may hinge upon the transactions of an hour.

You may milk a cow too often.

The most generous person may be worried into refusing to give at all. A man cannot always be giving. You may milk the cow oftener than is right, but you won't get any the more milk.

You may walk a long time behind a goose before you will pick up an ostrich feather.

And listen a long time to some talkers before you hear anything worth remembering.

You must contrive to bake with the flour you have.

If you cannot get all the materials you wish, you must work up those which are given you, and make the best of them. Be the flour what it may, let the bread-making be as good as good can be.

You must not throw your snails into your neighbour's garden.

You must put up with a great deal if you would put down a great deal.

The reformer must endure a world of misrepresentation, disappointment and enmity. You cannot vanquish "the armies of the aliens" without warfare and wounds. This work is for brave hearts only. "What man is there that is fearful and faint-hearted? let him go and return unto his house."—Deut. xx. 8.

You must spoil before you spin.

In learning any art we must expect some failures. Every speaker has his break-downs, as every potter has his broken pots.

You must take all the Bible or none.

It stands or falls together. He to whom it belongs will no more yield to its being divided, than the true mother, in Solomon's day, would consent to the dividing of the living child.

You mustn't tie up a hound with a string of sausages.

To try to check sin by a measure of indulgence in it is absurd.

You need iron nails to fight with a bear.

In such a conflict, hard must meet hard; and as we are not thus fashioned, we shun the contest with hard, unfeeling men.

You need not jump over the house to open the window.

Do not exert yourself more than is needed to effect your purpose. To accept a great and useful truth, it is not needful to become an all-knowing philosopher, and solve the secret of the unconditioned and the absolute.

You need not provide frogs for the well you have dug.

Nor mice for your barley-mow. They will come naturally. Neither need you instruct young men in vices, nor girls in follies.

You need not teach a bull to bellow.

That which nature teaches of itself you need not inculcate.

You plough with an ox that will not miss a furrow.

A good, careful, painstaking worker shirks nothing.

You pour water into a sieve.

When you give to a spendthrift, or invest in speculative companies. In trying to help shiftless ne'er-do-wells it is much the same.

You trust a great weight to a slender thread.

Especially if you trust your soul to a priest, or risk eternity on an uncertain to-morrow.

You want a little licking into shape.

It was the belief of the older naturalists that bears lick their whelps into proper form while they are yet young and tender. This is a fable; but it illustrates the duty of parents to fashion the crude mind; and it also shows how Providence does, in very deed, "shape our ends, rough-hew them how we will."

You want better bread than wheaten.

And better milk than cows can give. Some are never satisfied.

You were put out of the oven for nipping the pies.

Hislop parallels this with the charge which a vulgar street boy brought against another:—"You was put out of the work'us for eating the number off your plate."

You will find critics to be as common as crickets.

Fellows who cannot write a line will criticize a poem. Once a critic was a good judge; but now he is simply an unmerciful fault-finder, two steps above a fool, but a great many below a wise man. Alas! that, in reference to Holy Scripture, we should be pestered with fellows who criticize things which they cannot understand.

> For truth is precious and divine;
> Too rich a pearl for carnal swine.

You will never please everybody.

Remember the fable of "The Old Man and his Ass." If you please God always, and your wife generally, be quite content.

You will not be loved yourself if you love none but yourself.

You would talk a horse's hind leg off.

Or chatter a cat to death, or beat a magpie into fits.

> A dearth of words we need not fear;
> But 'tis a task to learn to hear.

You'd do well in Lubberland, where they have half-a-crown a day for sleeping.

. That is to say, you are a lazy fellow, not worth your salt.

You'll find it true,
The morning dew
Gives healthy hue.

It would be advisable to get up early and see if it be not so. It is due to the dew that we duly give it a fair trial.

You'll not put out the fire with tow.

Nor stay anger with provoking words.

You're in and out, like a dog at a fair.

> Said of a person who seems to be everywhere, and especially where he is not wanted.

You're worse than a brute if you treat brutes cruelly.

> None of my readers would do this himself; but it is also our duty never to let others do it without a vigorous protest.

Young idlers become old thieves.

Young people, like soft wax, soon take an impression.

> " Ere your boy has reached to seven,
> Teach him well the way to heaven ;
> Better still the work will thrive,
> If he learns before he's five."

Your choice of a wife will flavour your life.

Your dirty shoes are not welcome in my parlour.

> *You* are welcome, but not those boots which spoil my carpets.

Your geese are not swans.

> They are ordinary birds after all. Do not exaggerate, lest people should say, " He has a deal of thunder, and very little rain."

Your head should save your heels.

Your own legs are better than stilts.

> If you depend upon yourself, you will do better than if you get help from others. It also means that the natural is better than the artificial. Let the speaker use his own voice, manner, and matter, and they will suit him far better than those he imitates.

Your shoes will not fit everybody.

> Nor your ways, methods, and beliefs, suit all people. Do not try to force them upon others.

Your talk travels on, and on, and on ; and yet it goes no further than all round the gooseberry bush.

Your wit will never worry you.

> Very few need fret on that score.

Youth's too hot and bold ;
Age too weak and cold.

Sayings of a more Spiritual Sort.

Yokes are good for youthful shoulders.

> As with young bullock newly broke,
> Our neck must learn to bear the yoke.

You can be an honest man and not a Christian; but you cannot be a Christian and not be an honest man.

You cannot wrestle with God, and wrangle with your neighbour.

You have only one soul, give it to your one Saviour.

You may have much in little where others have little in much.

> A man's life consists not in what he possesses; fitness and content are all important.

> > A little hearth best fits a little fire,
> > A little chapel fits a little choir,
> > My little bell best fits my little spire.

You must be divorced from the law to be married to Christ.

> Yet some would be both under law and gospel at the same time: but the double marriage is contrary both to law and gospel. If it be of works, it cannot be of grace.

Your trust is worthy when you trust the trust-worthy.

> Look well to the ground of your faith, that it be strong enough to bear up your soul.

> > Little pillars, it is plain,
> > Cannot heavy weights sustain.

ZEAL and discretion are like the two lions which supported the throne of Solomon.

They make a fine pair; but are poor things apart. Zeal without discretion is wildfire, and discretion without zeal is cowardice.

Zeal is fit only for wise men, but is mostly found in fools.

The more's the pity if so it be.

Zeal is like fire; it needs both feeding and watching.

It is a good servant, but a bad master. In the one case it is earnestness; in the other fanaticism.

Zeal pleaseth God, for zeal is the love of God in man.

Zeal without knowledge is a runaway horse.

Nobody knows where it will go, or what mischief it will do. In these dull times we are almost eager to run the risk. We are overdone with rocking-horse without life or progress.

Zeal without knowledge is fire without light, and knowledge without zeal is light without fire.

Zeal without knowledge is like haste to a man in the dark.

It leads to blunders and accidents.

Zeal without knowledge soon becomes cold.

There is nothing to feed its fires, and so it dies down, and is very hard to re-kindle.

Alabaster, Passmore, & Sons, Printers, Fann Street, Aldersgate Street, E C.

TYPES AND EMBLEMS: A Collection of Sermons
preached on Sunday and Thursday Evenings at the Metropolitan Tabernacle. By C. H. Spurgeon. 3s.

"It will be sure to be a favourite. ' Types and Emblems' are attractive themes, and in Mr. Spurgeon's hands they neither lack suggestiveness nor power. All his well-known qualities as a preacher are in great force throughout this volume."—*General Baptist Magazine.*

TRUMPET CALLS TO CHRISTIAN ENERGY: A
Second Series of Sunday and Thursday Evening Sermons. 3s. 6d.

"The aim in each of these addresses is the simple one of rousing Christian men and women to renewed activity for God. Believing them to be eminently calculated to do good, we wish them a wide circulation."—*Rock.*

THE PRESENT TRUTH: A Third Series of Sunday
and Thursday Evening Sermons, 3s. 6d.

"Each discourse has the genuine gospel ring that proves it to have been coined in the mint of heaven. No better gift-book could be suggested for an unconverted or backsliding friend."—*The Christian.*

STORM SIGNALS: A Fourth Series of Sunday and
Thursday Evening Sermons at the Metropolitan Tabernacle. 3s. 6d.

"Discourses which come upon the soul as the trumpet blast of judgment, but always end with salvation. . . . These are some of the most useful sermons Mr. Spurgeon has ever preached."—*Christian Age.*

FARM SERMONS. By C. H. Spurgeon. New Illus-
trated Volume. Crown 8vo. 328 pp. 3s. 6d. cloth gilt.

"These sermons are as fresh and fragrant as the newly-ploughed soil, or the new-mown hay, and ought to be perused with pleasure and profit by many who know little or nothing of agricultural pursuits."—*The Christian.*

THE ROYAL WEDDING. The Banquet and the Guests.
By C. H. Spurgeon. Paper covers, 6d. Cloth, 1s.

"An elegant little book of 80 pages, illustrating the parable of the Wedding Garment, and worthy of the world-wide fame of the author."—*Baptist Messenger.*

Illustrative.

ILLUSTRATIONS AND MEDITATIONS; or, Flowers
from a Puritan's Garden. Distilled and Dispensed by C. H. Spurgeon. Price 2s. 6d.

"It is a Garden full of beautiful and useful things, which will yield its delights to many classes of readers."—*Christian World.*

FEATHERS FOR ARROWS; or, Illustrations for
Preachers and Teachers, from my Note Book. By C. H. Spurgeon. Price 2s. 6d. 29th Thousand.

"The collection is very varied, but all bearing on the highest themes, and fitted to help the highest purpose of the Christian ministry. There is an admirable index of subjects, and another of texts, which greatly add to the practical usefulness of the book: we cordially recommend it."—*Evangelical Magazine.*

Extracts.

FLASHES OF THOUGHT; being one Thousand Choice
Extracts from the Works of C. H. Spurgeon. Alphabetically arranged, and with a copious Index. Price 5s.

"A thousand extracts, bright with the light of heaven, sparkling with wit, rich in imagery, beautiful in their setting, forcible in style, and devoutly stimulating in tone, make up a volume of unique merit."—*General Baptist Magazine.*

SPURGEON'S GEMS: being Brilliant Passages Selected
from the Discourses of C. H. Spurgeon. Large Type, 4s.

GLEANINGS AMONG THE SHEAVES. By C. H.
Spurgeon. Cloth, price 1s.
"These extracts are quite Spurgeonic—racy, rich, and rare, both as to style and matter—full of exquisite consolation—faithful advice—clear analogies —poetic touches—and glorious old gospel."—*Weekly Review.*

SPURGEON'S BIRTHDAY BOOK. Cloth, 2s. 6d.,
Calf or Morocco, 5s., Russia, with Photograph, 10s. 6d.
"A metaphor, simile, allegory, or illustration for every day in the year, compiled from the works of C. H. Spurgeon. For thirty pence our readers may possess a book which is as useful as it is handsomely got up."—*Christian Age.*

Devotional.

MORNING BY MORNING; or, Daily Readings for the
Family or the Closet. By C. H. Spurgeon. 3s. 6d. Morocco, 7s. 6d.
"Those who have learned the value of morning devotion, will highly prize these helps. All who love a full-orbed gospel, vigorous, varied thought, and a racy style, will appreciate this volume."—*Rev. J. Angus, D.D.*

EVENING BY EVENING; or, Readings at Eventide for
the Family or the Closet. By C. H. Spurgeon. 3s. 6d. Morocco, 7s. 6d.
"On learning that 'Evening by Evening' was published, how gladly I bade it welcome! And I can humbly commend it in no higher terms than by simply saying that it will be found a fit companion, every way, for its forerunner of the morning."—*Charles J. Brown, D.D., Edinburgh.*

THE CHEQUE BOOK OF THE BANK OF FAITH;
Being Precious Promises arranged for Daily Use; with Brief Experimental Comments. 3s. 6d. Persian Morocco, red and gilt edges, 7s. 6d.
"'The Cheque Book of the Bank of Faith' is suitable for family use, or for solitary prayer. It consists of a series of texts from the Bible, both from the Old and New Testaments, with a short commentary upon them. There is one of these texts for each day in the year. Each of them contains a promise of God, which, as the writer remarks, may be compared to a cheque payable to order, to be endorsed by faith, and presented in due time. There is much that is comforting in the volume, which will, doubtless, be largely used in households."
The Morning Post.

For Students.

LECTURES TO MY STUDENTS; A Selection from
Addresses delivered to the Students of the Pastors' College, Metropolitan Tabernacle. By C. H. Spurgeon, President. First and Second Series. Price 3s. 6d. each.
"We have read this work with a feeling very nearly approaching to delight. Nothing that Mr. Spurgeon has printed has so thoroughly pleased us, and few of his works are calculated to be of greater practical service. It abounds in words of wisdom; it is rich in humour, but richer in human and spiritual experience."—*Nonconformist.*

COMMENTING AND COMMENTARIES: Two Lec-
tures addressed to the Students of the Pastors' College, together with a Catalogue of Bible Commentaries and Expositions. Price 3s. 6d.
"Every candid reader will admit that, in impartiality, in terse and telling brevity, in wisdom sharpened into wit, in unaffected zeal for Christ's cause, and, above all, in robust common sense, this volume has few equals, if any."
Literary World.

MY SERMON-NOTES. A Selection from Outlines of

Discourses delivered at the Metropolitan Tabernacle. Part I. Genesis to Proverbs—I. to LXIV. Part II. Ecclesiastes to Malachi—LXV. to CXXIX. 2s. 6d. each. Parts I. and II. bound together in one Volume, Cloth, 5s. Part III. Matthew to Acts—CXXX. to CXCV. Part IV. Romans to Revelation. CXCVI. to CCLXIV. 2s. 6d. each. Parts III. and IV. bound together in one volume, price 5s.

" When a preacher, be he lay or regular, finds himself severely pressed for a subject, he will find here an outline clearly drawn, a good deal of filling up and a little lot of stories or pithy bits to season the whole.

SPEECHES by C. H. SPURGEON AT HOME and

Abroad. In Paper covers, 1s. Cloth, 2s.

The pieces are in the main given as they originally appeared ; in the majority of instances the author is made to speak in the first person ; but this is not the case throughout. The reader will also find that the principal subjects are admirably reported.

Periodical.

THE SWORD AND THE TROWEL: A Monthly

Magazine, Price 3d. Yearly vols., 5s. Cases for binding, 1s. 4d.

It commands a large circulation among almost all classes of Christians, and as a religious periodical, it now occupies a position second to none. It records the works of faith and labours of love which are the honour of the various sections of the Church, and it contends most unsparingly against the errors of the times. It is an accurate record of the religious movements which emanate from the Metropolitan Tabernacle, but its advocacy is far from being confined within that area. No pains will be spared to render the Magazine growingly worthy of the widest circulation.—Editor, C. H. SPURGEON.

Historical.

THE METROPOLITAN TABERNACLE: its History

and Work. With 33 Illustrations. By C. H. SPURGEON. Price, in paper covers, 1s. Bound in cloth, 2s.

" Profusely illustrated with portraits, *fac-similes* of forgotten caricatures, and other engravings, quaint and otherwise, is likely to rival 'John Ploughman' in popularity. Containing between one and two hundred octavo pages, the matter might easily have been spread out into a five or six shilling volume ; but, as Mr. Spurgeon desires to write for the people, he publishes his works at prices to suit the pockets even of the poor."—*Christian World*.

MEMORIAL VOLUME. Containing Sermons and

Addresses delivered on the completion of the Twenty-fifth year of the Pastorate of C. H. SPURGEON. Price 1s., cloth.

Popular.

JOHN PLOUGHMAN'S TALK; or, Plain Advice for

Plain People. Illustrated. By C. H. SPURGEON. In stiff covers, 1s. Cloth, gilt edges, 2s. 360th Thousand

" Racy and pungent; very plain, and to the purpose. No fear as to whether it will be read or not by those into whose hands it may fall. If Mr. Spurgeon goes on at this rate in his multiform publications, he will leave nothing racy unsaid."—*Watchman*.

JOHN PLOUGHMAN'S PICTURES; or, More of his

Plain Talk for Plain People. In stiff covers, 1s.; cloth, gilt edges, 2s. 130th Thousand.

"Every page is full of sayings well calculated to teach the people the charms of religion, and the happiness attending sober industry."—*Christian World.*

SPURGEON'S SHILLING SERIES. Bound in Cloth.

No. 1.—Christ's Glorious Achievements. | No. 4.—The Mourner's Comforter.
„ 2.—Seven Wonders of Grace. | „ 5.—The Bible and the Newspaper.
„ 3.—The Spare Half-Hour; | „ 6.—Eccentric Preachers.
No. 7.—Good Cheer.

"Promises to form a valuable library of religious literature."—*Christian Mag.*

THE CLUE OF THE MAZE. By C. H. Spurgeon. 1s.

It is the author's desire that it may strengthen the faith of many, and recover others out of the snare of the enemy.

"Heartily do we thank Mr. Spurgeon for the work, and commend the book as just what is often required for a present; it will be found to be acceptable by the uncultured and the cultured as well."—*The Freeman.*

ALL OF GRACE. An Earnest Word with those who

are seeking Salvation by the Lord Jesus Christ. By C. H. SPURGEON. Price 1s. Persian Morocco, gilt edges, 2s. Thirtieth Thousand.

"Every word is weighted with precious truth, and truth so simply and convincingly put that none can fail to understand God's way of salvation. Powerful illustrations, apt and original similes, and the one affectionate desire to win for Christ and to Christ, make it a gospel treasury of priceless worth."
The Christian.

ACCORDING TO PROMISE; or, The Method of the

Lord's Dealing with His Chosen People. A Companion Volume to "All of Grace." Cloth 1s. Morocco, gilt edges, 2s. Twentieth Thousand.

"It is an eminently practical volume, the fruit of a ripe experience; as simple in its form as it is searching in its exposure of counterfeit religion; and we have no doubt that many will have reason to rejoice that they made its acquaintance. As Mr. Spurgeon remarks in one of his homely sentences, 'he who looked into his accounts and found that his business was a losing one was saved from bankruptcy.'"—*Christian Leader.*

TEN YEARS OF MY LIFE in the Service of the

Book Fund: Being a Grateful Record of my Experience of the Lord's Ways, and Work, and Wages. By Mrs. C. H. SPURGEON. Third Edition, handsomely bound, 3s. 6d. Also in bevelled boards, gilt edges, with New Portrait and Autograph, 5s.

"A deeply interesting narrative of a beneficent and courageously sustained effort. Mrs. Spurgeon has much of the style of her husband's writing, and this autobiographic sketch might in many respects have proceeded from his pen."—*Daily Telegraph.*

WORKS BY OTHER AUTHORS.

A BODY OF DIVINITY, contained in Sermons upon the

Assembly's Catechism. By the Rev. THOMAS WATSON, Rector of St. Stephen's, Walbrook. A new and complete edition, revised and adapted to modern readers by the Rev. GEORGE ROGERS, Camberwell. With a Preface and Appendix by Pastor C. H. SPURGEON. Price 6s.

"Every divine of Calvinistic views should read it, and every private Christian also. We can heartily recommend it to all lovers of sound doctrine, among whom we hope for a large sale."—*C. H. Spurgeon.*

"THEOPNEUSTIA:" The Plenary Inspiration of the
Holy Scriptures. By L. Gaussen, D.D. With Prefatory Note by C. H. Spurgeon. Price 3s. 6d.

"We have now issued a new edition of this grand work. Every Christian should read it, and scatter it. It is one of *the* books for the period."—C. H. Spurgeon, in *The Sword and the Trowel*.

ELISHA COLES ON DIVINE SOVEREIGNTY. With
Preface by C. H. Spurgeon. 2s. 6d.

Romaine says of this book: "The doctrines of grace, of which this book treats, are the truths of God: our author has defended them in a masterly manner. He has not only proved them to be plainly revealed in the Scriptures, but has also shown that they are of such constant use to the children of God, that without the steadfast belief of them, they cannot go on their way rejoicing. In the practical view of these points Elisha Coles is singularly excellent."

HENRY'S OUTLINES OF CHURCH HISTORY: A
Brief Sketch of the Christian Church from the First Century. By Joseph Fernandez, LL.D. 2s. 6d.

"The Church Histories hitherto in vogue are too cumbersome, too verbose, too involved to be used in schools and colleges, and we entertain the hope that the present work will remedy that evil, and supply a work which all our friends who are tutors can use with pleasure and safety."—*C. H. Spurgeon*.

GLIMPSES OF JESUS; or, Christ Exalted in the Affec-
tions of his People. By W. P. Balfern. Eighth Thousand. Fcp. 8vo. Cloth 3s.

"I hailed with pleasure the advent of this precious volume. I sat down to read it, and soon discovered its beauty; it was a feast of fat things, a season long to be remembered. I have read it again and again, and would desire to adore the Holy Spirit for that gracious unction which rested on me in its perusal."—*C. H. Spurgeon*.

THE BEAUTY OF THE GREAT KING, and other
Poems for the Heart and Home. By W. P. Balfern, Author of "Glimpses of Jesus." Second Edition. 2s. 6d.

"We strongly recommend this book to the attention of our readers. No child of God can read it without pleasure and profit. It has been written in the furnace, and will comfort such as are in it."—*C. H. Spurgeon*.

Pastor C. H. SPURGEON: his Life and Work to his
Fiftieth Birthday; with an Account of his Ancestors for 200 Years. By George J. Stevenson, M.A. Paper covers, 1s., cloth, 2s.

SKETCH OF THE LIFE OF Rev. C. H. SPURGEON,
with Thirteen Portraits and Engravings. 2d.

THE PATHOS OF LIFE; or, Touching Incidents Illus-
trative of the Truth of the Gospel. By W. Poole Balfern. Second Edition. 2s. 6d.

"The book will be highly valued by the Sunday-school teacher, by the minister of the gospel, and by all who know anything of Mr. Balfern and his writings, or who can appreciate earnest and deep-toned, yet cheerful spirituality."—*Literary World*.

BOOKSELLERS AND BOOKBUYERS in Byeways and Highways. By C. H. Spurgeon, Samuel Manning, LL.D., and G. Holden Pike. With a Preface by the Right Hon. the Earl of Shaftesbury, K.G. Cloth, gilt edges, 1s. 6d.

"Externally this is an attractive book. It is brought out with the view of creating and increasing public interest in Colportage."—*C. H. Spurgeon.*

THE PULPIT BY THE HEARTH. Being Plain Chapters for Sabbath Reading. By Arthur Mursell. Price 2s. 6d.

CONFERENCE ADDRESSES, being a Selection from Addresses delivered at the Annual Conferences of the Pastors' College, by the Rev. George Rogers. With a recommendation by C. H. Spurgeon. Cloth 2s. 6d.

"Twelve such addresses it would be very hard to find anywhere else. We firmly believe that every student and minister who heard them will be anxious at once to possess a copy, and we shall be greatly surprised if the volume does not command a host of readers. Mother-wit is blended with fatherly wisdom, and the whole is sanctified by zeal for the cause of God. We cannot too heartily command the volume to our subscribers."—*C. H. Spurgeon.*

A COLLECTION OF RARE JEWELS. From the Mines of William Gurnall. (1680.) Dug up and deposited in a Casket, by Arthur Augustus Rees (1853). Second Edition. Price 2s.

"Of all the Puritans, Gurnall is the best adapted for quoting. He is sententious, and withal pictorial, and both in a high degree. Mr. Rees has made his selections with a discerning eye; they are not mere clippings at random, but extracts chosen with judgment."—*C. H. Spurgeon.*

STRAY LEAVES FROM MY LIFE STORY. By J. Manton Smith. Cloth, 2s. 6d.

"Mr. Smith is always merry; indeed, we had better say 'jolly,' for that is the more classical word. He is earnest up to the eyes, and he is tenderness itself; but from quite unexpected corners of his nature humour wells up, and floods the rest of his being; hence in this life story there is no lack of fun, albeit that the spirit and object are deeply serious. We recommend the publishers to print a large edition, for these 'Stray Leaves' are sure to be blown about by every wind, and so they will circulate in every quarter."— C. H. Spurgeon in *The Sword and the Trowel.*

FRONDED PALMS. A Collection of Pointed Papers on a wide range of subjects. By W. Y. Fullerton. With over one hundred Illustrations. Cloth, 2s. 6d.

"Vivacious, witty, sensible, gracious tales here abound. May God bless the book and the writer!"—*C. H. Spurgeon.*

"Well printed, and abounding in capital illustrations. The book is one likely to be of great spiritual benefit to young people."—*Literary World.*

FOUR LETTERS TO THE CHRISTIANS CALLED "BRETHREN" on the subject of Ministry. By Arthur Augustus Rees. Price Sixpence.

WAYMARKS FOR WANDERERS. Being Five Addresses delivered in the Metropolitan Tabernacle. By W. Y. Fullerton, Evangelist. Price 1s.

"A little book upon the prodigal son. The theme has been often descanted on, but this treatise is not a repetition; it is full of freshness and originality. What is better, its earnest pleadings and plain gospel statements are sure to be useful to seeking souls, and we commend it for wide distribution by those who wish to lead others to the home above."—*C. H. Spurgeon.*

BUNYAN'S WATER OF LIFE. Preface by C. H.
SPURGEON. 1s. This is a tasteful little book, very suitable for a present, and
likely to be made useful wherever it may be circulated. It is written in
Bunyan's best style; it is simple, forcible, pleasing, and full of illustration.

BAPTIST CONFESSION OF FAITH. Thirty-two
Articles on Christian Faith and Practice, with Scripture Proofs, adopted by
the Ministers and Messengers of the General Assembly, which met in
London in 1689. Preface by C. H. SPURGEON. Paper covers, 4d. Post
free, 5 stamps.

BAPTISM DISCOVERED PLAINLY AND FAITH-
fully according to the Word of God. By JOHN NORCOTT. A New
Edition, corrected and somewhat altered by C. H. SPURGEON. Price
2d. In large type, paper covers, 6d.; cloth, 1s.

LECTURES ON BAPTISM. By the Late WILLIAM
SHIRREFF, Minister of the Gospel, Glasgow. With a Preface by C. H.
SPURGEON. Cloth, 2s. 6d.
"The Lectures are, to our mind, singularly likely to conciliate and win those
who already hold sound views upon the great doctrines of the gospel. They
were clearly meant to be an appeal to the author's old friends, the Presbyterians.
They are thorough and uncompromising, but, at the same time, calm and
judicious."—C. H. Spurgeon.

FOR EVER AND EVER. A College Lecture upon the
Duration of Future Punishment. By Rev. GEORGE ROGERS. Price 2d.

FUTURE PUNISHMENT. A Lecture Delivered to
the Students of the Metropolitan Tabernacle College, in reply to a series
of letters in "The Christian World," from the Rev. Edward White. By
the Rev. GEORGE ROGERS. Price 1d.

MURSELL'S LECTURES TO WORKING MEN. De-
livered at the Lambeth Baths, Westminster Bridge Road. Price One
Penny each; or 10d. the series in wrapper. Post free.

WHAT'S YOUR NAME?	COLOURS OF THE RAINBOW.
TEMPLE BAR.	RIPPLES ON THE RIVER.
THE CRYSTAL PALACE.	FACES IN THE FIRE.
SUGAR-COATED PILLS.	CRIES FROM THE CRADLE.

WASHED AWAY.

A LAY OF TWO CITIES. By "Jesharelah." Crown
8vo. French Morocco, gilt edges. Price 2s.
"This book is very prettily got up, as it deserved to be. The jewel is worthy
of the setting. Babylon and Jerusalem (not the old cities, but those of which
they were the types) are the subjects of the lays of Jesharelah. With true
devotion and shrewd sense he mingles a sufficiency of the poetic spirit to com-
mand the reader's attention. It must be a high pleasure to a man of business,
like our author, to rise into other regions than those of our grimy city, to
think of high and holy themes, and then to cast into musical verse the result
of his contemplations. If Jesharelah cannot ride the winged horse of Milton,
he can amble at a fair pace along a pleasant way; and his tracks may guide
others along that narrow way which leads to the City which hath foundations."
C. H. Spurgeon.

PASSMORE & ALABASTER, PATERNOSTER BUILDINGS.

CPSIA information can be obtained
at www.ICGtesting.com
Printed in the USA
LVHW04s1232190518
577803LV00028B/398/P